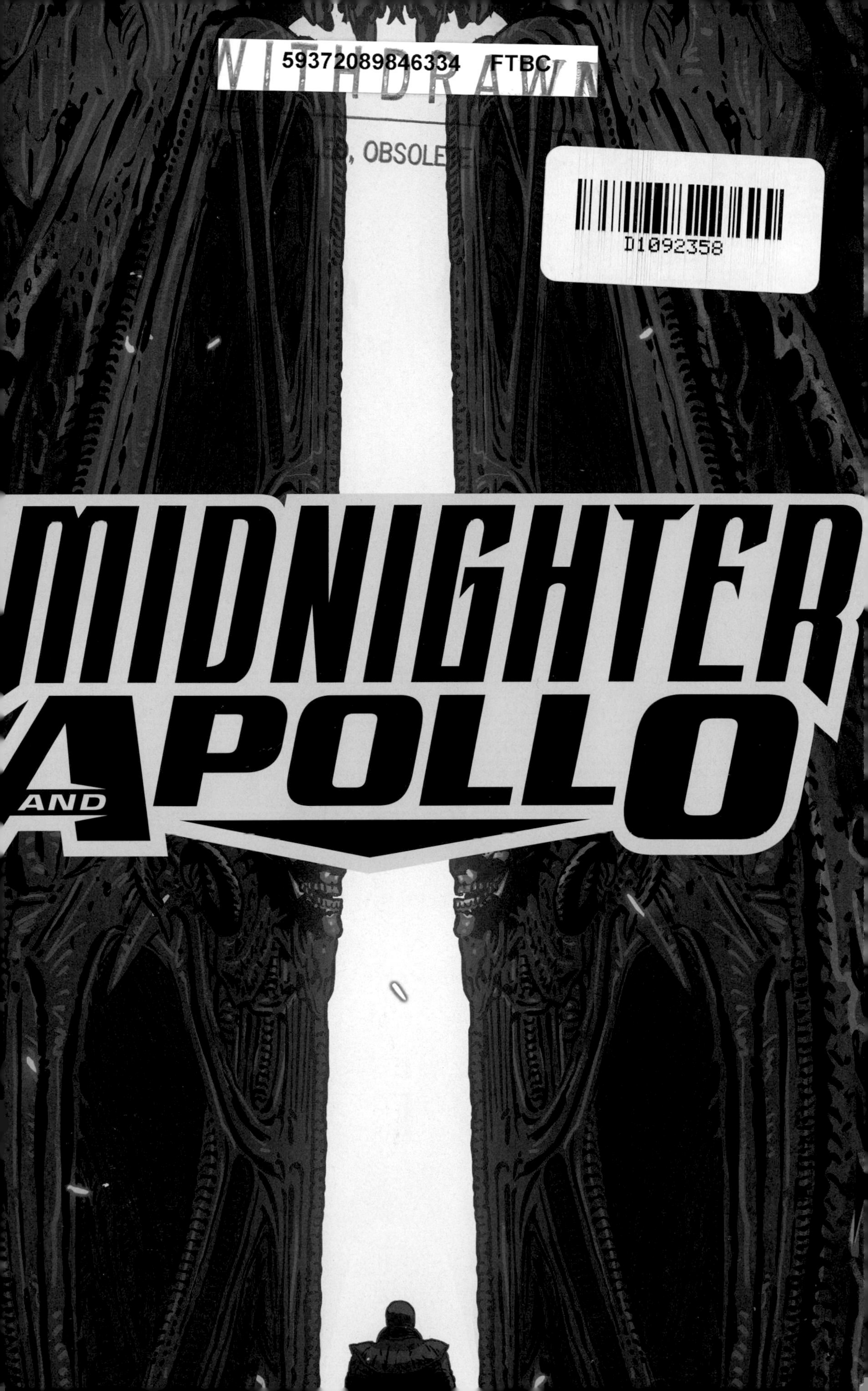
MIDNIGHTER
AND
APOLLO

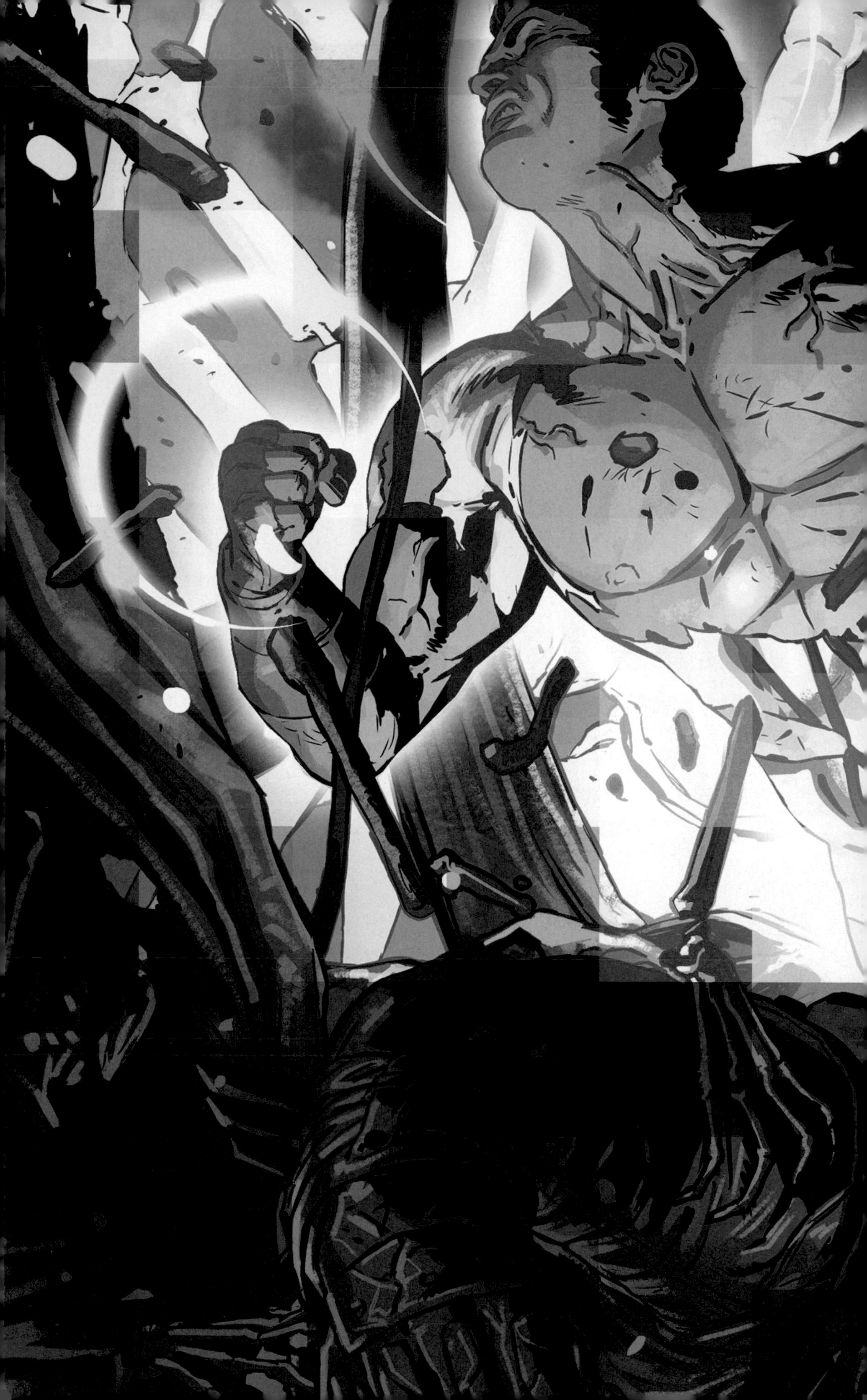

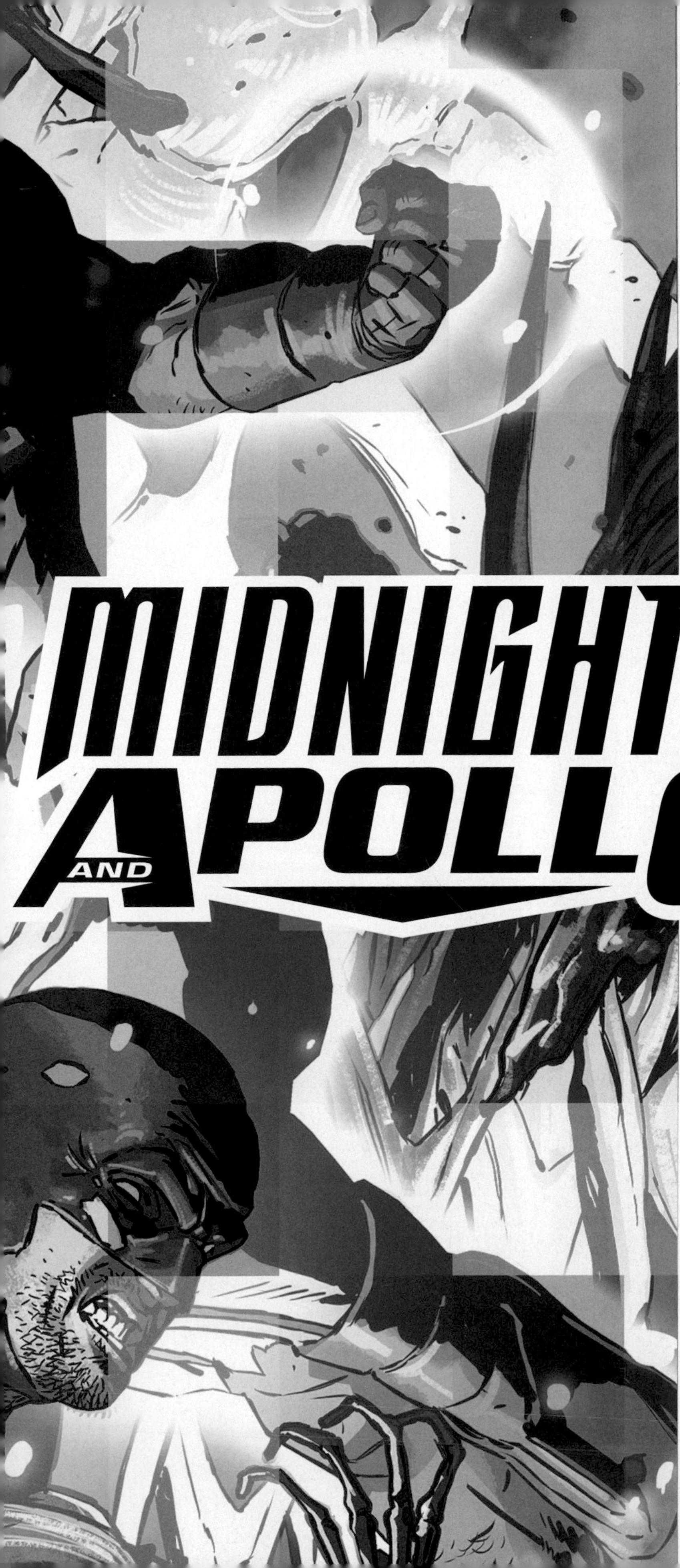

MIDNIGHTER AND APOLLO

STEVE ORLANDO
writer

FERNANDO BLANCO
artist

ROMULO FAJARDO JR.
JOHN RAUCH
colorists

JOSH REED
letterer

ACO
ROMULO FAJARDO JR.
original series and collection cover artists

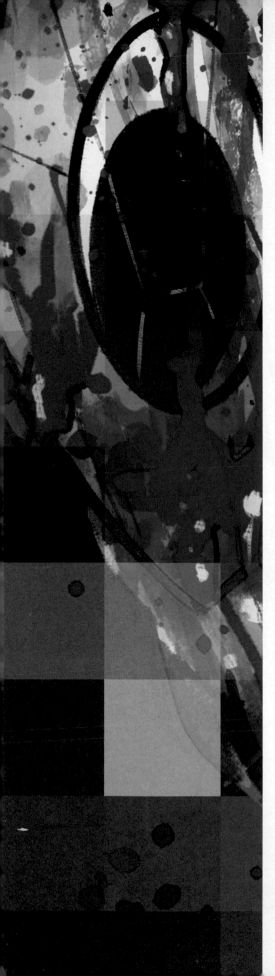

CHRIS CONROY Editor - Original Series
DAVE WIELGOSZ Assistant Editor - Original Series
JEB WOODARD Group Editor - Collected Editions
ERIKA ROTHBERG Editor - Collected Edition
STEVE COOK Design Director - Books
MONIQUE GRUSPE Publication Design

BOB HARRAS Senior VP - Editor-in-Chief, DC Comics

DIANE NELSON President
DAN DiDIO Publisher
JIM LEE Publisher
GEOFF JOHNS President & Chief Creative Officer
AMIT DESAI Executive VP - Business & Marketing Strategy,
Direct to Consumer & Global Franchise Management
SAM ADES Senior VP - Direct to Consumer
BOBBIE CHASE VP - Talent Development
MARK CHIARELLO Senior VP - Art, Design & Collected Editions
JOHN CUNNINGHAM Senior VP - Sales & Trade Marketing
ANNE DePIES Senior VP - Business Strategy, Finance & Administration
DON FALLETTI VP - Manufacturing Operations
LAWRENCE GANEM VP - Editorial Administration & Talent Relations
ALISON GILL Senior VP - Manufacturing & Operations
HANK KANALZ Senior VP - Editorial Strategy & Administration
JAY KOGAN VP - Legal Affairs
THOMAS LOFTUS VP - Business Affairs
JACK MAHAN VP - Business Affairs
NICK J. NAPOLITANO VP - Manufacturing Administration
EDDIE SCANNELL VP - Consumer Marketing
COURTNEY SIMMONS Senior VP - Publicity & Communications
JIM (SKI) SOKOLOWSKI VP - Comic Book Specialty Sales & Trade Marketing
NANCY SPEARS VP - Mass, Book, Digital Sales & Trade Marketing

MIDNIGHTER AND APOLLO

DC Comics, 2900 West Alameda Ave., Burbank, CA 91505
Printed by LSC Communications, Salem, VA, USA. 6/16/17. First Printing.
ISBN: 978-1-4012-7201-2

Library of Congress Cataloging-in-Publication Data is available.

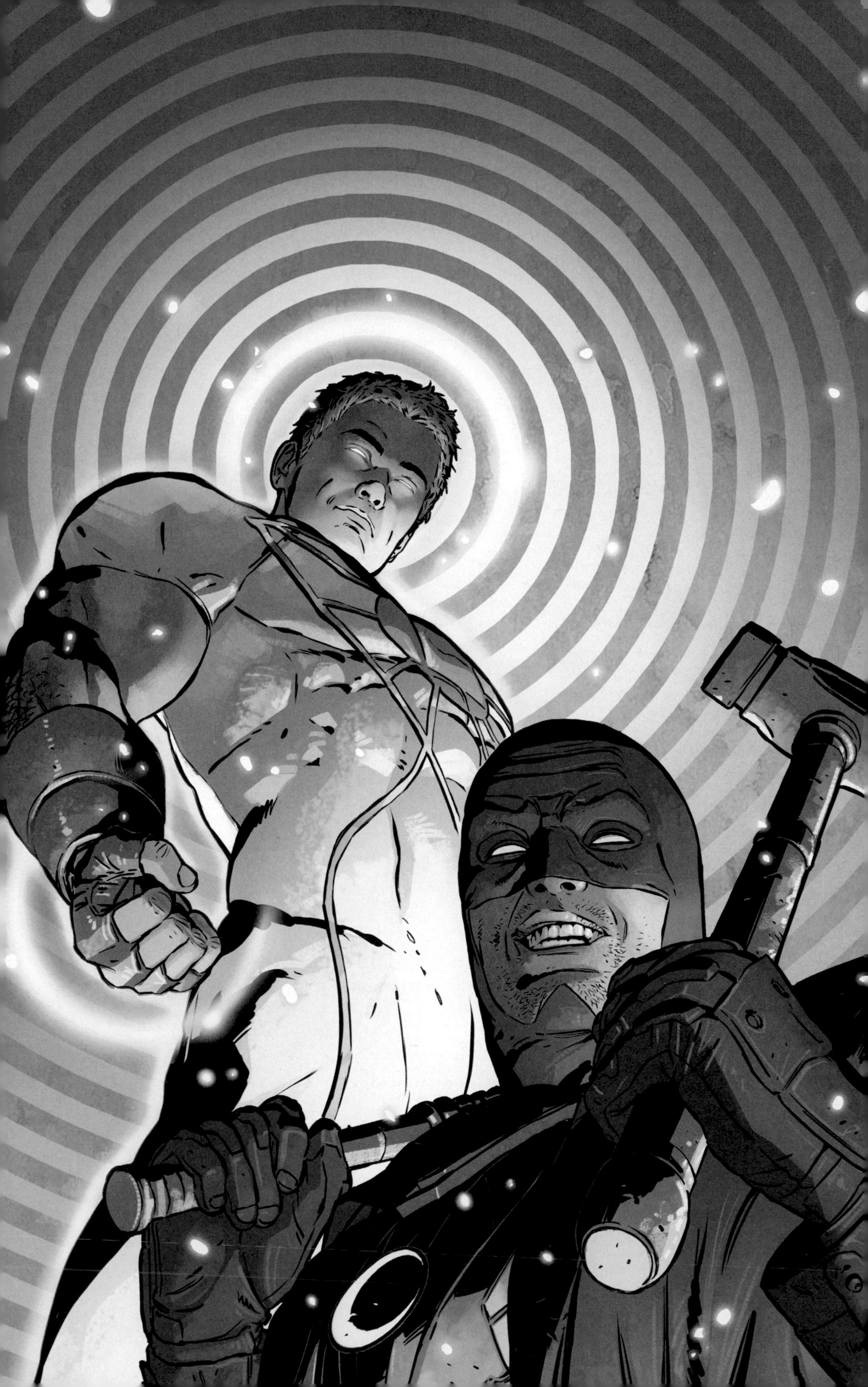

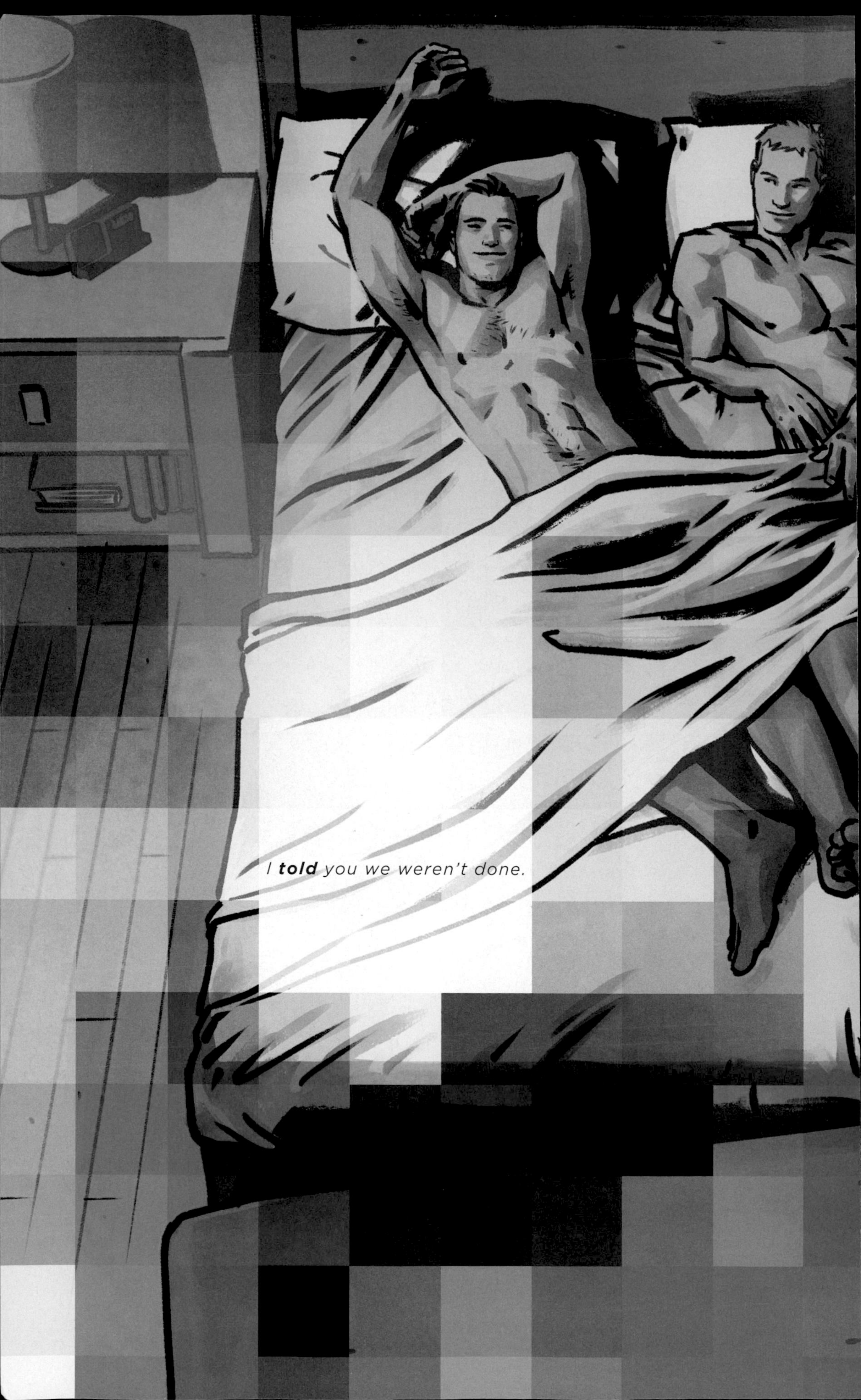
I ***told*** you we weren't done.

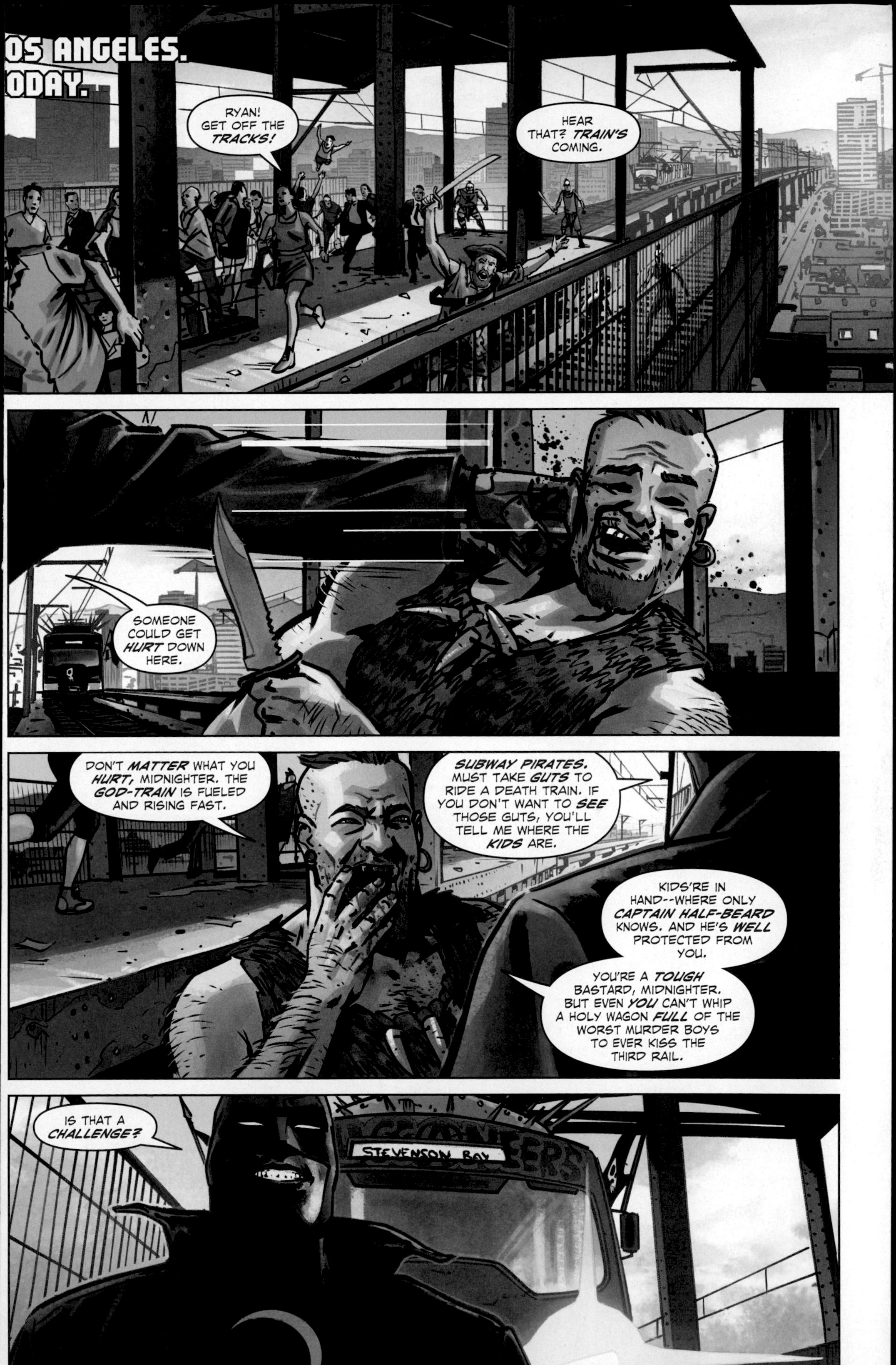
OS ANGELES.
ODAY.
RYAN! GET OFF THE TRACKS!
HEAR THAT? TRAIN'S COMING.
SOMEONE COULD GET HURT DOWN HERE.
DON'T MATTER WHAT YOU HURT, MIDNIGHTER. THE GOD-TRAIN IS FUELED AND RISING FAST.
SUBWAY PIRATES. MUST TAKE GUTS TO RIDE A DEATH TRAIN. IF YOU DON'T WANT TO SEE THOSE GUTS, YOU'LL TELL ME WHERE THE KIDS ARE.
KIDS'RE IN HAND--WHERE ONLY CAPTAIN HALF-BEARD KNOWS. AND HE'S WELL PROTECTED FROM YOU.
YOU'RE A TOUGH BASTARD, MIDNIGHTER. BUT EVEN YOU CAN'T WHIP A HOLY WAGON FULL OF THE WORST MURDER BOYS TO EVER KISS THE THIRD RAIL.
IS THAT A CHALLENGE?
STEVENSON BAY

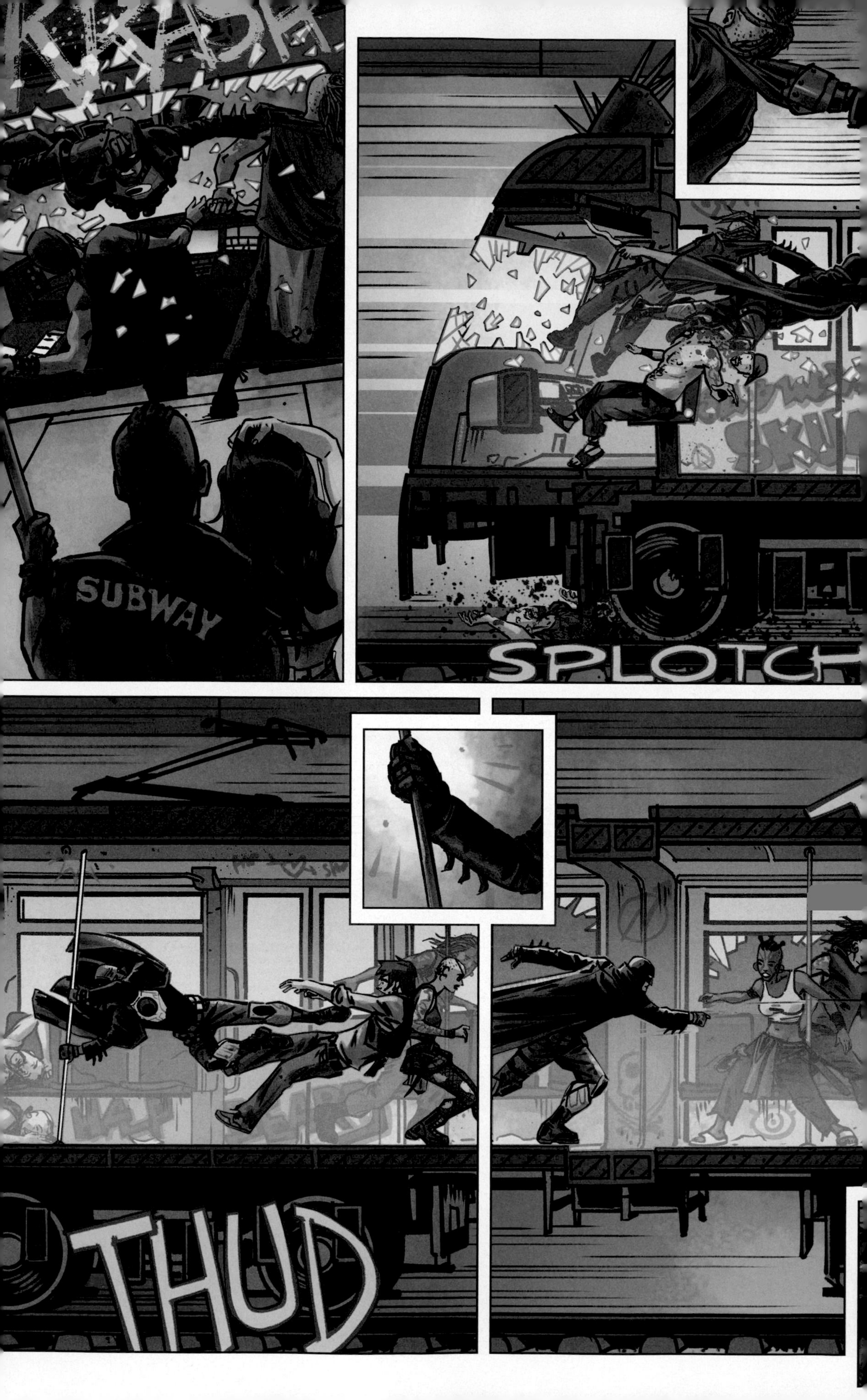
KRASH
SUBWAY
SPLOTCH
THUD

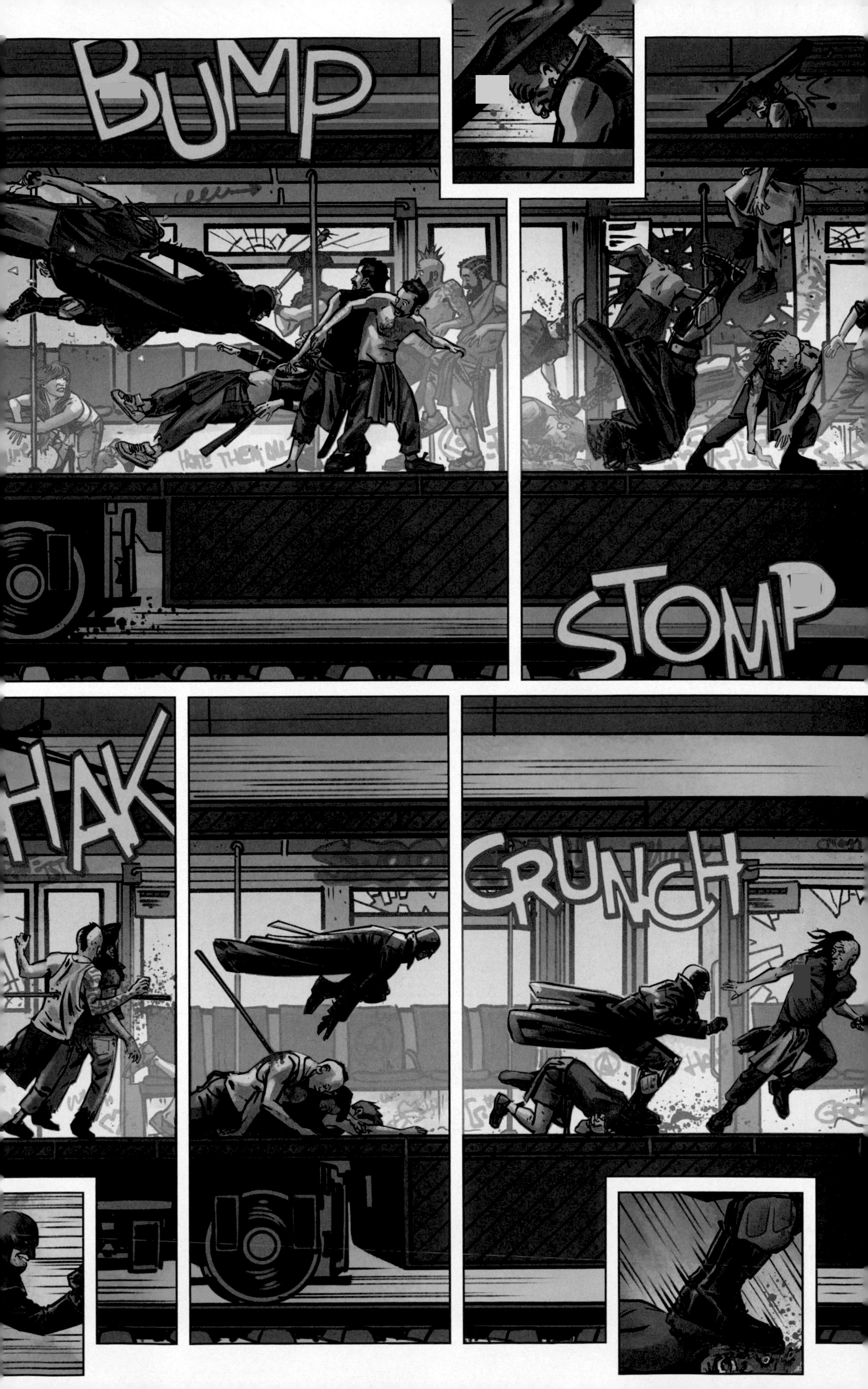

BUMP
STOMP
HAK
CRUNCH

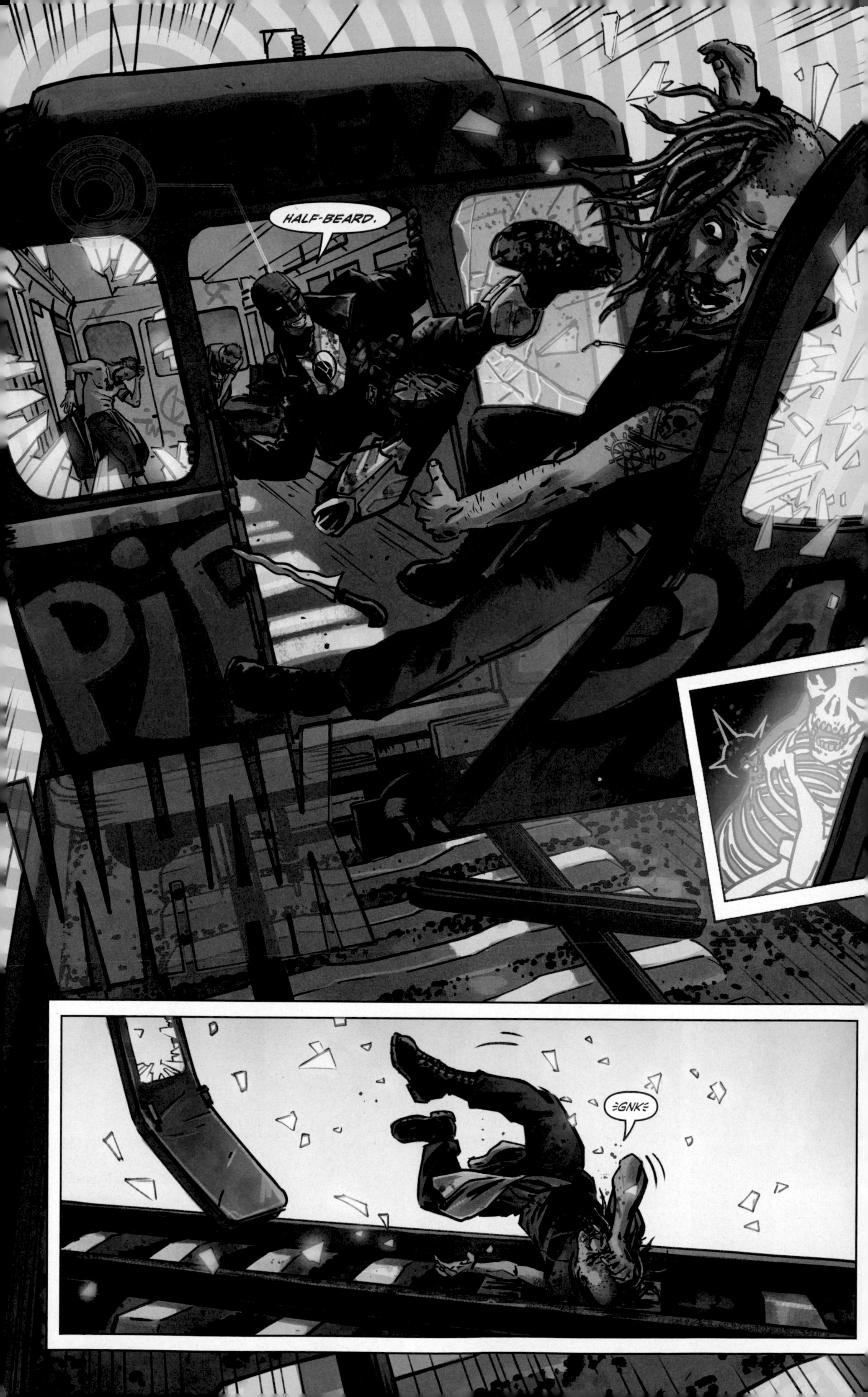
HALF-BEARD.
GNK

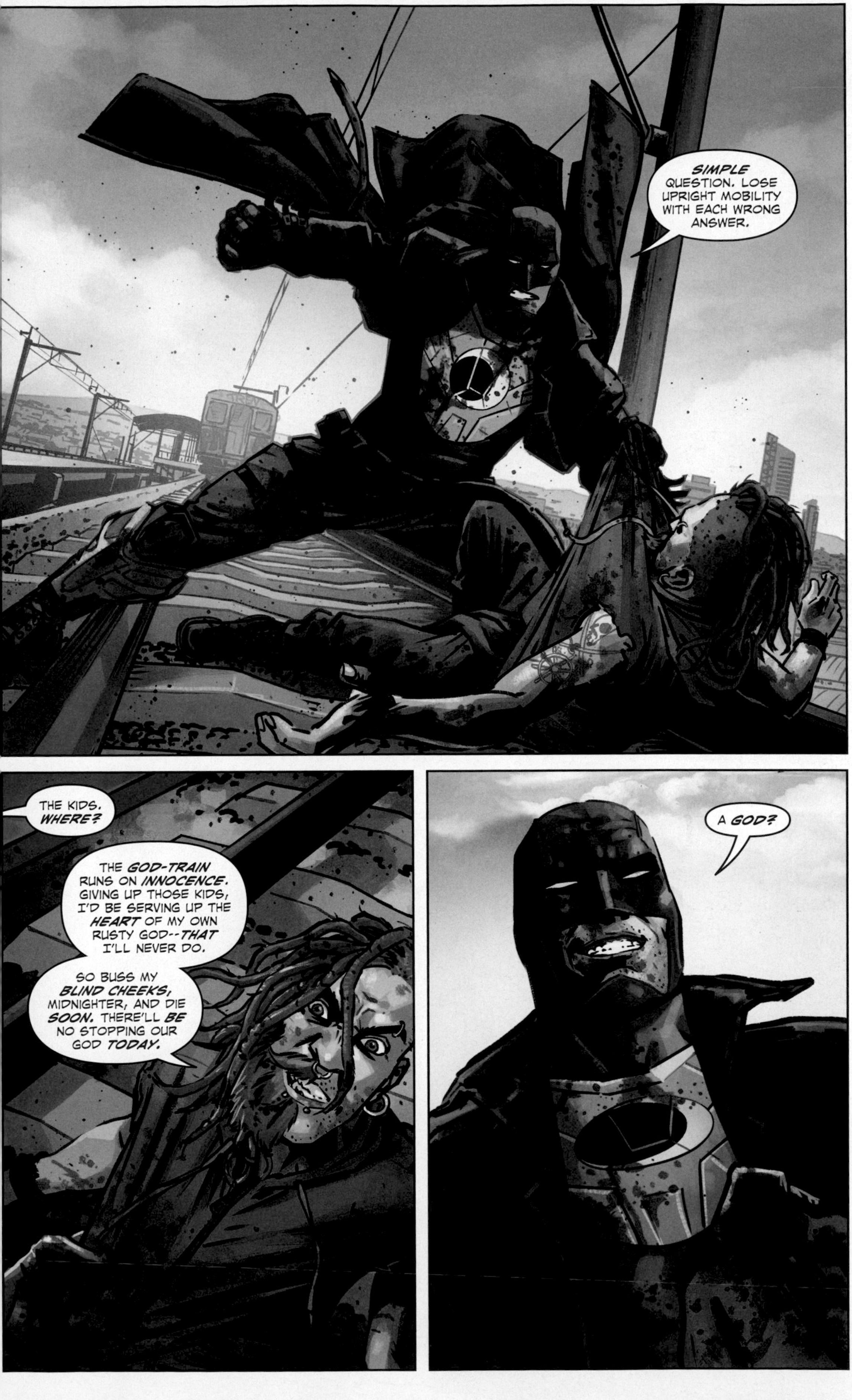
SIMPLE QUESTION. LOSE UPRIGHT MOBILITY WITH EACH WRONG ANSWER.
THE KIDS. WHERE?
THE GOD-TRAIN RUNS ON INNOCENCE. GIVING UP THOSE KIDS, I'D BE SERVING UP THE HEART OF MY OWN RUSTY GOD--THAT I'LL NEVER DO.
SO BUSS MY BLIND CHEEKS, MIDNIGHTER, AND DIE SOON. THERE'LL BE NO STOPPING OUR GOD TODAY.
A GOD?

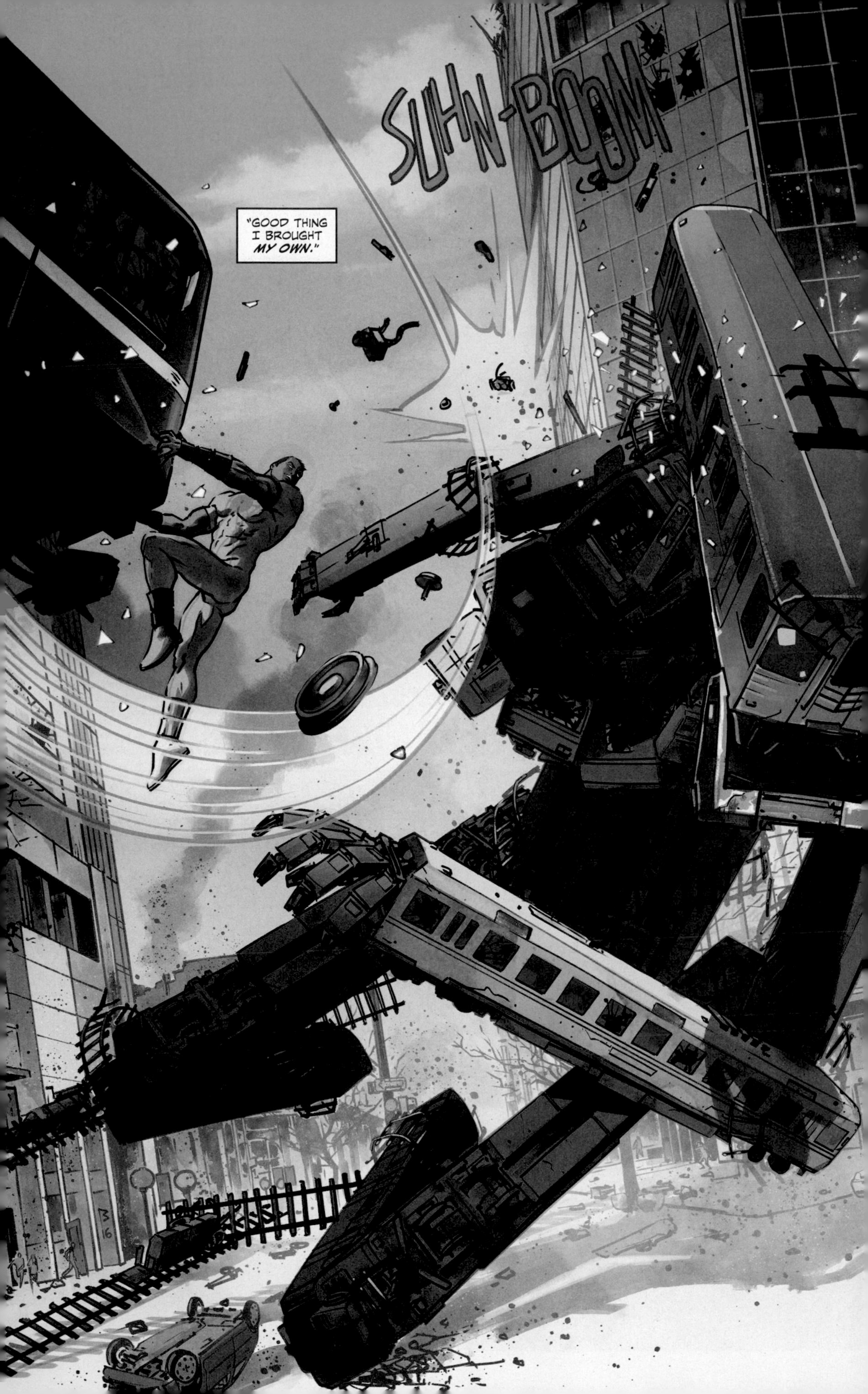
"GOOD THING I BROUGHT *MY OWN.*"
SUHN-BOOM

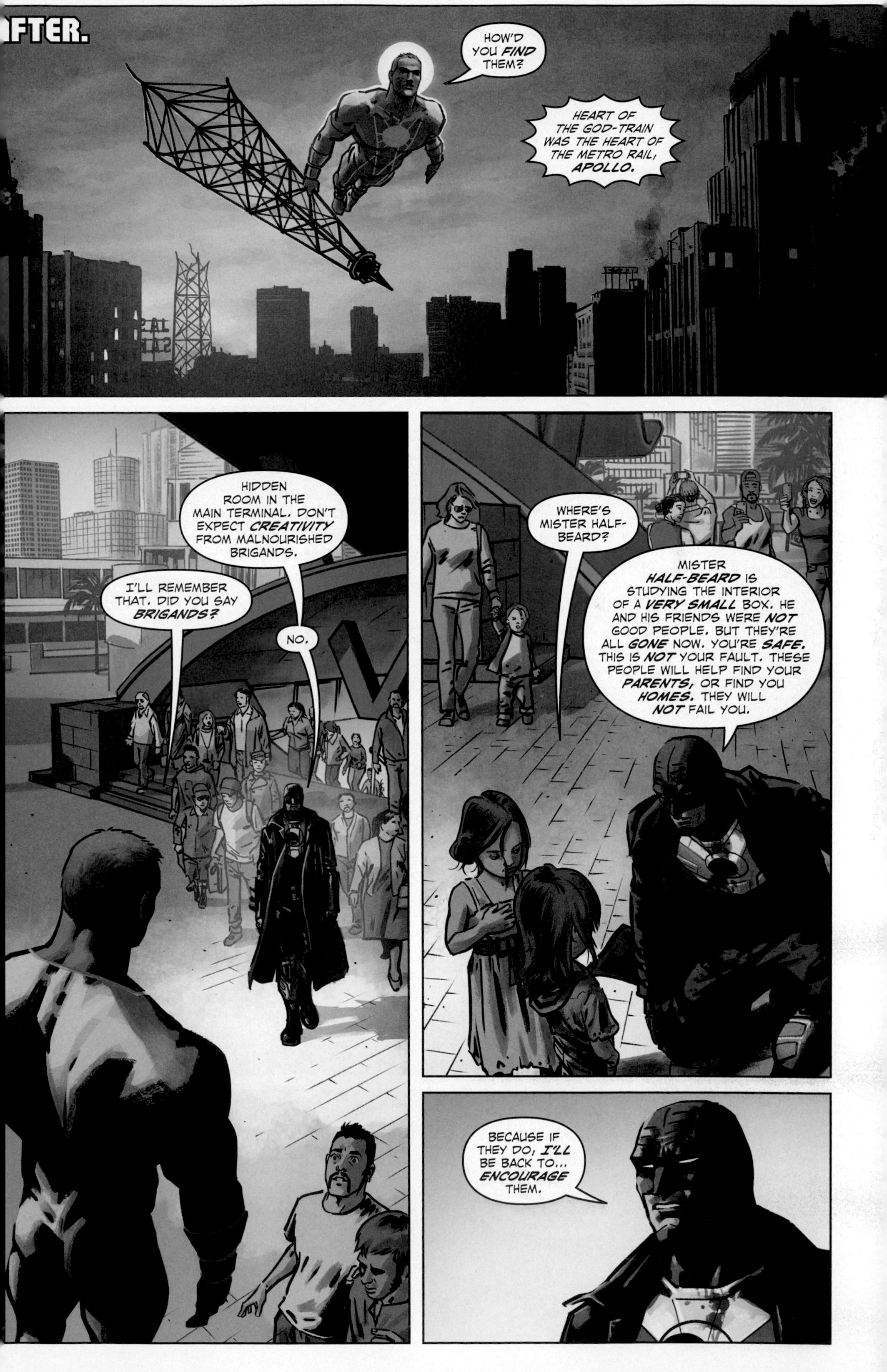
FTER.
HOW'D YOU FIND THEM?
HEART OF THE GOD-TRAIN WAS THE HEART OF THE METRO RAIL, APOLLO.
HIDDEN ROOM IN THE MAIN TERMINAL. DON'T EXPECT CREATIVITY FROM MALNOURISHED BRIGANDS.
I'LL REMEMBER THAT. DID YOU SAY BRIGANDS?
NO.
WHERE'S MISTER HALF-BEARD?
MISTER HALF-BEARD IS STUDYING THE INTERIOR OF A VERY SMALL BOX. HE AND HIS FRIENDS WERE NOT GOOD PEOPLE. BUT THEY'RE ALL GONE NOW. YOU'RE SAFE. THIS IS NOT YOUR FAULT. THESE PEOPLE WILL HELP FIND YOUR PARENTS, OR FIND YOU HOMES. THEY WILL NOT FAIL YOU.
BECAUSE IF THEY DO, I'LL BE BACK TO... ENCOURAGE THEM.

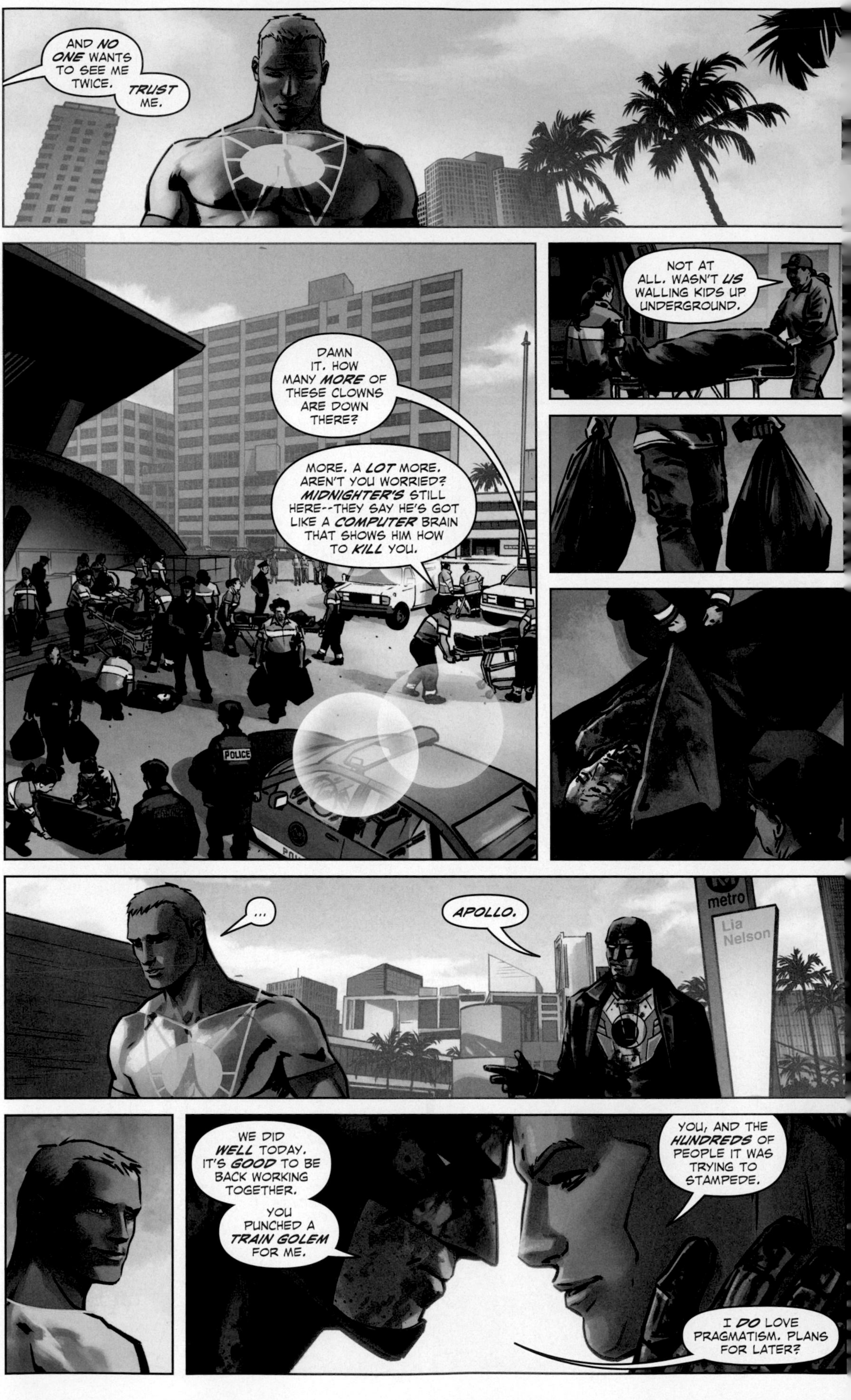
AND NO ONE WANTS TO SEE ME TWICE.
TRUST ME.
DAMN IT. HOW MANY MORE OF THESE CLOWNS ARE DOWN THERE?
MORE. A LOT MORE. AREN'T YOU WORRIED? MIDNIGHTER'S STILL HERE--THEY SAY HE'S GOT LIKE A COMPUTER BRAIN THAT SHOWS HIM HOW TO KILL YOU.
POLICE
NOT AT ALL. WASN'T US WALLING KIDS UP UNDERGROUND.
...
APOLLO.
metro
Lia Nelson
WE DID WELL TODAY. IT'S GOOD TO BE BACK WORKING TOGETHER.
YOU PUNCHED A TRAIN GOLEM FOR ME.
YOU, AND THE HUNDREDS OF PEOPLE IT WAS TRYING TO STAMPEDE.
I DO LOVE PRAGMATISM. PLANS FOR LATER?

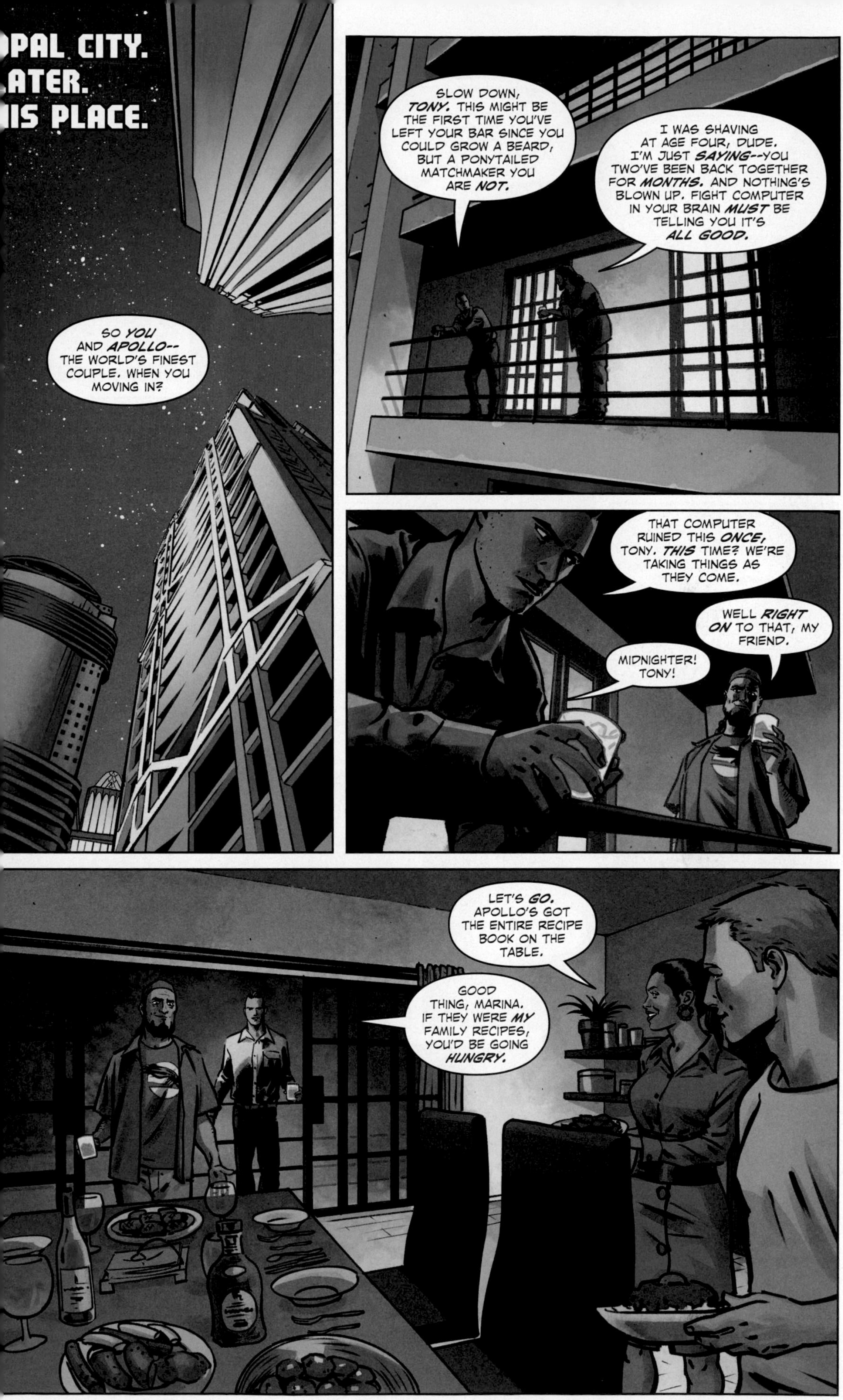
PAL CITY.
ATER.
IS PLACE.
SO YOU AND APOLLO-- THE WORLD'S FINEST COUPLE. WHEN YOU MOVING IN?
SLOW DOWN, TONY. THIS MIGHT BE THE FIRST TIME YOU'VE LEFT YOUR BAR SINCE YOU COULD GROW A BEARD, BUT A PONYTAILED MATCHMAKER YOU ARE NOT.
I WAS SHAVING AT AGE FOUR, DUDE. I'M JUST SAYING--YOU TWO'VE BEEN BACK TOGETHER FOR MONTHS. AND NOTHING'S BLOWN UP. FIGHT COMPUTER IN YOUR BRAIN MUST BE TELLING YOU IT'S ALL GOOD.
THAT COMPUTER RUINED THIS ONCE, TONY. THIS TIME? WE'RE TAKING THINGS AS THEY COME.
WELL RIGHT ON TO THAT, MY FRIEND.
MIDNIGHTER! TONY!
LET'S GO. APOLLO'S GOT THE ENTIRE RECIPE BOOK ON THE TABLE.
GOOD THING, MARINA. IF THEY WERE MY FAMILY RECIPES, YOU'D BE GOING HUNGRY.

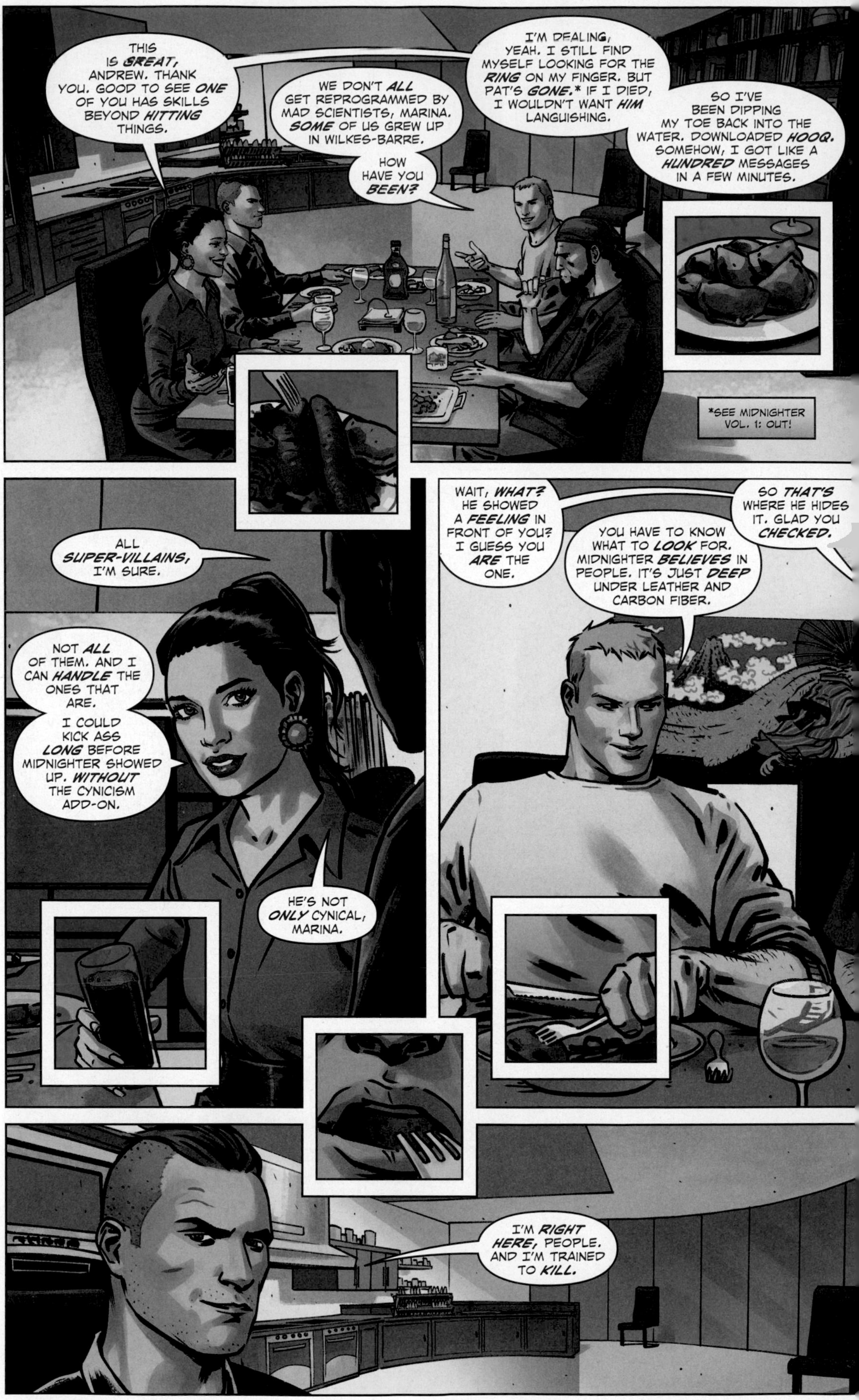
THIS IS GREAT, ANDREW. THANK YOU. GOOD TO SEE ONE OF YOU HAS SKILLS BEYOND HITTING THINGS.
WE DON'T ALL GET REPROGRAMMED BY MAD SCIENTISTS, MARINA. SOME OF US GREW UP IN WILKES-BARRE.
HOW HAVE YOU BEEN?
I'M DEALING, YEAH. I STILL FIND MYSELF LOOKING FOR THE RING ON MY FINGER. BUT PAT'S GONE.* IF I DIED, I WOULDN'T WANT HIM LANGUISHING.
SO I'VE BEEN DIPPING MY TOE BACK INTO THE WATER. DOWNLOADED HOOQ. SOMEHOW, I GOT LIKE A HUNDRED MESSAGES IN A FEW MINUTES.
*SEE MIDNIGHTER VOL. 1: OUT!
ALL SUPER-VILLAINS, I'M SURE.
NOT ALL OF THEM. AND I CAN HANDLE THE ONES THAT ARE.
I COULD KICK ASS LONG BEFORE MIDNIGHTER SHOWED UP. WITHOUT THE CYNICISM ADD-ON.
HE'S NOT ONLY CYNICAL, MARINA.
WAIT, WHAT? HE SHOWED A FEELING IN FRONT OF YOU? I GUESS YOU ARE THE ONE.
YOU HAVE TO KNOW WHAT TO LOOK FOR. MIDNIGHTER BELIEVES IN PEOPLE. IT'S JUST DEEP UNDER LEATHER AND CARBON FIBER.
SO THAT'S WHERE HE HIDES IT. GLAD YOU CHECKED.
I'M RIGHT HERE, PEOPLE. AND I'M TRAINED TO KILL.

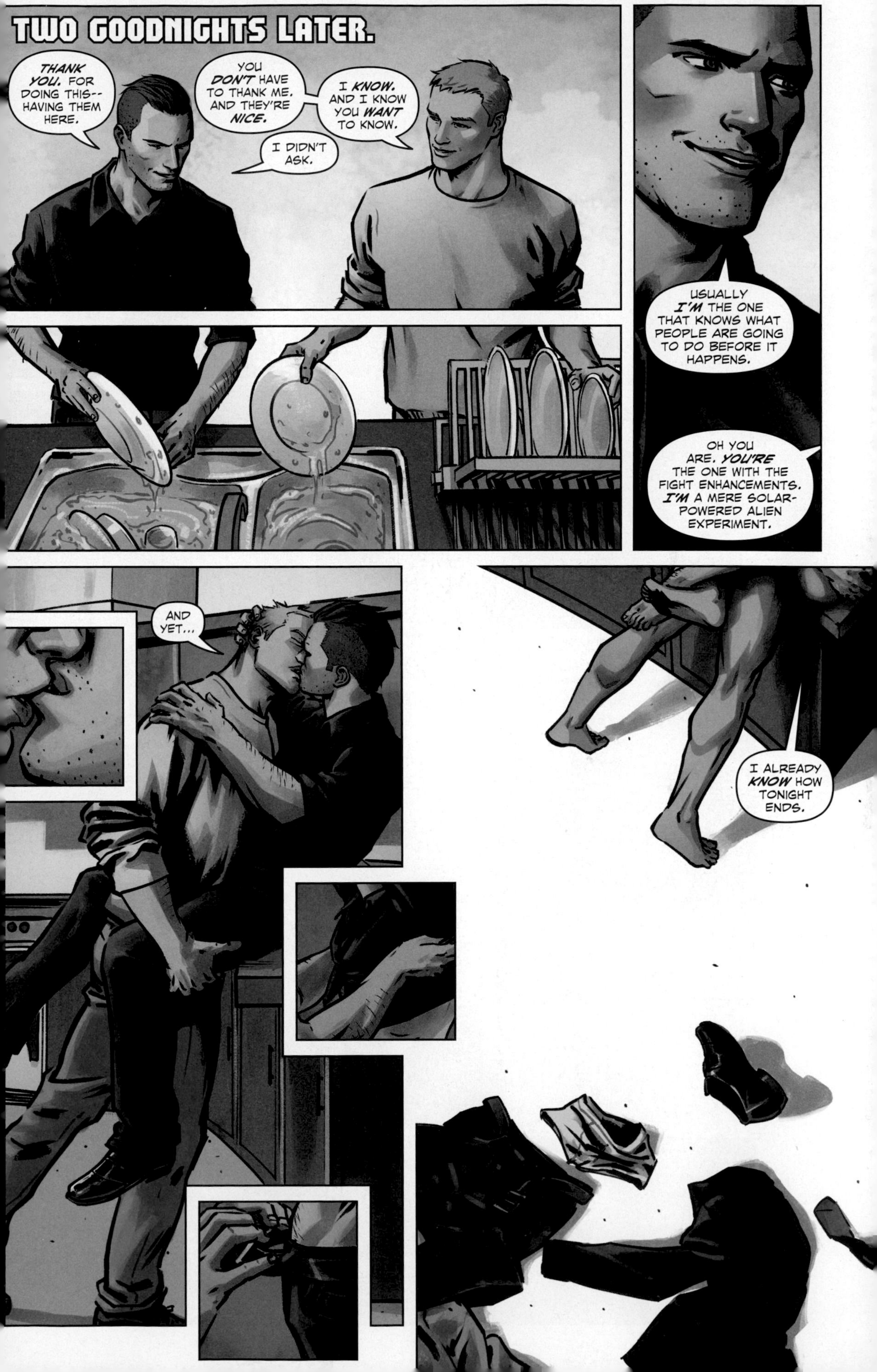
TWO GOODNIGHTS LATER.
THANK YOU. FOR DOING THIS-- HAVING THEM HERE.
YOU DON'T HAVE TO THANK ME. AND THEY'RE NICE.
I KNOW. AND I KNOW YOU WANT TO KNOW.
I DIDN'T ASK.
USUALLY I'M THE ONE THAT KNOWS WHAT PEOPLE ARE GOING TO DO BEFORE IT HAPPENS.
OH YOU ARE. YOU'RE THE ONE WITH THE FIGHT ENHANCEMENTS. I'M A MERE SOLAR-POWERED ALIEN EXPERIMENT.
AND YET...
I ALREADY KNOW HOW TONIGHT ENDS.

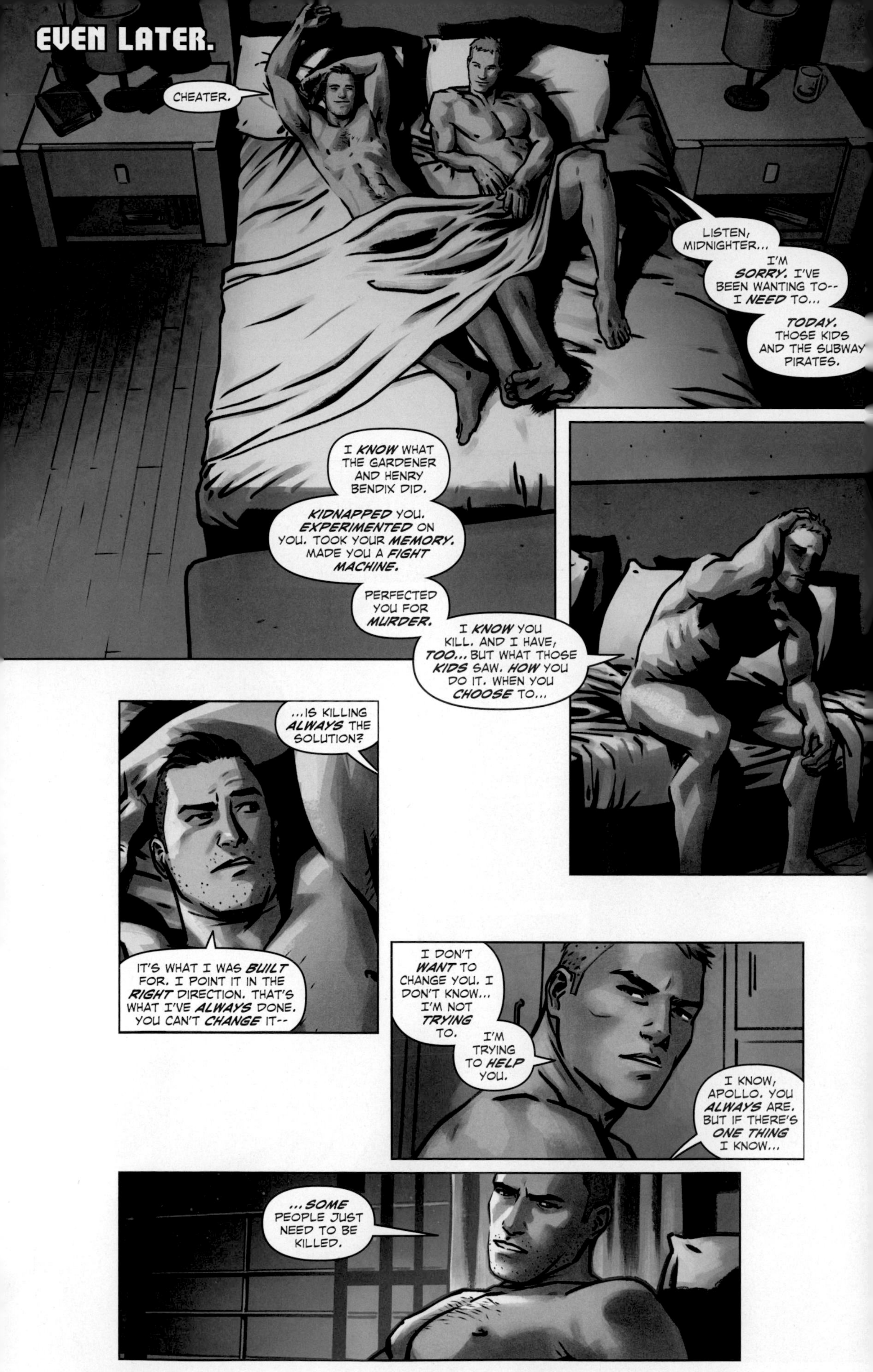
EVEN LATER.
CHEATER.
LISTEN, MIDNIGHTER...
I'M SORRY. I'VE BEEN WANTING TO-- I NEED TO...
TODAY. THOSE KIDS AND THE SUBWAY PIRATES.
I KNOW WHAT THE GARDENER AND HENRY BENDIX DID.
KIDNAPPED YOU. EXPERIMENTED ON YOU. TOOK YOUR MEMORY. MADE YOU A FIGHT MACHINE.
PERFECTED YOU FOR MURDER.
I KNOW YOU KILL. AND I HAVE, TOO... BUT WHAT THOSE KIDS SAW. HOW YOU DO IT. WHEN YOU CHOOSE TO...
...IS KILLING ALWAYS THE SOLUTION?
IT'S WHAT I WAS BUILT FOR. I POINT IT IN THE RIGHT DIRECTION. THAT'S WHAT I'VE ALWAYS DONE. YOU CAN'T CHANGE IT--
I DON'T WANT TO CHANGE YOU. I DON'T KNOW... I'M NOT TRYING TO.
I'M TRYING TO HELP YOU.
I KNOW, APOLLO. YOU ALWAYS ARE. BUT IF THERE'S ONE THING I KNOW...
...SOME PEOPLE JUST NEED TO BE KILLED.

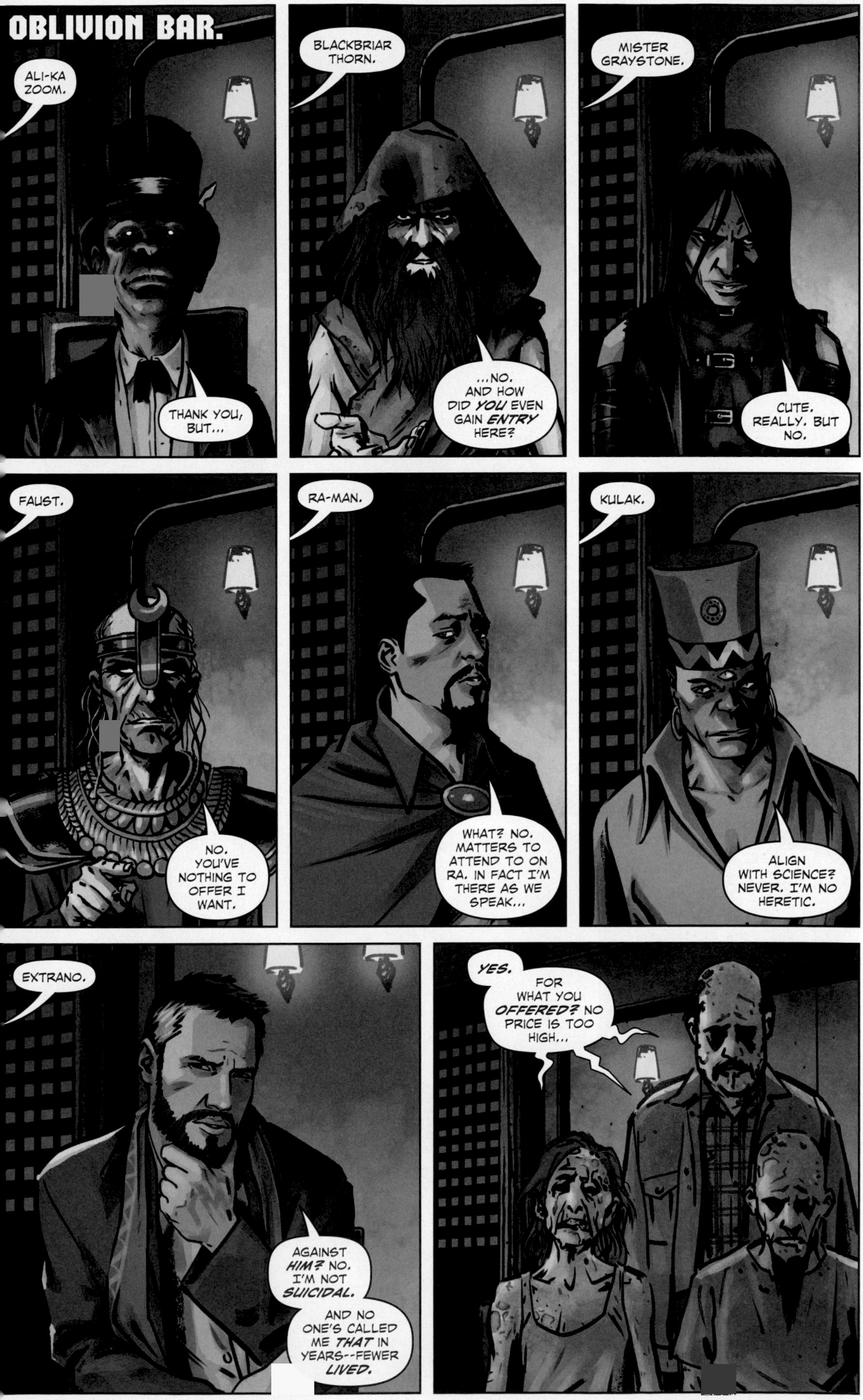
OBLIVION BAR.
ALI-KA ZOOM.
THANK YOU, BUT...
BLACKBRIAR THORN.
...NO. AND HOW DID YOU EVEN GAIN ENTRY HERE?
MISTER GRAYSTONE.
CUTE. REALLY. BUT NO.
FAUST.
NO. YOU'VE NOTHING TO OFFER I WANT.
RA-MAN.
WHAT? NO. MATTERS TO ATTEND TO ON RA. IN FACT I'M THERE AS WE SPEAK...
KULAK.
ALIGN WITH SCIENCE? NEVER. I'M NO HERETIC.
EXTRANO.
AGAINST HIM? NO. I'M NOT SUICIDAL.
AND NO ONE'S CALLED ME THAT IN YEARS--FEWER LIVED.
YES.
FOR WHAT YOU OFFERED? NO PRICE IS TOO HIGH...

MISTER **BENDIX.**

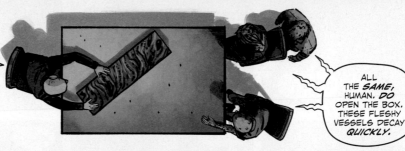

GOOD. AS WE **AGREED**-- THE **PACKAGE.** THE GOTHAM MUSEUM OF ANTIQUITIES MAY BE ABLE TO KEEP **YOU** OUT. BUT **MAGIC** WARDS MEAN **NOTHING** TO MY **TELEPORT DOORS.**

ALL THE **SAME,** HUMAN. **DO** OPEN THE BOX. THESE FLESHY VESSELS DECAY **QUICKLY.**

AT **MY** PACE-- I THINK YOU'LL SEE **EVERYTHING** IS IN ORDER.

CRAFTED BY A MAD **TEXAS RANGER** FROM THE STEEL OF A HALO, THE BONES OF SAINTS, INFERNAL GEMSTONES...

...THE **ACE** OF **WINCHESTERS.**

YOU'RE **WELCOME.** NOW THE **LORDS OF THE GUN** CONTROL THE **ONLY** POSSIBLE INSTRUMENT OF THEIR **UNDOING.**

AND SO WE **DO,** HENRY BENDIX.

BARGAINS ARE THE LOW LANGUAGE OF HELL. WE WILL **KEEP** THIS ONE.

MIDNIGHTER AND **APOLLO** WILL SUFFER.

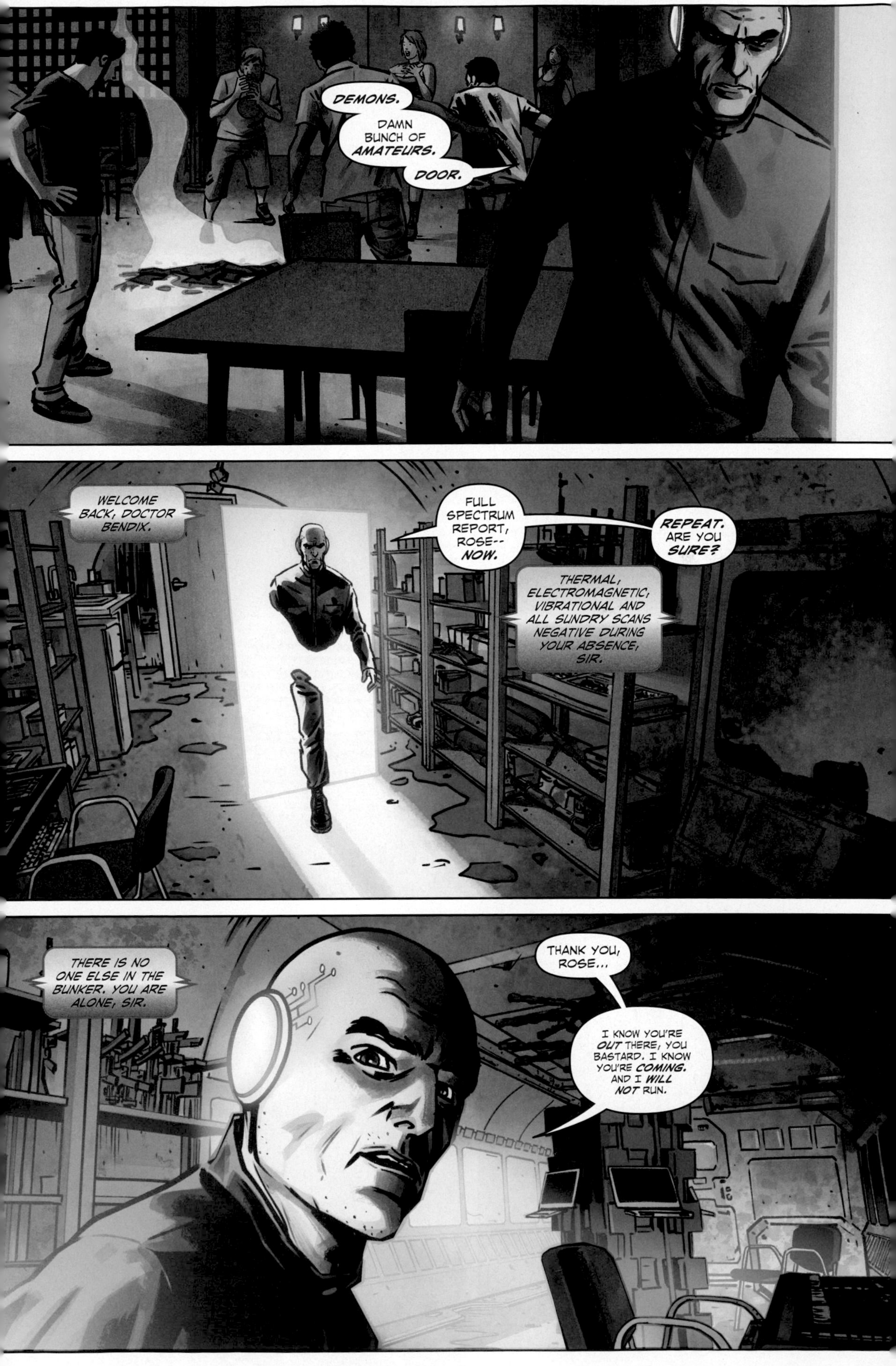
DEMONS.
DAMN BUNCH OF AMATEURS.
DOOR.
WELCOME BACK, DOCTOR BENDIX.
FULL SPECTRUM REPORT, ROSE-- NOW.
REPEAT. ARE YOU SURE?
THERMAL, ELECTROMAGNETIC, VIBRATIONAL AND ALL SUNDRY SCANS NEGATIVE DURING YOUR ABSENCE, SIR.
THERE IS NO ONE ELSE IN THE BUNKER. YOU ARE ALONE, SIR.
THANK YOU, ROSE...
I KNOW YOU'RE OUT THERE, YOU BASTARD. I KNOW YOU'RE COMING. AND I WILL NOT RUN.

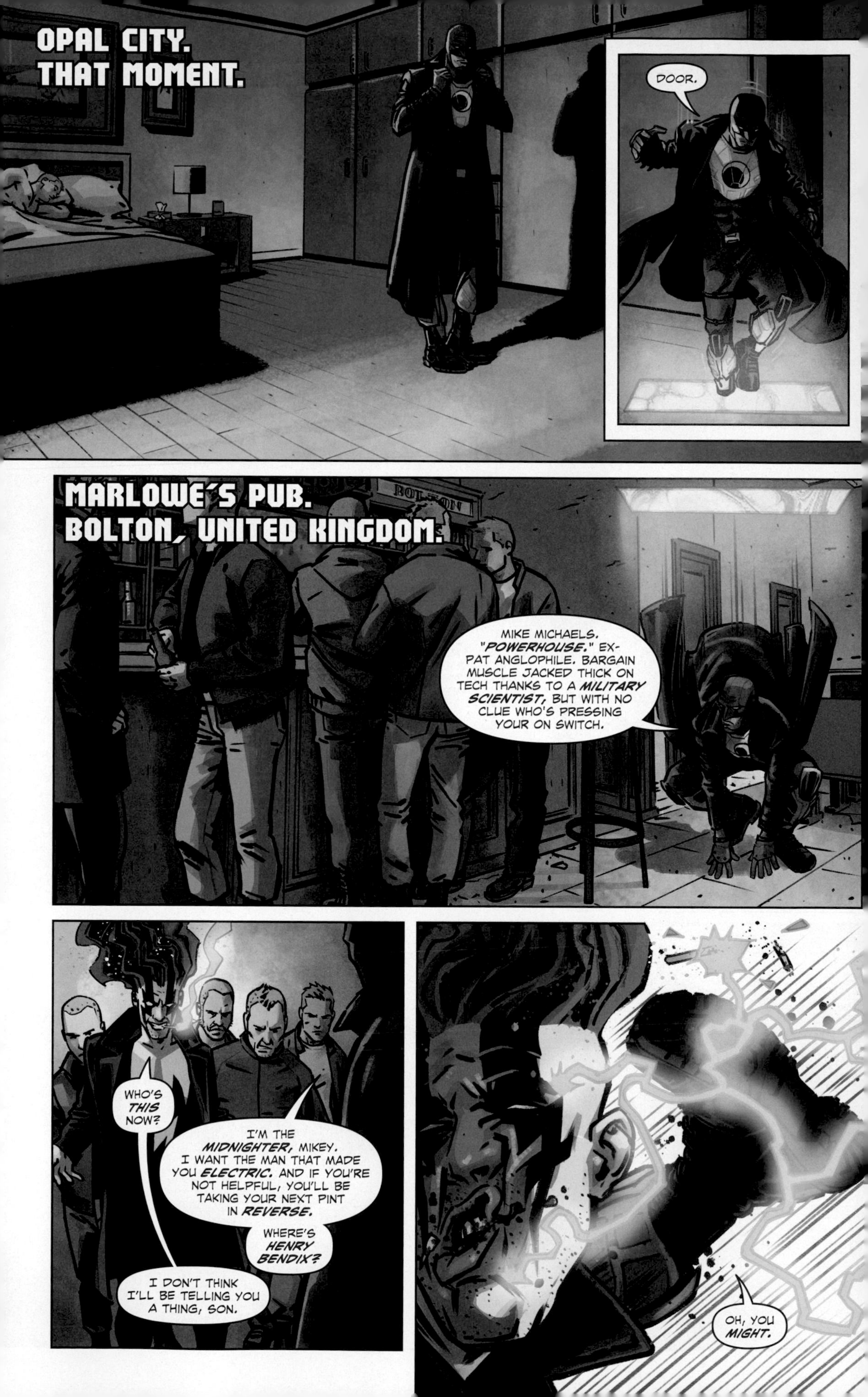
OPAL CITY.
THAT MOMENT.
DOOR.
MARLOWE'S PUB.
BOLTON, UNITED KINGDOM.
MIKE MICHAELS. "POWERHOUSE." EX-PAT ANGLOPHILE. BARGAIN MUSCLE JACKED THICK ON TECH THANKS TO A MILITARY SCIENTIST, BUT WITH NO CLUE WHO'S PRESSING YOUR ON SWITCH.
WHO'S THIS NOW?
I'M THE MIDNIGHTER, MIKEY. I WANT THE MAN THAT MADE YOU ELECTRIC. AND IF YOU'RE NOT HELPFUL, YOU'LL BE TAKING YOUR NEXT PINT IN REVERSE.
WHERE'S HENRY BENDIX?
I DON'T THINK I'LL BE TELLING YOU A THING, SON.
OH, YOU MIGHT.

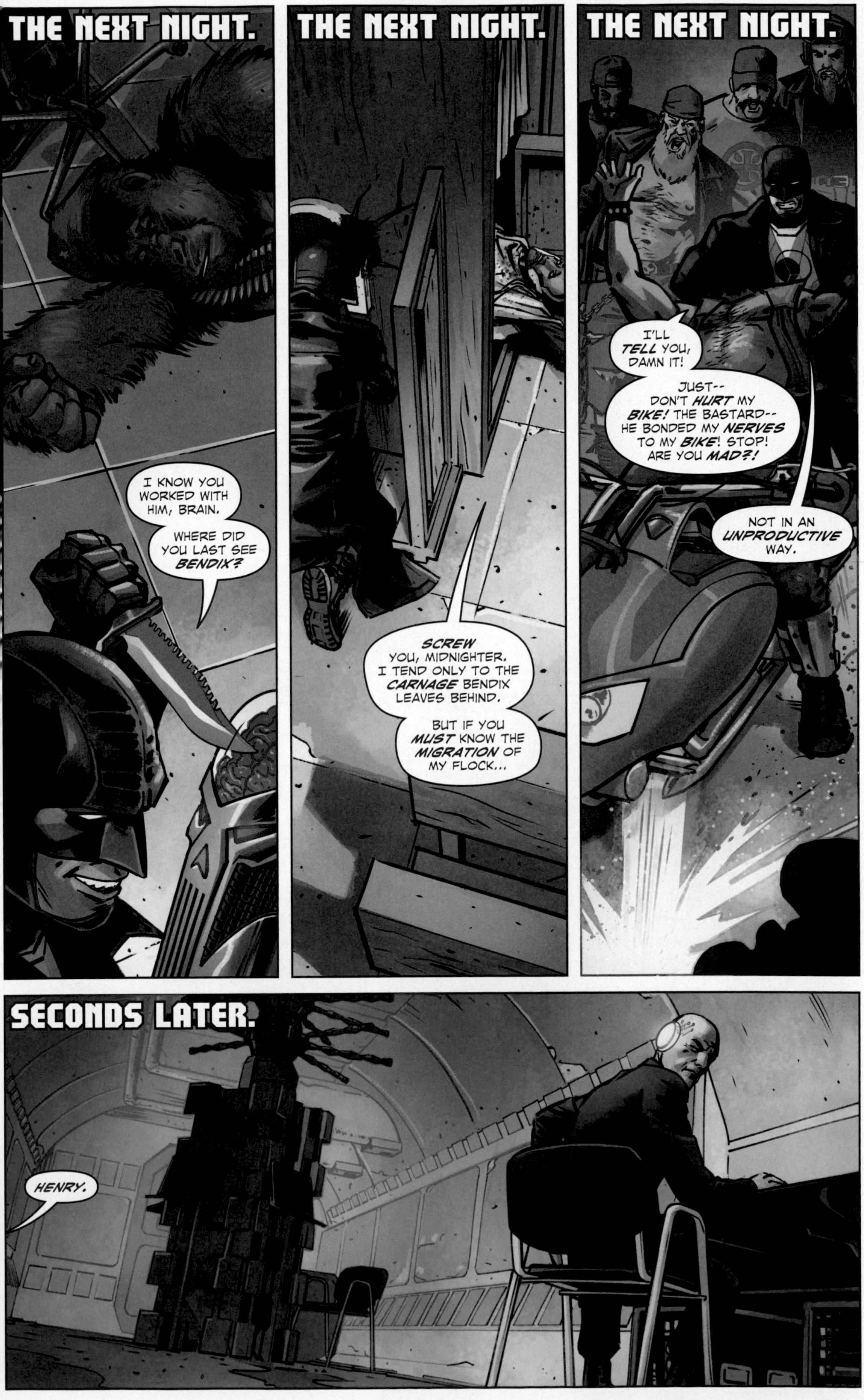
THE NEXT NIGHT.
I KNOW YOU WORKED WITH HIM, BRAIN.
WHERE DID YOU LAST SEE BENDIX?
THE NEXT NIGHT.
SCREW YOU, MIDNIGHTER. I TEND ONLY TO THE CARNAGE BENDIX LEAVES BEHIND.
BUT IF YOU MUST KNOW THE MIGRATION OF MY FLOCK...
THE NEXT NIGHT.
I'LL TELL YOU, DAMN IT!
JUST-- DON'T HURT MY BIKE! THE BASTARD-- HE BONDED MY NERVES TO MY BIKE! STOP! ARE YOU MAD?!
NOT IN AN UNPRODUCTIVE WAY.
SECONDS LATER.
HENRY.

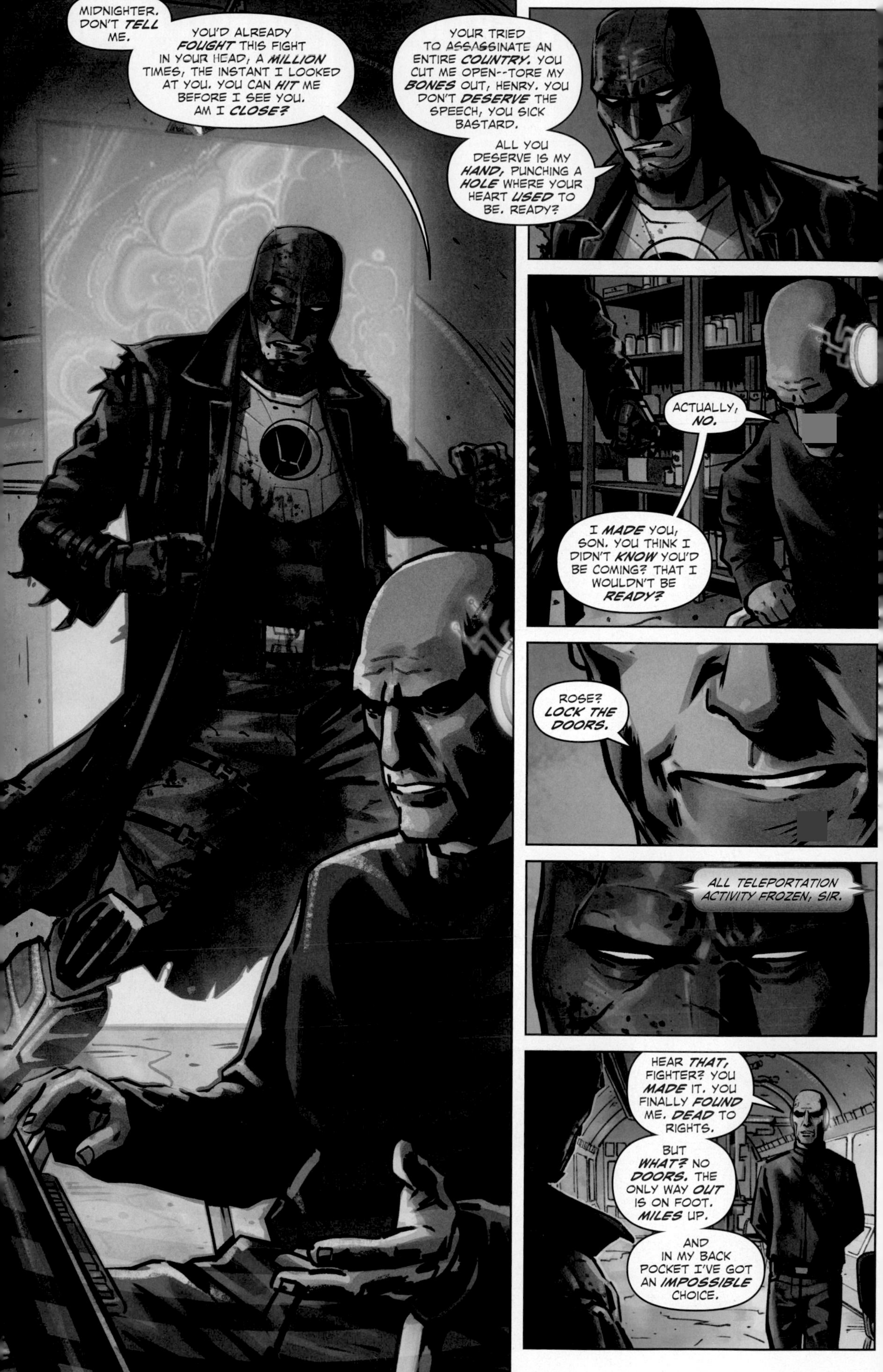
MIDNIGHTER. DON'T TELL ME.
YOU'D ALREADY FOUGHT THIS FIGHT IN YOUR HEAD, A MILLION TIMES, THE INSTANT I LOOKED AT YOU. YOU CAN HIT ME BEFORE I SEE YOU. AM I CLOSE?
YOUR TRIED TO ASSASSINATE AN ENTIRE COUNTRY. YOU CUT ME OPEN--TORE MY BONES OUT, HENRY. YOU DON'T DESERVE THE SPEECH, YOU SICK BASTARD.
ALL YOU DESERVE IS MY HAND, PUNCHING A HOLE WHERE YOUR HEART USED TO BE. READY?
ACTUALLY, NO.
I MADE YOU, SON. YOU THINK I DIDN'T KNOW YOU'D BE COMING? THAT I WOULDN'T BE READY?
ROSE? LOCK THE DOORS.
ALL TELEPORTATION ACTIVITY FROZEN, SIR.
HEAR THAT, FIGHTER? YOU MADE IT. YOU FINALLY FOUND ME. DEAD TO RIGHTS.
BUT WHAT? NO DOORS. THE ONLY WAY OUT IS ON FOOT. MILES UP.
AND IN MY BACK POCKET I'VE GOT AN IMPOSSIBLE CHOICE.

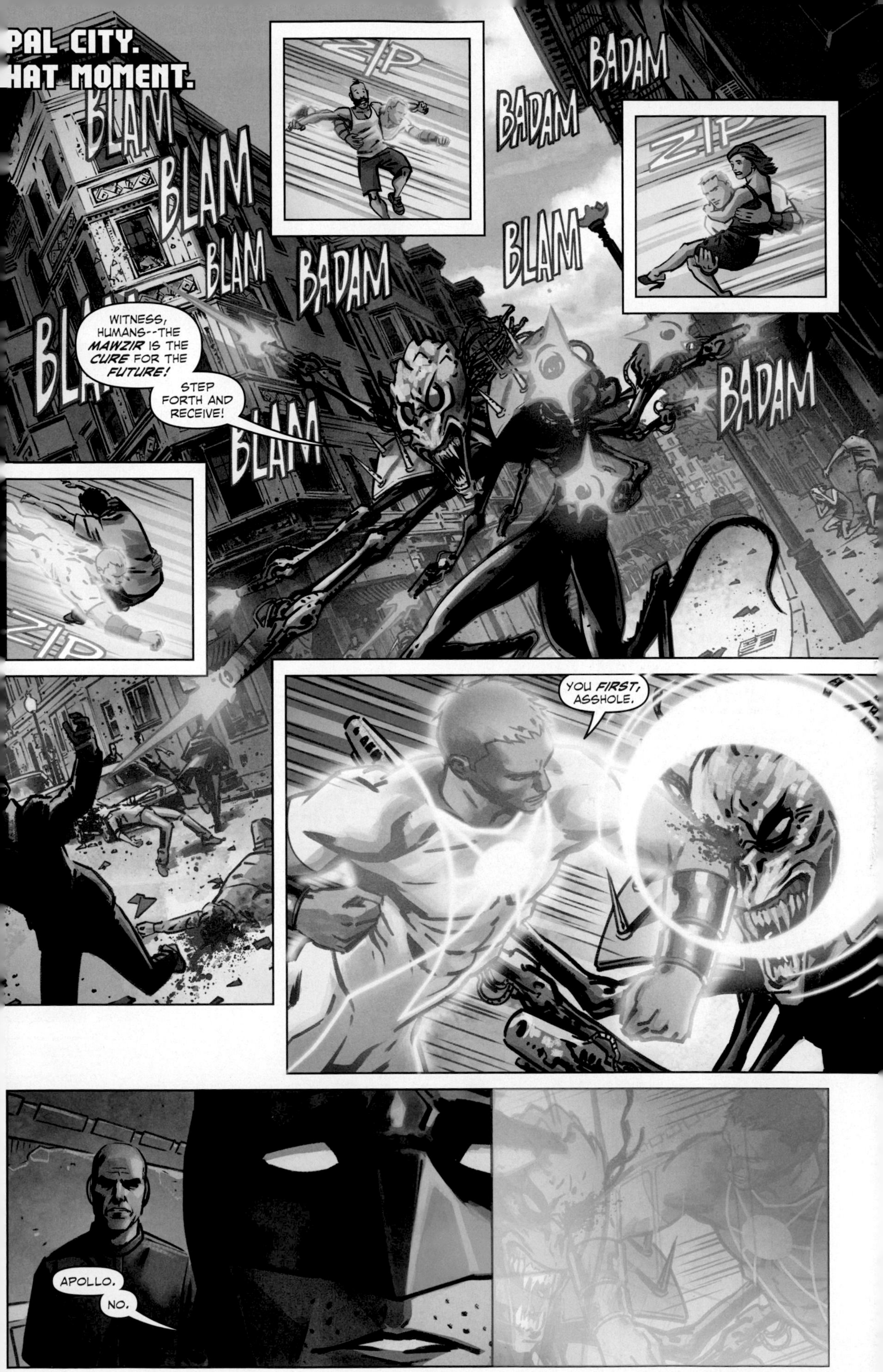
PAL CITY.
HAT MOMENT.
ZIP
BLAM
BLAM
BLAM
BADAM
BADAM
BADAM
ZIP
BLAM
BLAM
WITNESS, HUMANS--THE MAWZIR IS THE CURE FOR THE FUTURE!
STEP FORTH AND RECEIVE!
BADAM
BLAM
ZIP
YOU FIRST, ASSHOLE.
APOLLO.
NO.

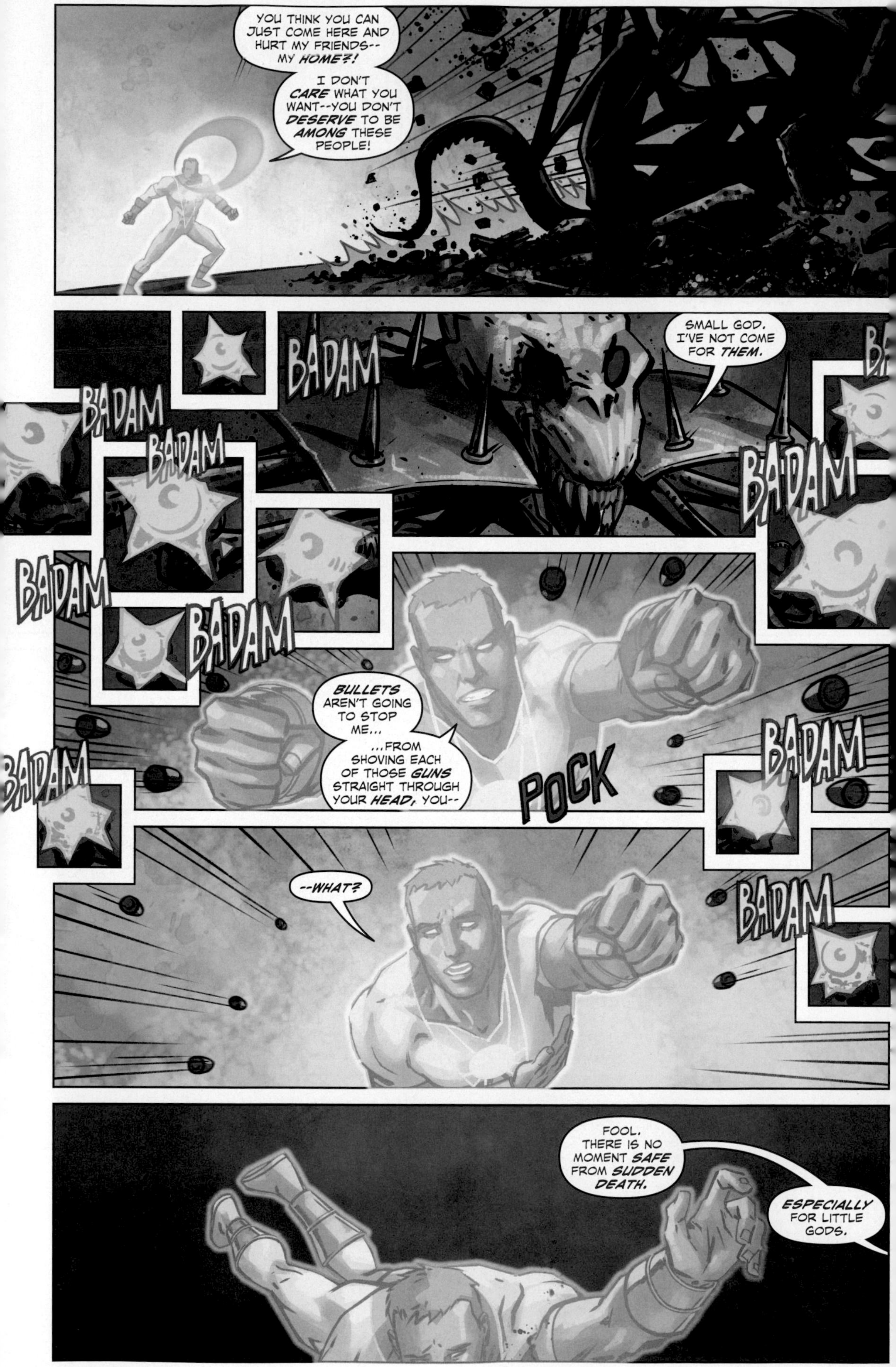
YOU THINK YOU CAN JUST COME HERE AND HURT MY FRIENDS-- MY HOME?!
I DON'T CARE WHAT YOU WANT--YOU DON'T DESERVE TO BE AMONG THESE PEOPLE!
BADAM
SMALL GOD. I'VE NOT COME FOR THEM.
BADAM
BADAM
BADAM
BADAM
BADAM
BULLETS AREN'T GOING TO STOP ME...
...FROM SHOVING EACH OF THOSE GUNS STRAIGHT THROUGH YOUR HEAD, YOU--
POCK
BADAM
BADAM
BADAM
--WHAT?
FOOL. THERE IS NO MOMENT SAFE FROM SUDDEN DEATH.
ESPECIALLY FOR LITTLE GODS.

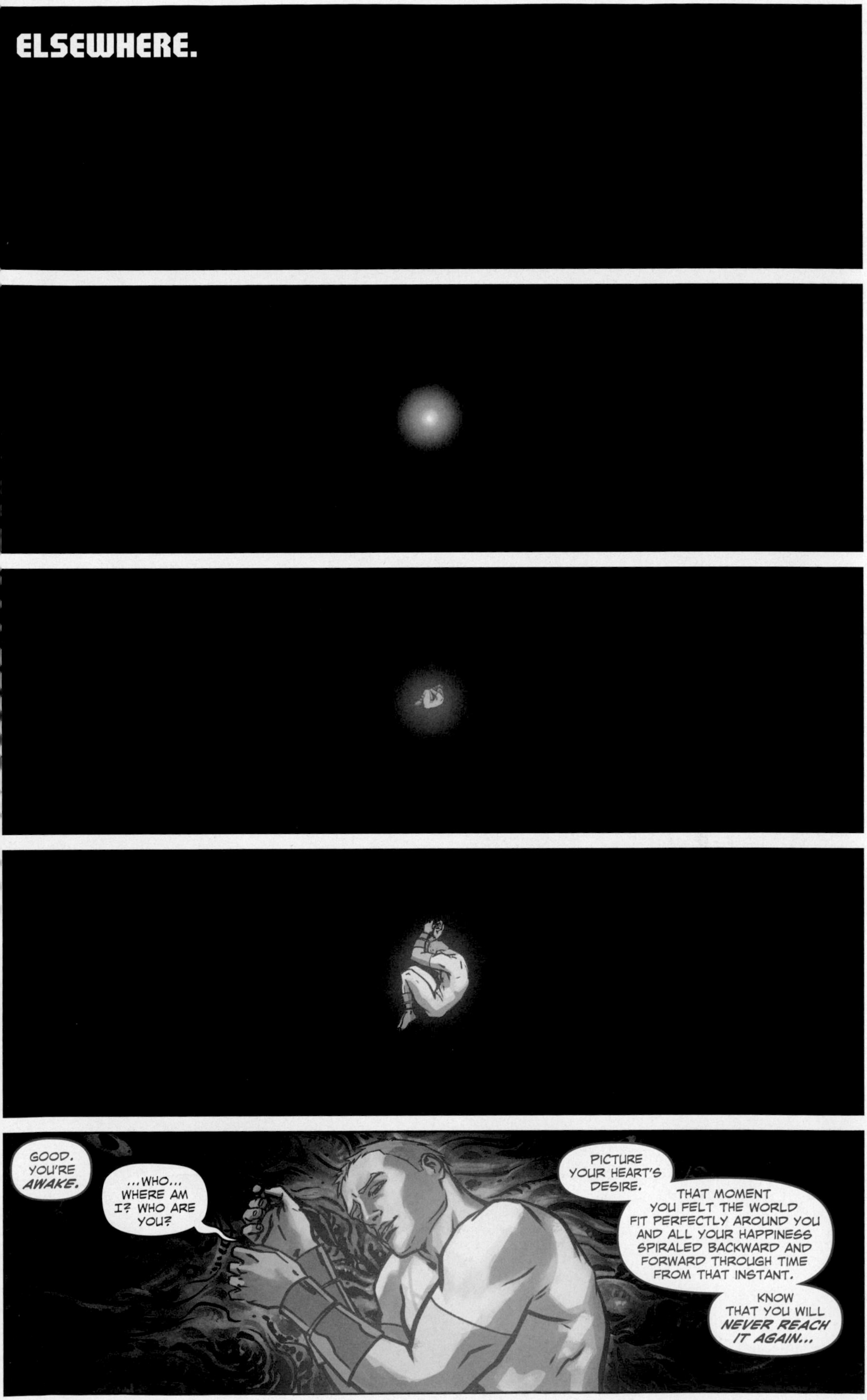
ELSEWHERE.
GOOD. YOU'RE *AWAKE.*
...WHO... WHERE AM I? WHO ARE YOU?
PICTURE YOUR HEART'S DESIRE.
THAT MOMENT YOU FELT THE WORLD FIT PERFECTLY AROUND YOU AND ALL YOUR HAPPINESS SPIRALED BACKWARD AND FORWARD THROUGH TIME FROM THAT INSTANT.
KNOW THAT YOU WILL *NEVER REACH IT AGAIN...*

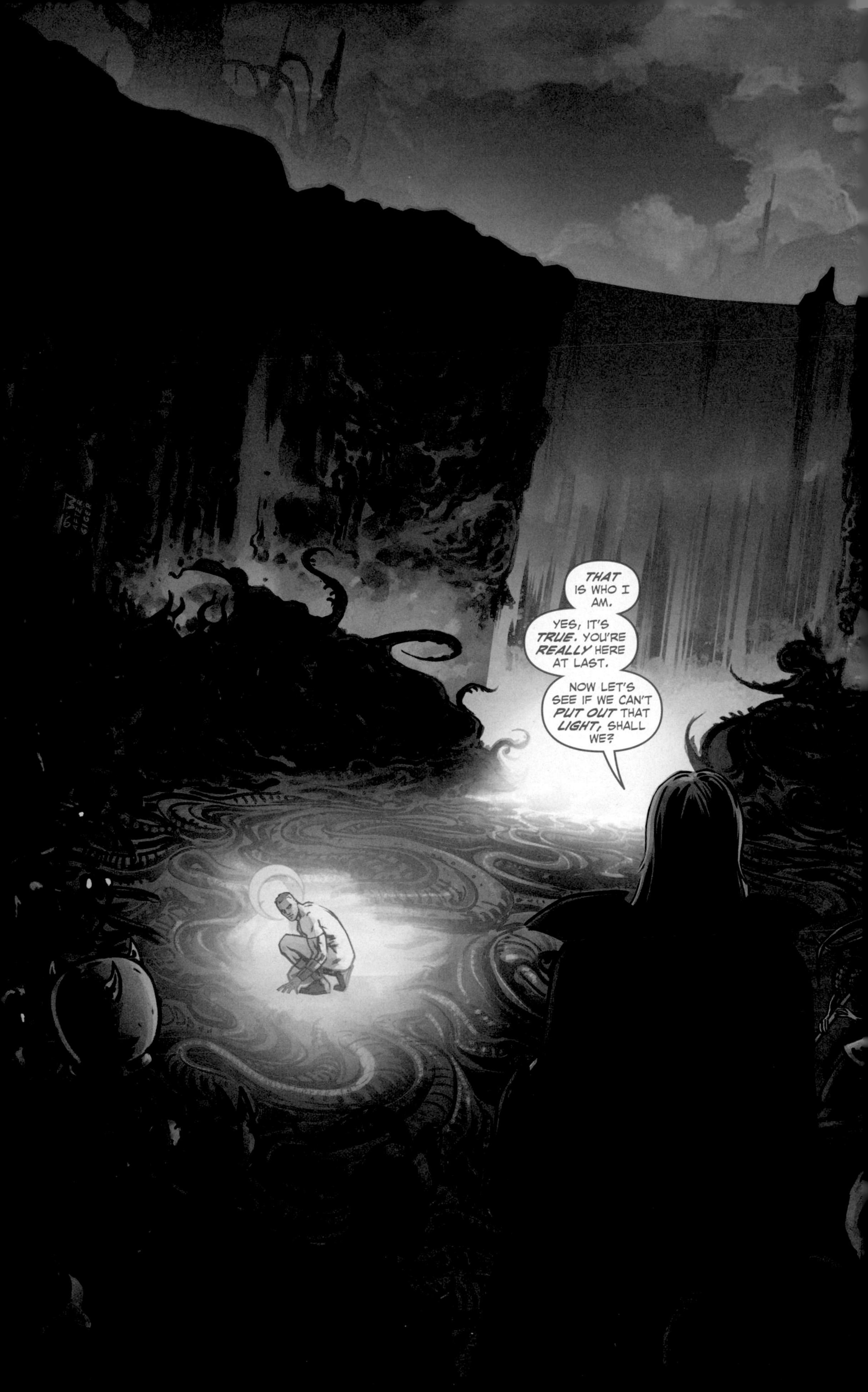
THAT IS WHO I AM.
YES, IT'S TRUE. YOU'RE REALLY HERE AT LAST.
NOW LET'S SEE IF WE CAN'T PUT OUT THAT LIGHT, SHALL WE?

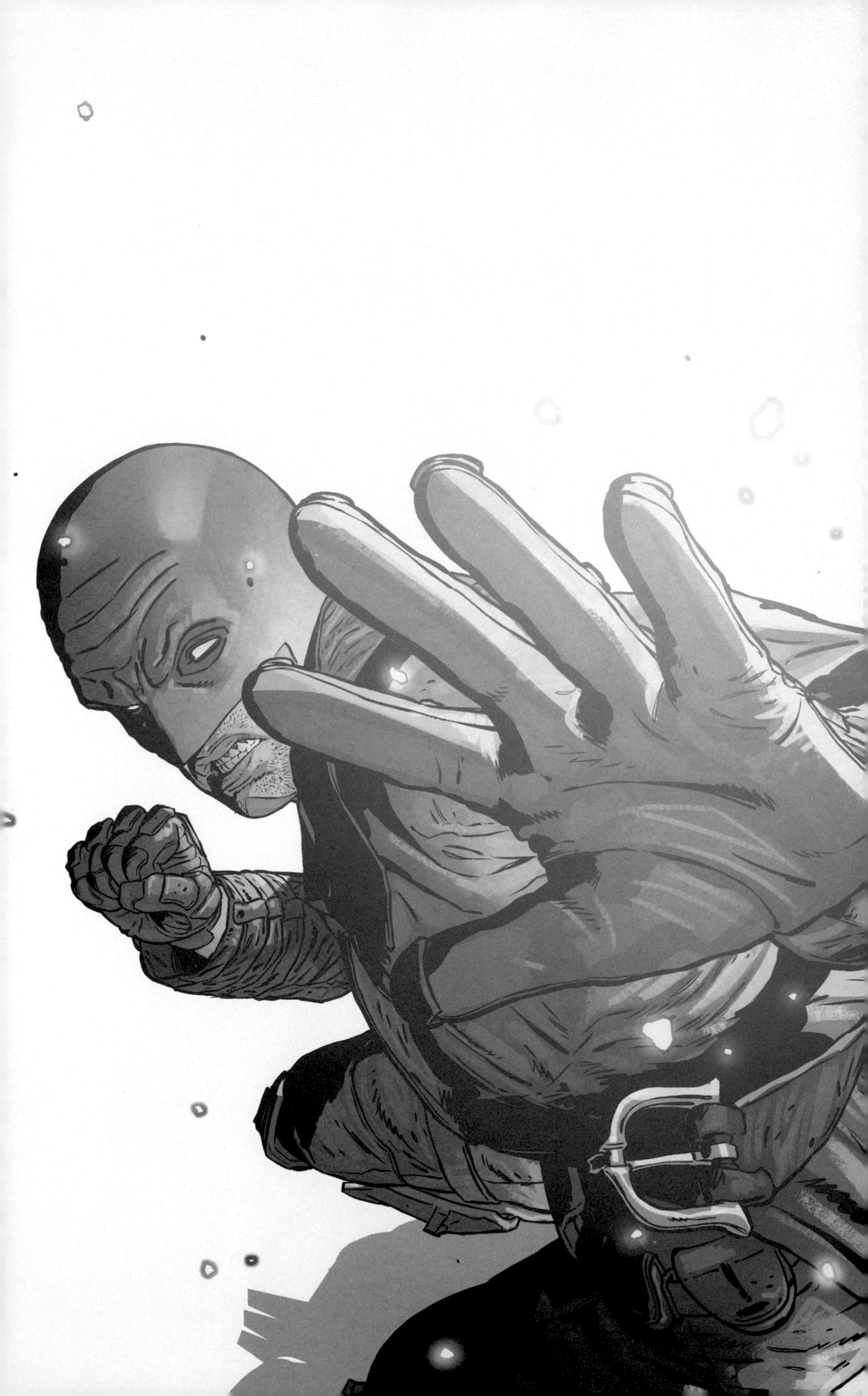

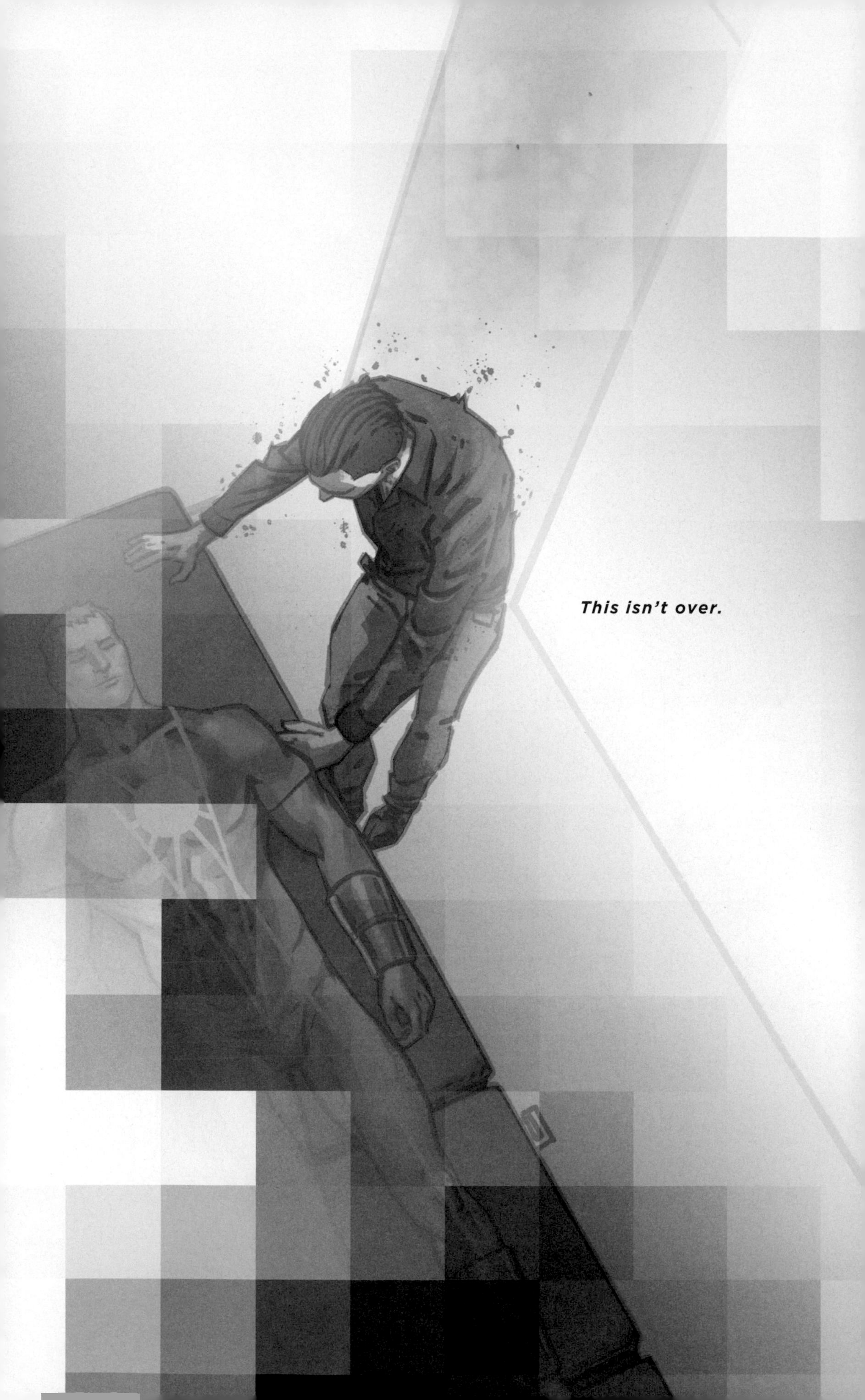
This isn't over.

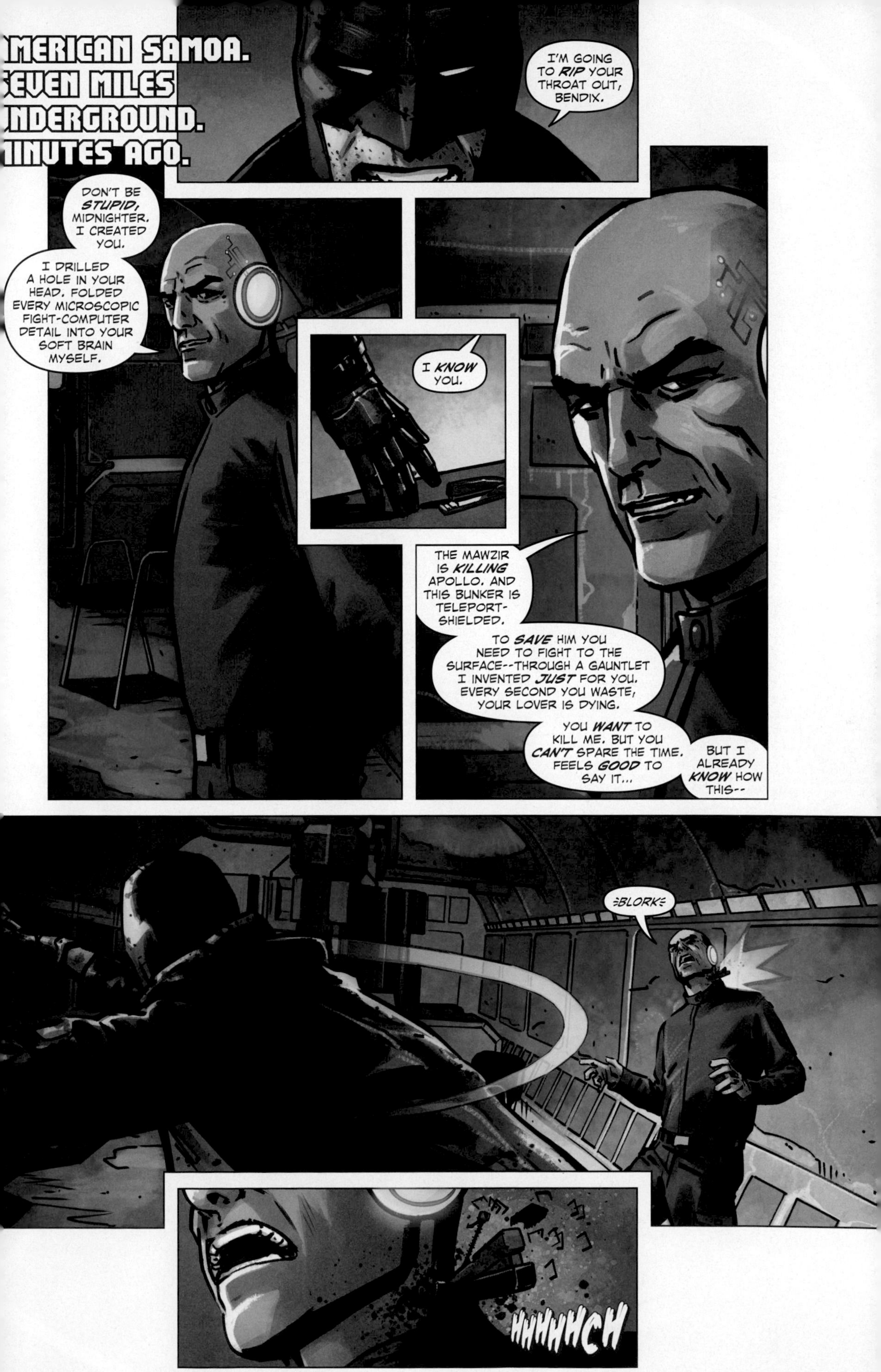
MERICAN SAMOA.
EVEN MILES
NDERGROUND.
IINUTES AGO.
I'M GOING TO RIP YOUR THROAT OUT, BENDIX.
DON'T BE STUPID, MIDNIGHTER. I CREATED YOU.
I DRILLED A HOLE IN YOUR HEAD. FOLDED EVERY MICROSCOPIC FIGHT-COMPUTER DETAIL INTO YOUR SOFT BRAIN MYSELF.
I KNOW YOU.
THE MAWZIR IS KILLING APOLLO. AND THIS BUNKER IS TELEPORT-SHIELDED.
TO SAVE HIM YOU NEED TO FIGHT TO THE SURFACE--THROUGH A GAUNTLET I INVENTED JUST FOR YOU. EVERY SECOND YOU WASTE, YOUR LOVER IS DYING.
YOU WANT TO KILL ME. BUT YOU CAN'T SPARE THE TIME. FEELS GOOD TO SAY IT...
BUT I ALREADY KNOW HOW THIS--
=BLORK=
HHHHHCH

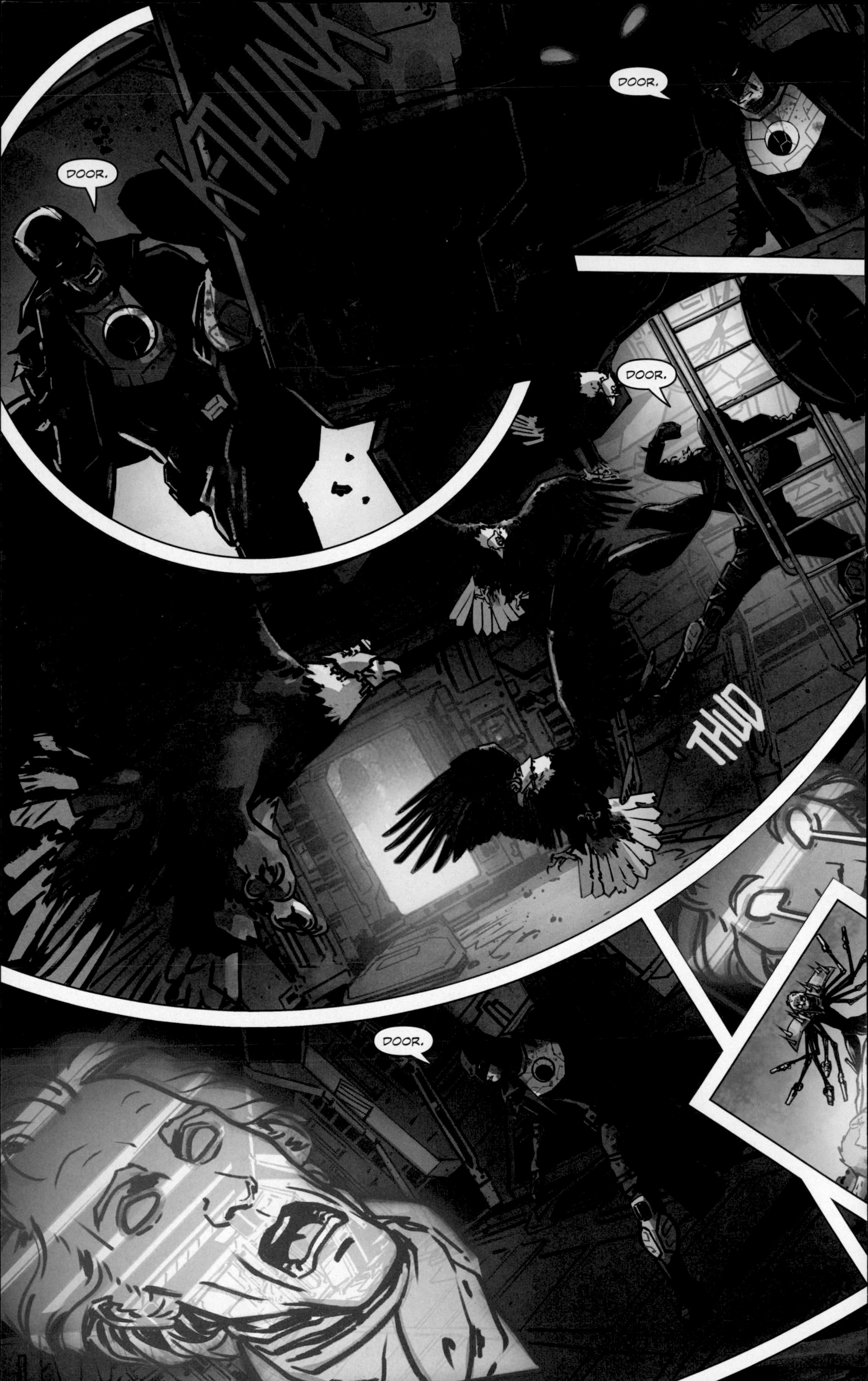
DOOR.
KTHUNK
DOOR.
DOOR.
THUD
DOOR.

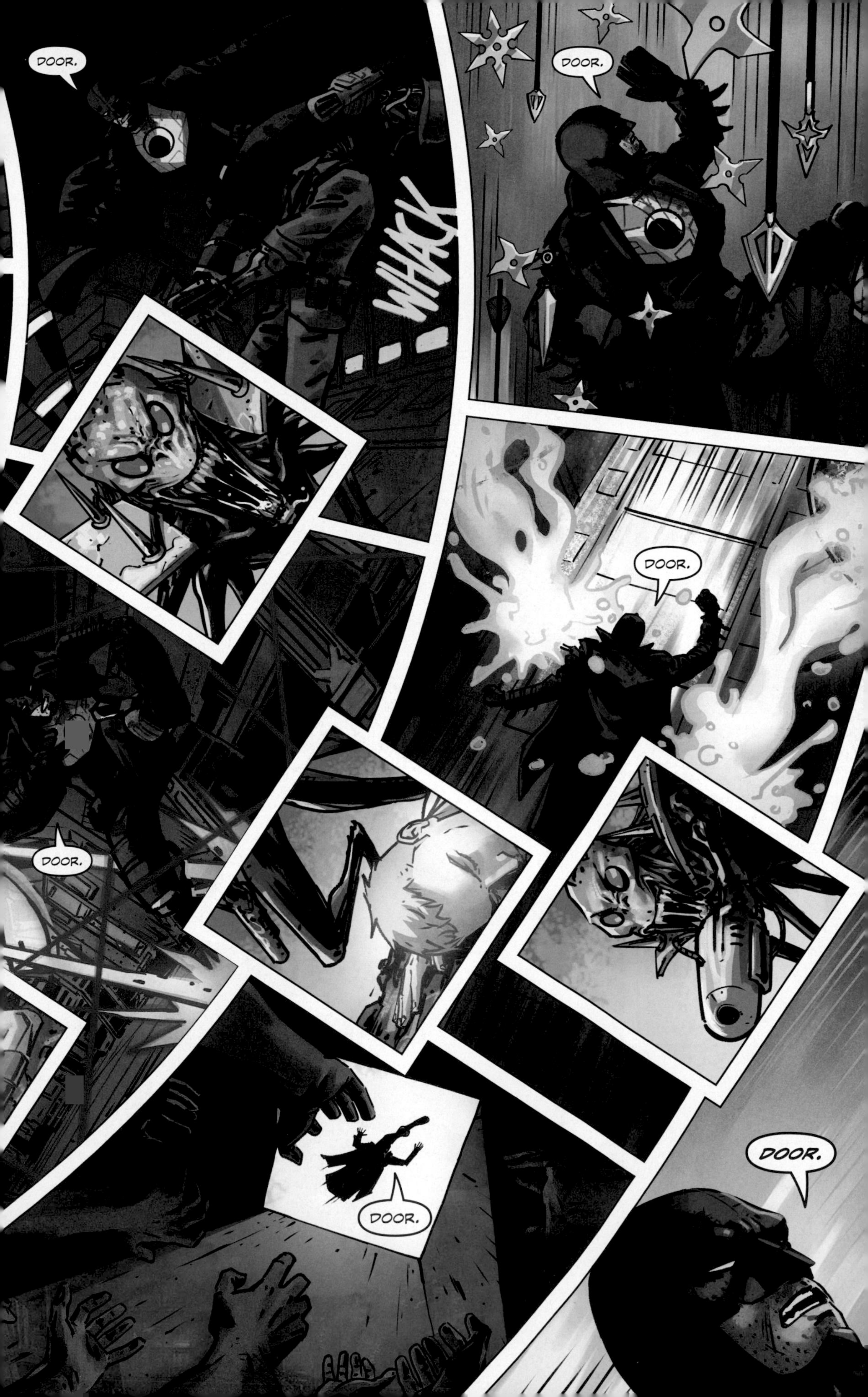
DOOR.
WHACK
DOOR.
DOOR.
DOOR.
DOOR.
DOOR.

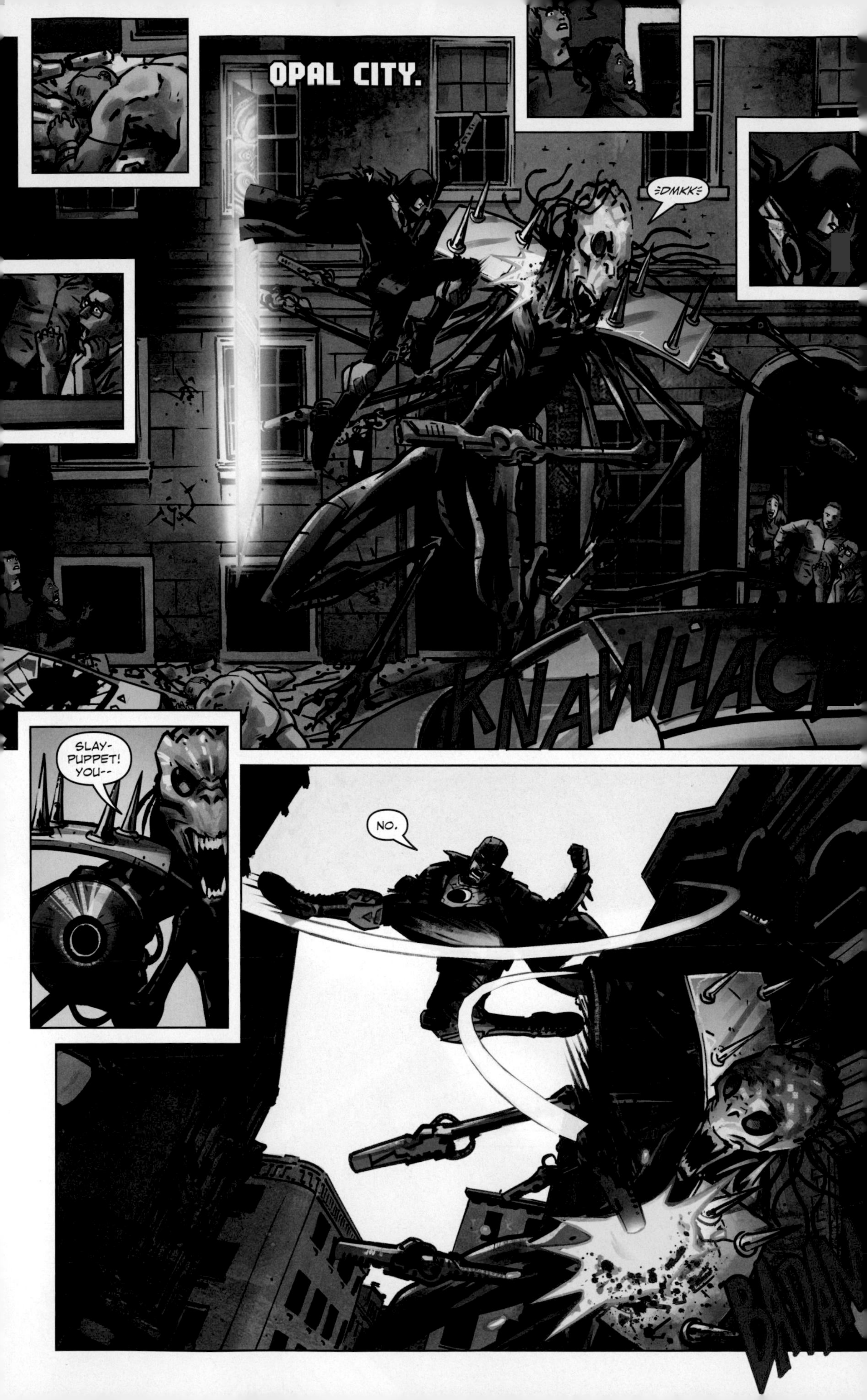
OPAL CITY.
DMKK
KNAWHACK
SLAY-PUPPET! YOU--
NO.

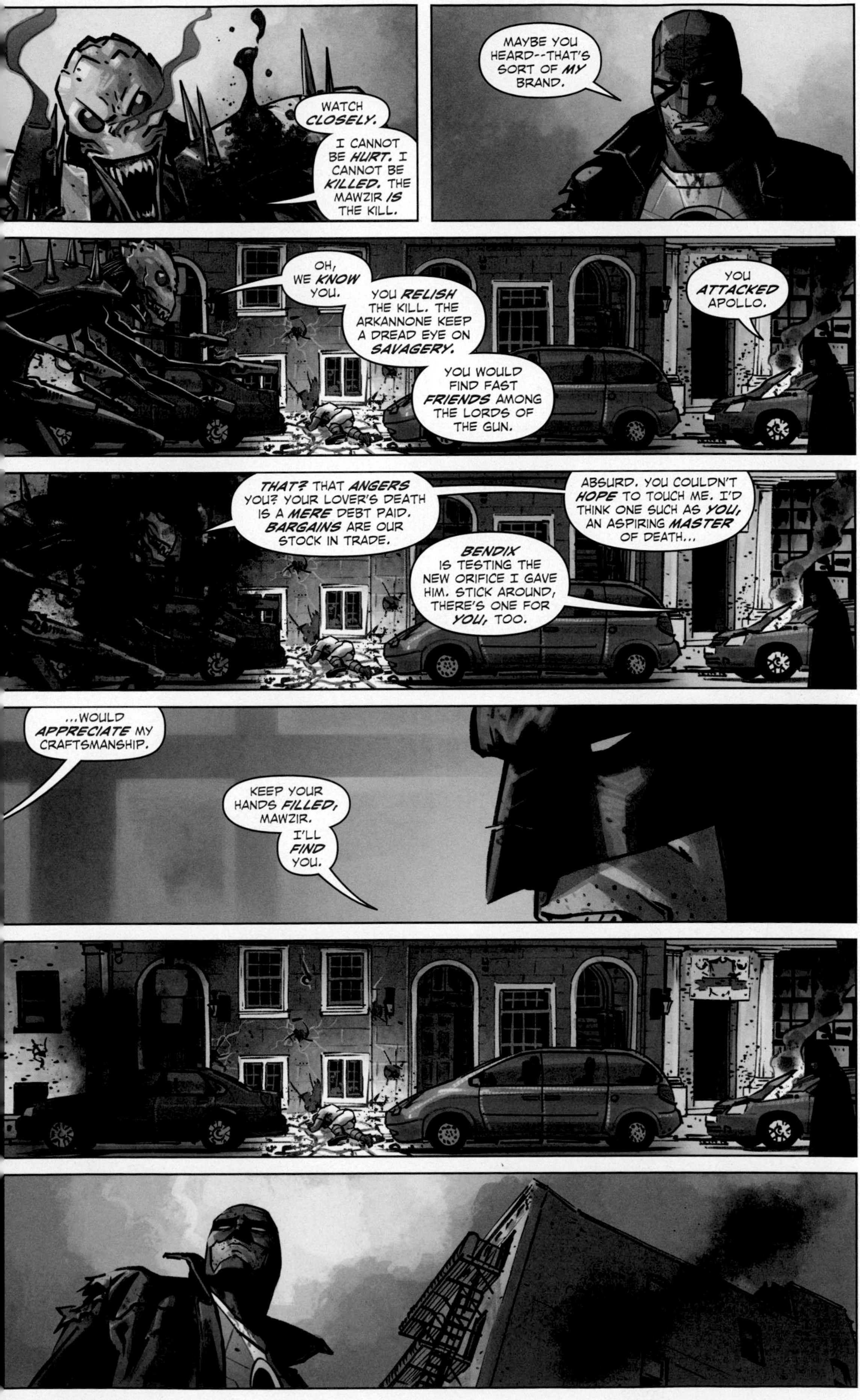
WATCH CLOSELY.
I CANNOT BE HURT. I CANNOT BE KILLED. THE MAWZIR IS THE KILL.
MAYBE YOU HEARD--THAT'S SORT OF MY BRAND.
OH, WE KNOW YOU.
YOU RELISH THE KILL. THE ARKANNONE KEEP A DREAD EYE ON SAVAGERY.
YOU WOULD FIND FAST FRIENDS AMONG THE LORDS OF THE GUN.
YOU ATTACKED APOLLO.
THAT? THAT ANGERS YOU? YOUR LOVER'S DEATH IS A MERE DEBT PAID. BARGAINS ARE OUR STOCK IN TRADE.
BENDIX IS TESTING THE NEW ORIFICE I GAVE HIM. STICK AROUND, THERE'S ONE FOR YOU, TOO.
ABSURD. YOU COULDN'T HOPE TO TOUCH ME. I'D THINK ONE SUCH AS YOU, AN ASPIRING MASTER OF DEATH...
...WOULD APPRECIATE MY CRAFTSMANSHIP.
KEEP YOUR HANDS FILLED, MAWZIR.
I'LL FIND YOU.

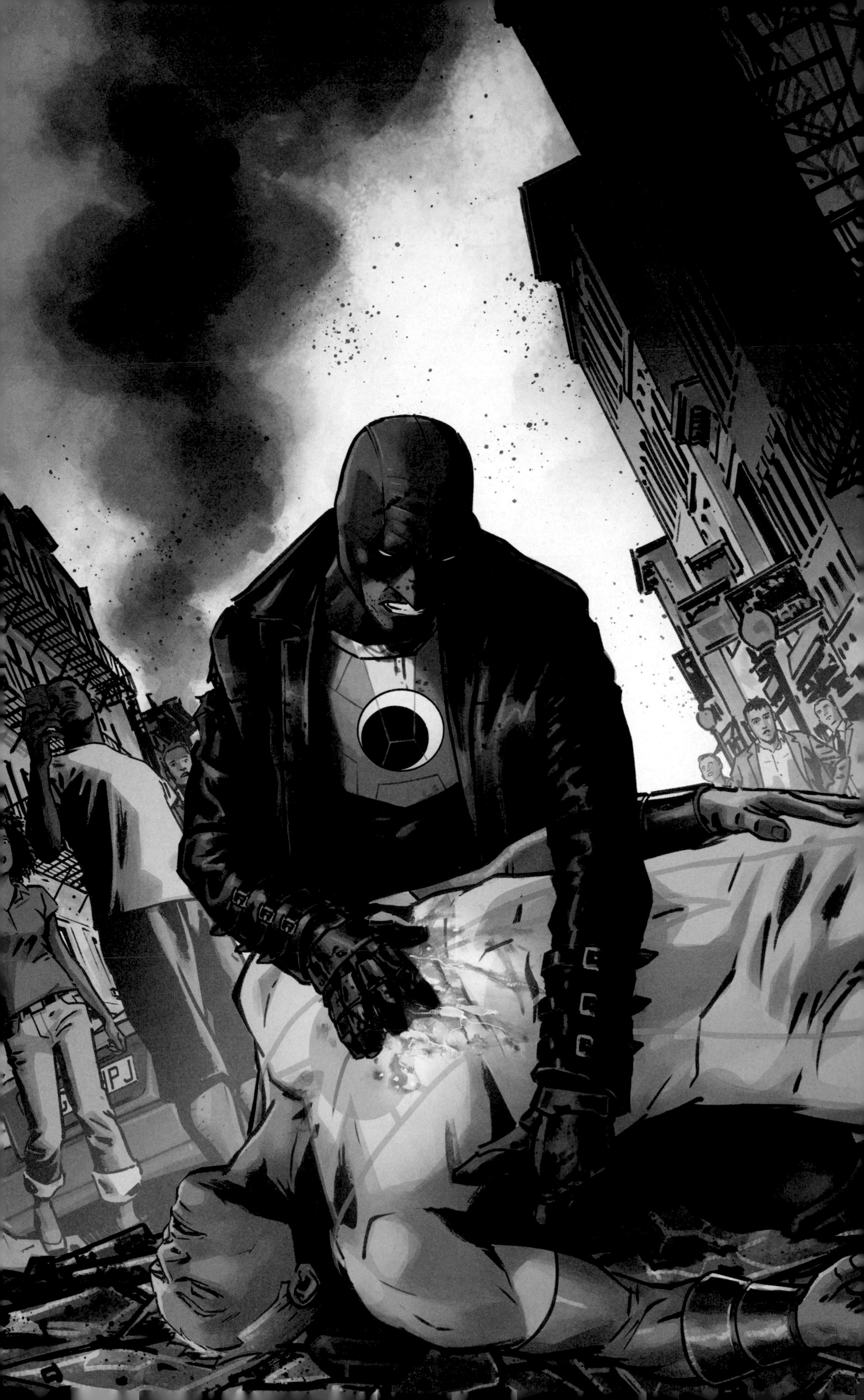

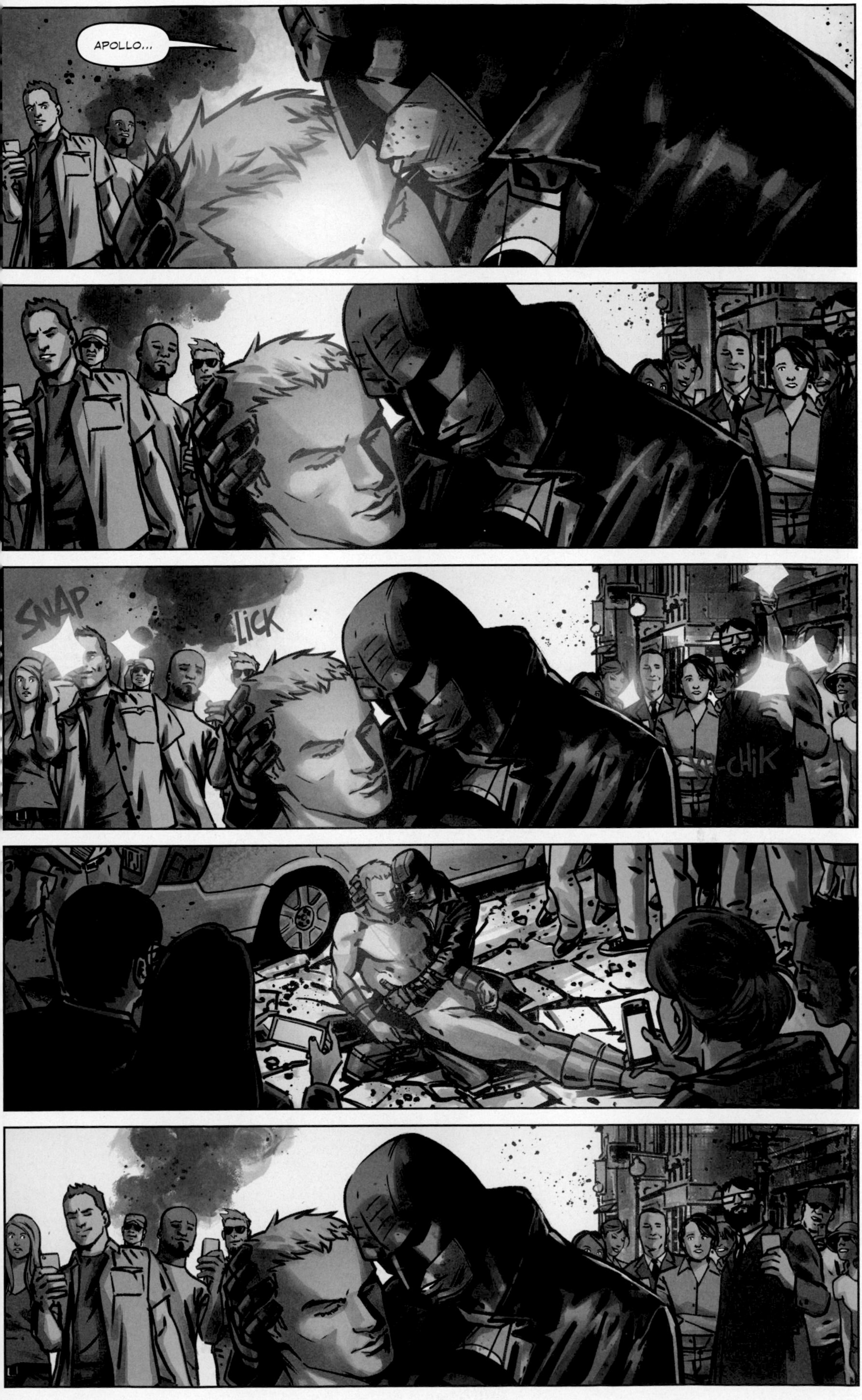
APOLLO...
SNAP
LICK
CHIK

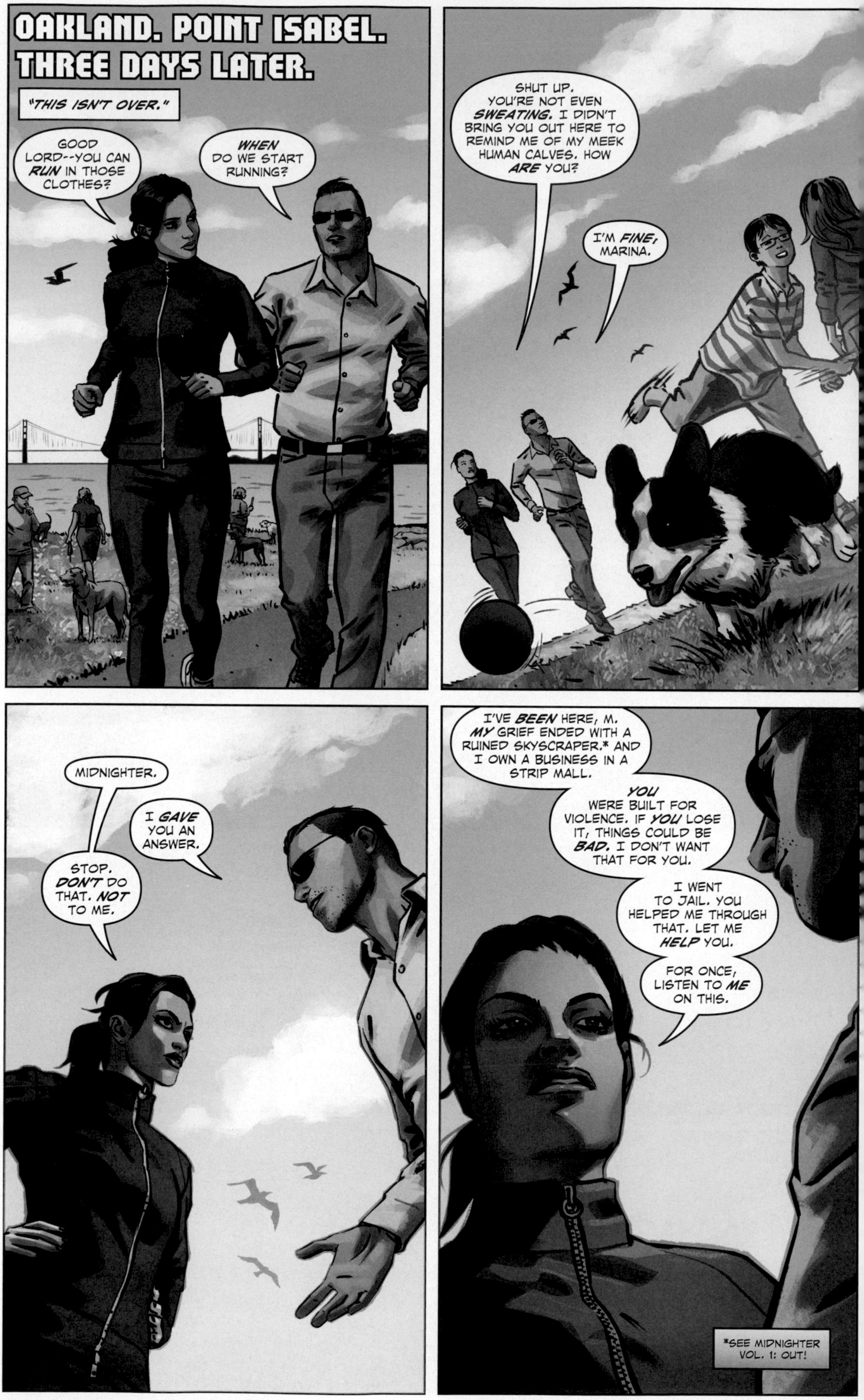
OAKLAND. POINT ISABEL. THREE DAYS LATER.
"THIS ISN'T OVER."
GOOD LORD--YOU CAN RUN IN THOSE CLOTHES?
WHEN DO WE START RUNNING?
SHUT UP. YOU'RE NOT EVEN SWEATING. I DIDN'T BRING YOU OUT HERE TO REMIND ME OF MY MEEK HUMAN CALVES. HOW ARE YOU?
I'M FINE, MARINA.
MIDNIGHTER.
I GAVE YOU AN ANSWER.
STOP. DON'T DO THAT. NOT TO ME.
I'VE BEEN HERE, M. MY GRIEF ENDED WITH A RUINED SKYSCRAPER.* AND I OWN A BUSINESS IN A STRIP MALL.
YOU WERE BUILT FOR VIOLENCE. IF YOU LOSE IT, THINGS COULD BE BAD. I DON'T WANT THAT FOR YOU.
I WENT TO JAIL. YOU HELPED ME THROUGH THAT. LET ME HELP YOU.
FOR ONCE, LISTEN TO ME ON THIS.
*SEE MIDNIGHTER VOL. 1: OUT!

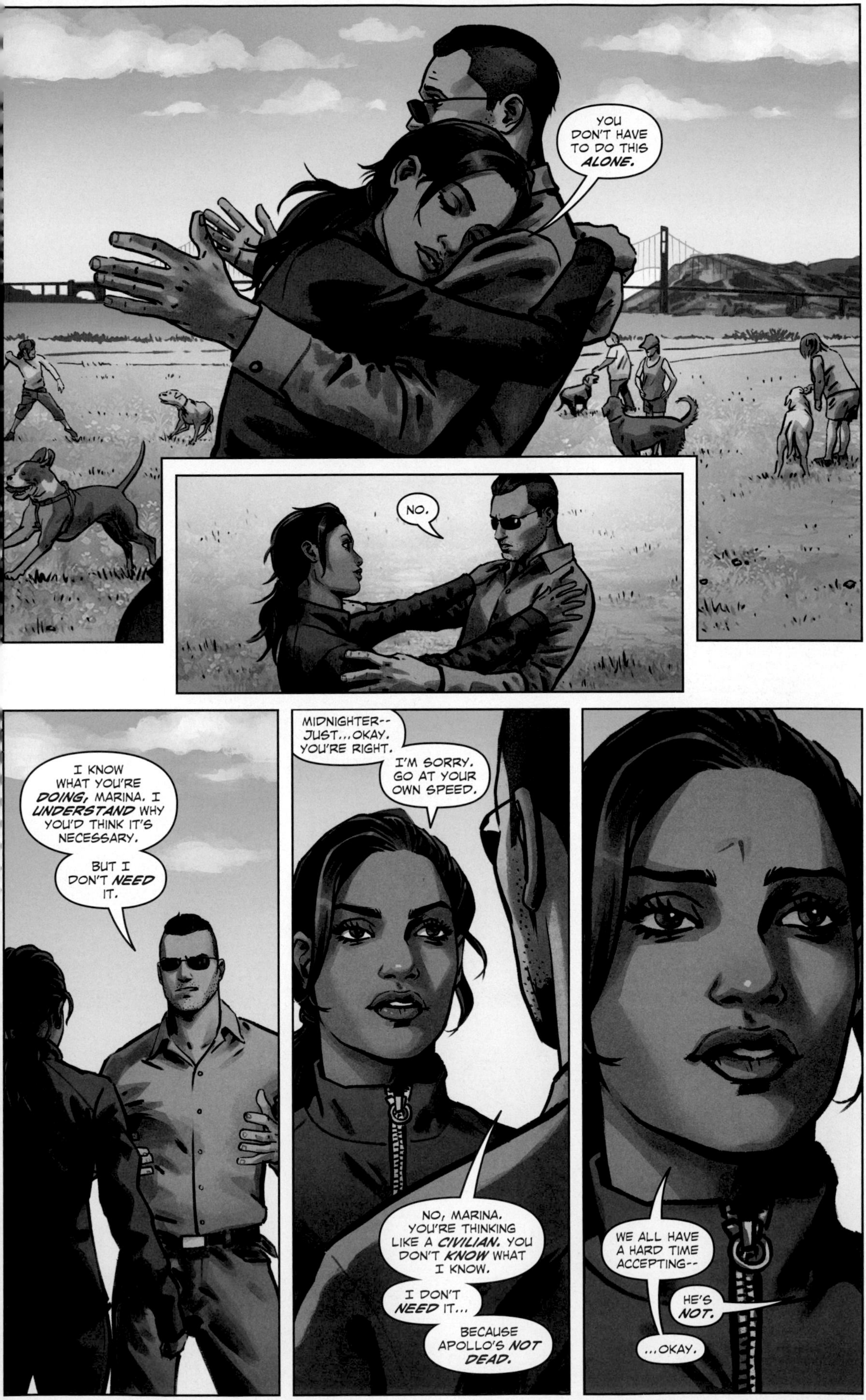
YOU DON'T HAVE TO DO THIS ALONE.
NO.
I KNOW WHAT YOU'RE DOING, MARINA. I UNDERSTAND WHY YOU'D THINK IT'S NECESSARY.
BUT I DON'T NEED IT.
MIDNIGHTER-- JUST...OKAY. YOU'RE RIGHT.
I'M SORRY. GO AT YOUR OWN SPEED.
NO, MARINA. YOU'RE THINKING LIKE A CIVILIAN. YOU DON'T KNOW WHAT I KNOW.
I DON'T NEED IT...
BECAUSE APOLLO'S NOT DEAD.
WE ALL HAVE A HARD TIME ACCEPTING--
HE'S NOT.
...OKAY.

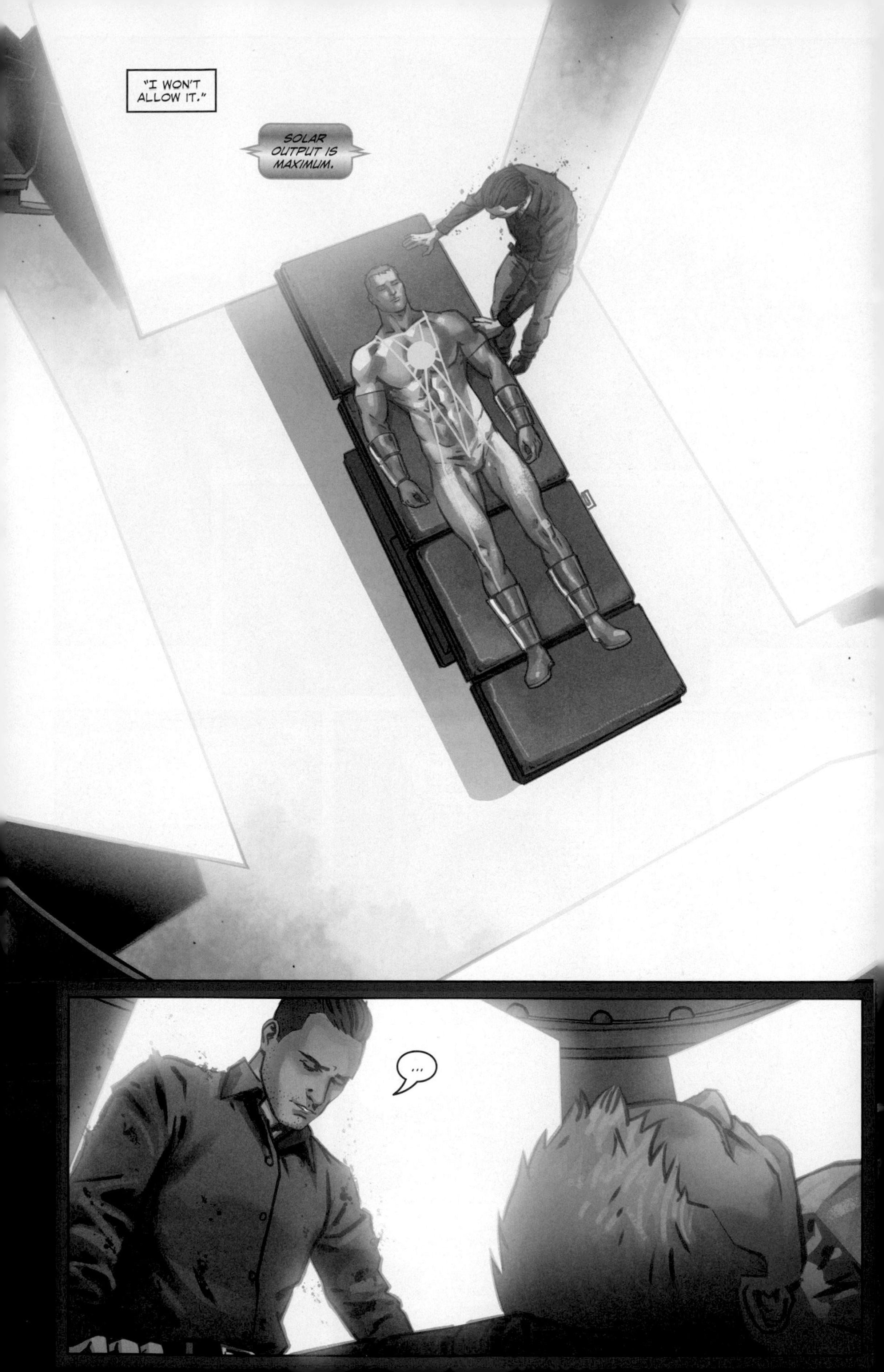
"I WON'T ALLOW IT."
SOLAR OUTPUT IS MAXIMUM.
...

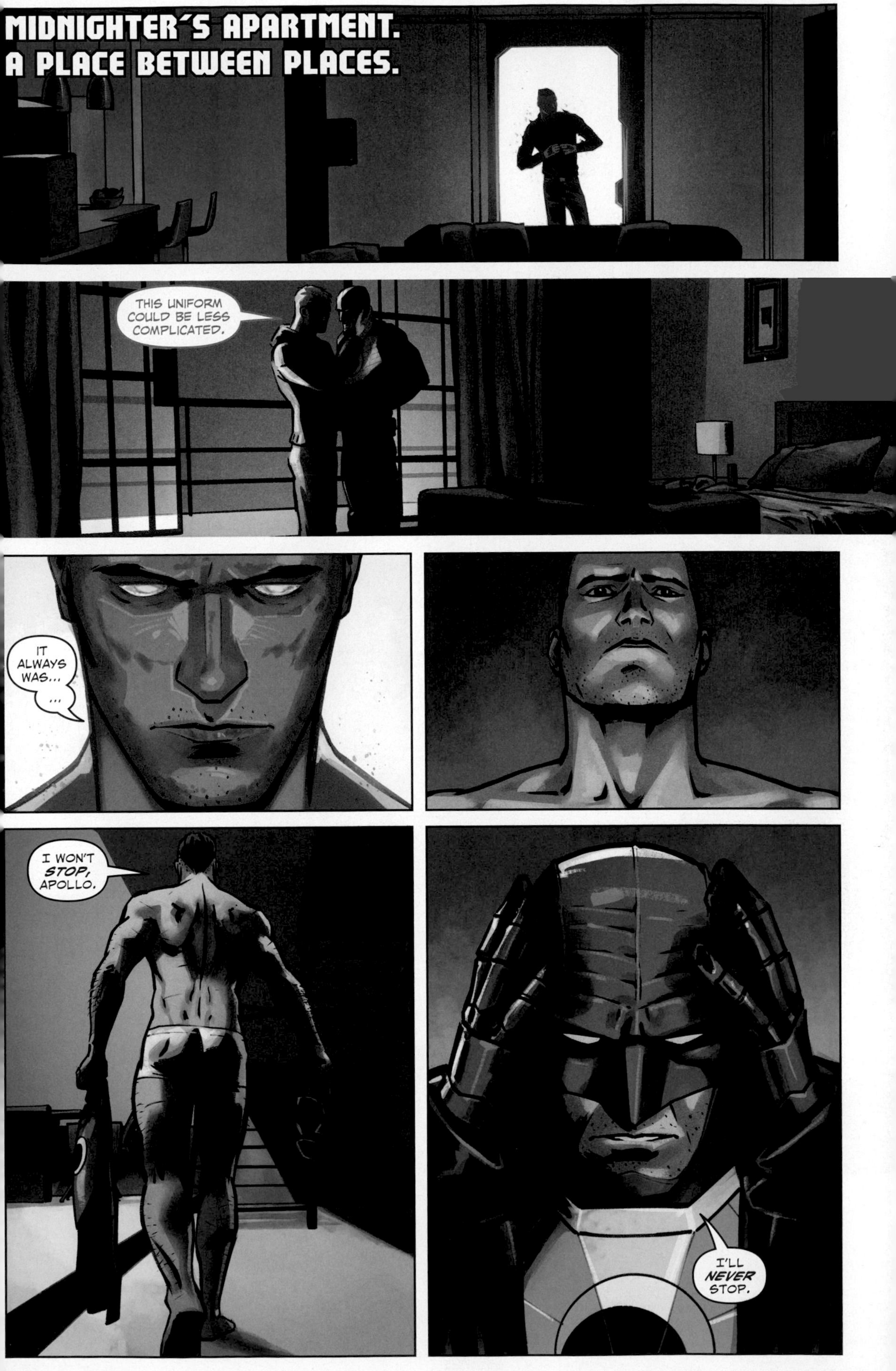
MIDNIGHTER'S APARTMENT.
A PLACE BETWEEN PLACES.
THIS UNIFORM COULD BE LESS COMPLICATED.
IT ALWAYS WAS...
...
I WON'T *STOP,* APOLLO.
I'LL *NEVER* STOP.

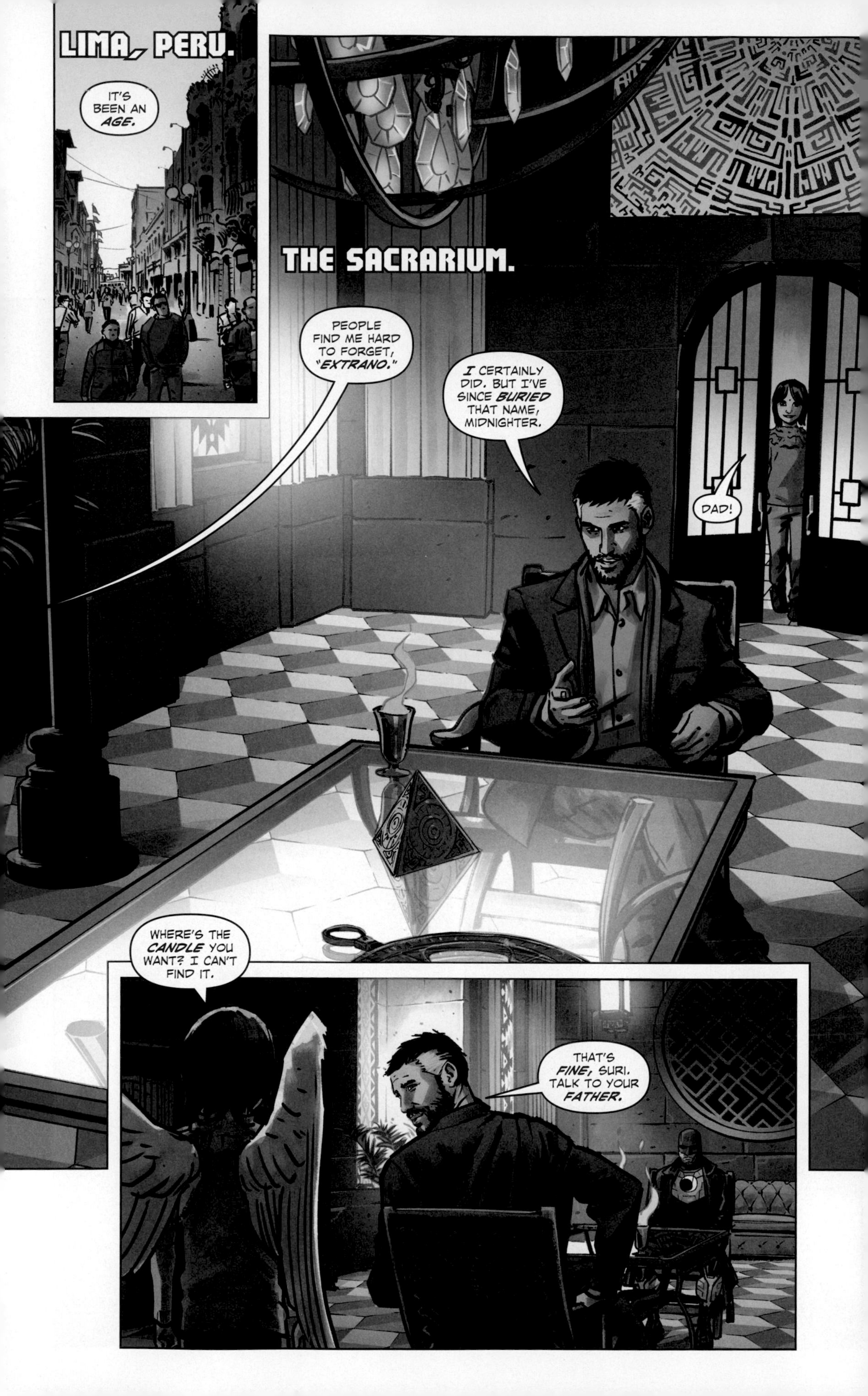
LIMA, PERU.
IT'S BEEN AN AGE.
THE SACRARIUM.
PEOPLE FIND ME HARD TO FORGET, "EXTRANO."
I CERTAINLY DID. BUT I'VE SINCE BURIED THAT NAME, MIDNIGHTER.
DAD!
WHERE'S THE CANDLE YOU WANT? I CAN'T FIND IT.
THAT'S FINE, SURI. TALK TO YOUR FATHER.

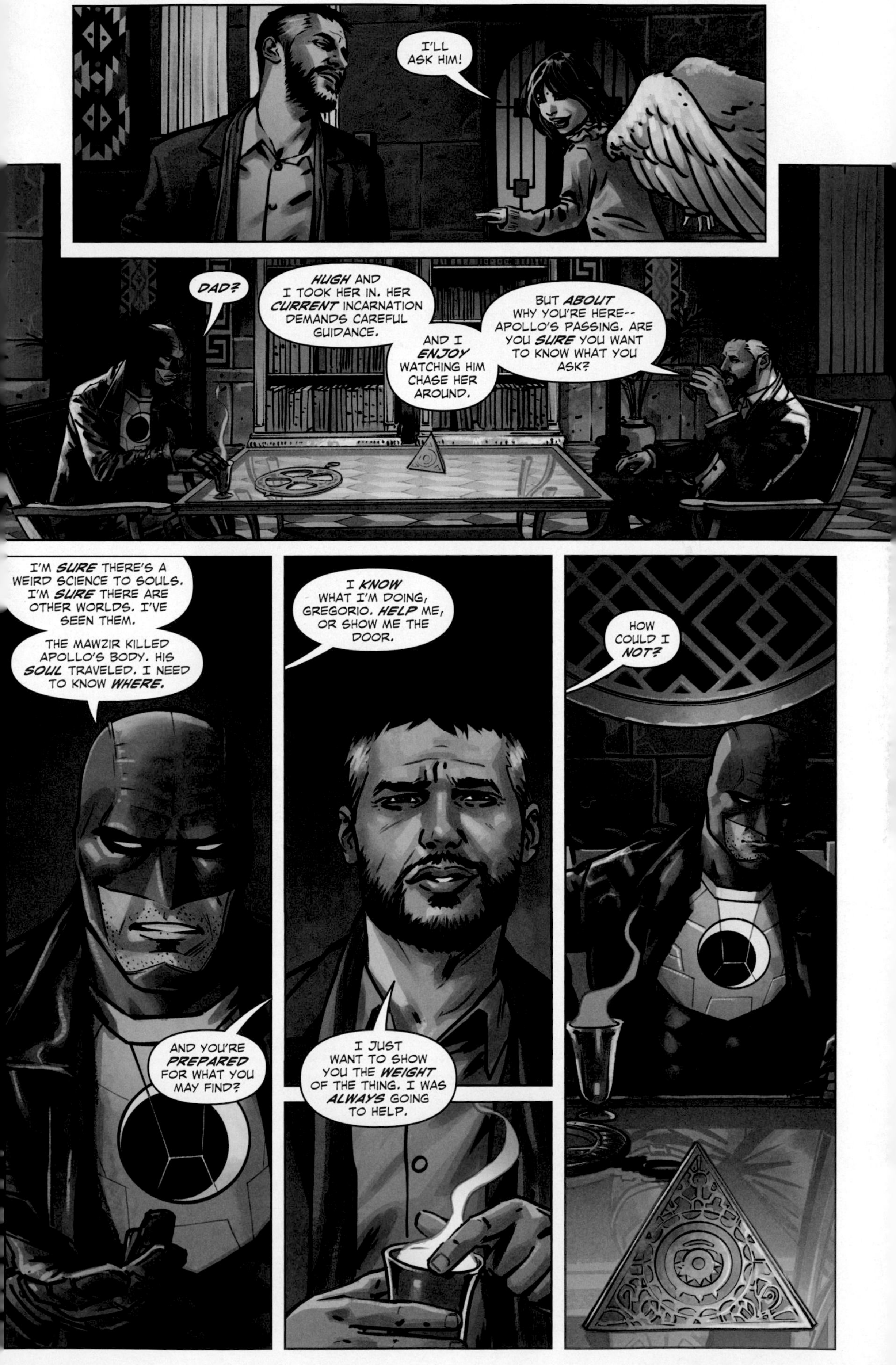
I'LL ASK HIM!
DAD?
HUGH AND I TOOK HER IN. HER CURRENT INCARNATION DEMANDS CAREFUL GUIDANCE.
AND I ENJOY WATCHING HIM CHASE HER AROUND.
BUT ABOUT WHY YOU'RE HERE-- APOLLO'S PASSING. ARE YOU SURE YOU WANT TO KNOW WHAT YOU ASK?
I'M SURE THERE'S A WEIRD SCIENCE TO SOULS. I'M SURE THERE ARE OTHER WORLDS. I'VE SEEN THEM.
THE MAWZIR KILLED APOLLO'S BODY. HIS SOUL TRAVELED. I NEED TO KNOW WHERE.
AND YOU'RE PREPARED FOR WHAT YOU MAY FIND?
I KNOW WHAT I'M DOING, GREGORIO. HELP ME, OR SHOW ME THE DOOR.
I JUST WANT TO SHOW YOU THE WEIGHT OF THE THING. I WAS ALWAYS GOING TO HELP.
HOW COULD I NOT?

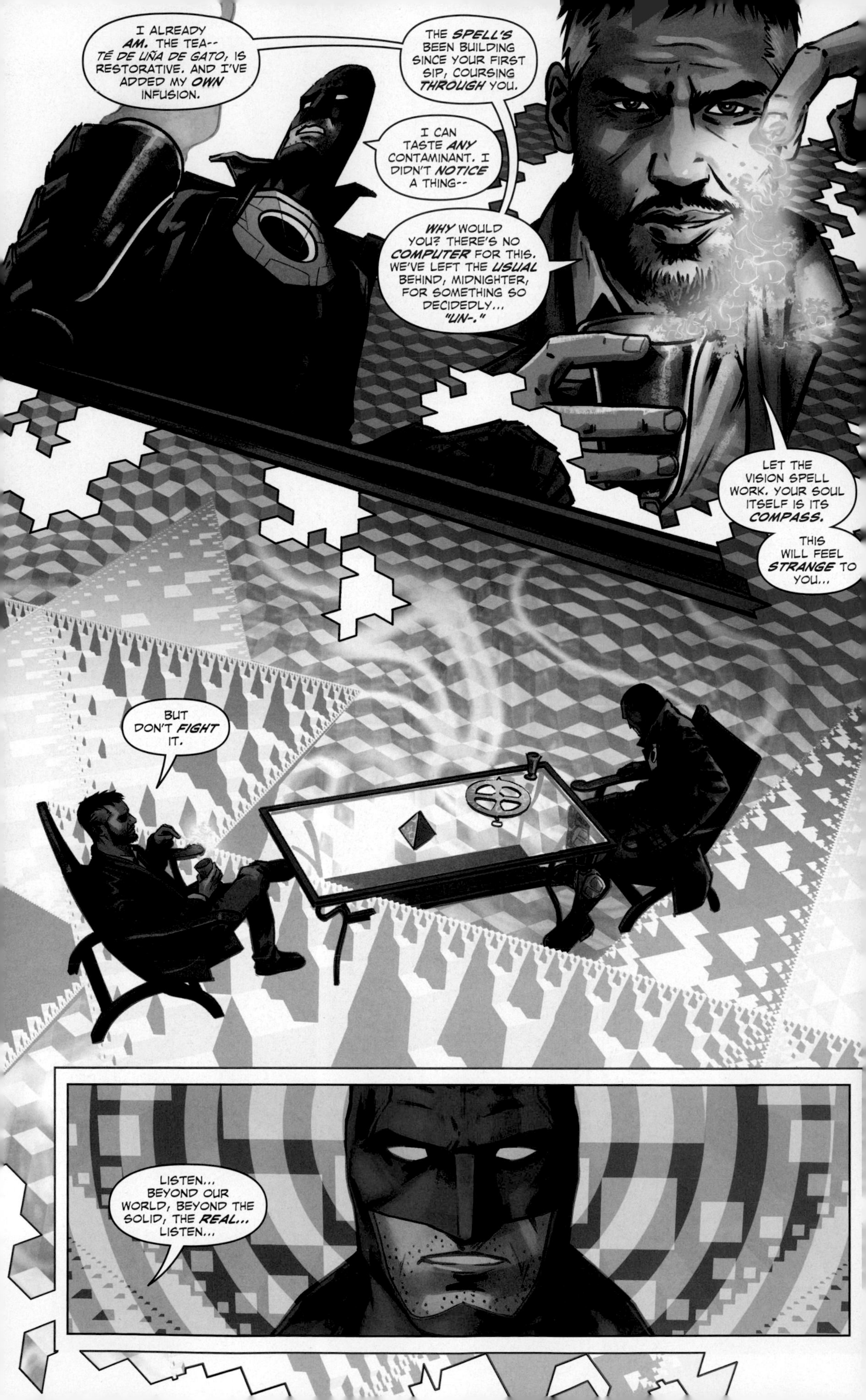
I ALREADY AM. THE TEA-- TÉ DE UÑA DE GATO, IS RESTORATIVE. AND I'VE ADDED MY OWN INFUSION.
THE SPELL'S BEEN BUILDING SINCE YOUR FIRST SIP, COURSING THROUGH YOU.
I CAN TASTE ANY CONTAMINANT. I DIDN'T NOTICE A THING--
WHY WOULD YOU? THERE'S NO COMPUTER FOR THIS. WE'VE LEFT THE USUAL BEHIND, MIDNIGHTER, FOR SOMETHING SO DECIDEDLY... "UN-."
LET THE VISION SPELL WORK. YOUR SOUL ITSELF IS ITS COMPASS.
THIS WILL FEEL STRANGE TO YOU...
BUT DON'T FIGHT IT.
LISTEN... BEYOND OUR WORLD, BEYOND THE SOLID, THE REAL... LISTEN...

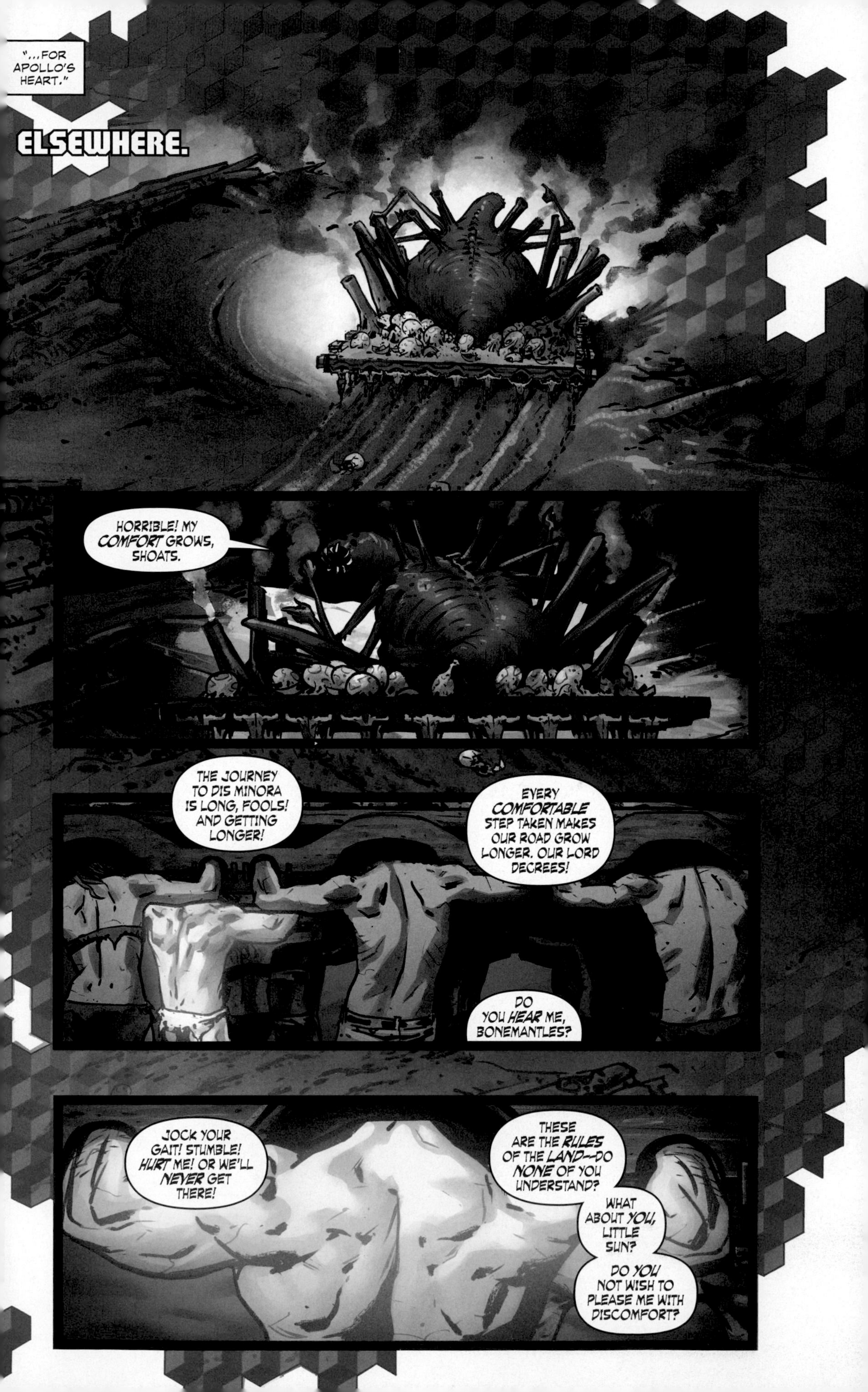
"...FOR APOLLO'S HEART."
ELSEWHERE.
HORRIBLE! MY *COMFORT* GROWS, SHOATS.
THE JOURNEY TO DIS MINORA IS LONG, FOOLS! AND GETTING LONGER!
EVERY *COMFORTABLE* STEP TAKEN MAKES OUR ROAD GROW LONGER. OUR LORD DECREES!
DO YOU *HEAR* ME, BONEMANTLES?
JOCK YOUR GAIT! STUMBLE! *HURT* ME! OR WE'LL *NEVER* GET THERE!
THESE ARE THE *RULES* OF THE *LAND*--DO *NONE* OF YOU UNDERSTAND?
WHAT ABOUT *YOU*, LITTLE SUN?
DO YOU NOT WISH TO PLEASE ME WITH DISCOMFORT?

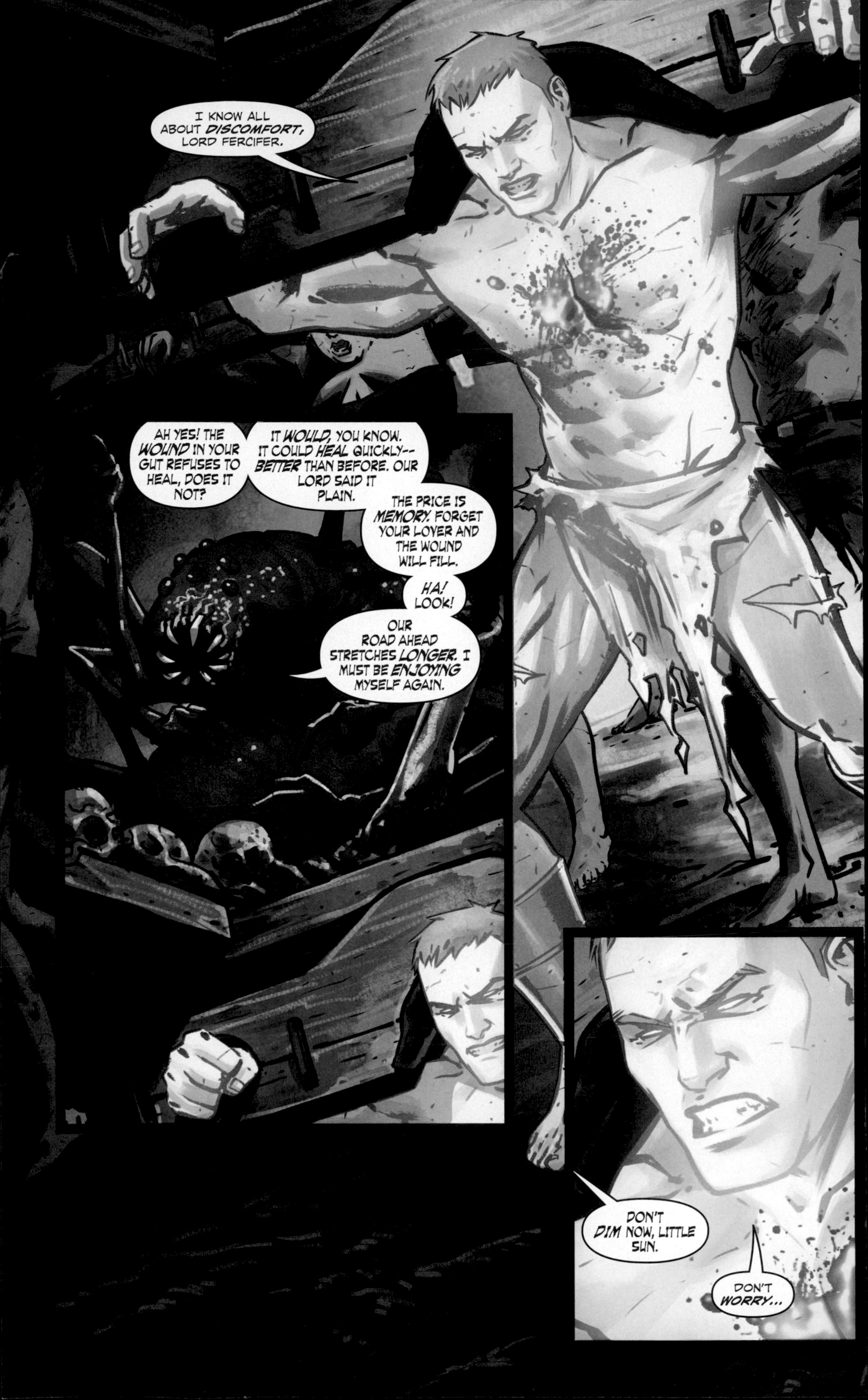
I KNOW ALL ABOUT DISCOMFORT, LORD FERCIFER.
AH YES! THE WOUND IN YOUR GUT REFUSES TO HEAL, DOES IT NOT?
IT WOULD, YOU KNOW. IT COULD HEAL QUICKLY-- BETTER THAN BEFORE. OUR LORD SAID IT PLAIN.
THE PRICE IS MEMORY. FORGET YOUR LOVER AND THE WOUND WILL FILL.
HA! LOOK!
OUR ROAD AHEAD STRETCHES LONGER. I MUST BE ENJOYING MYSELF AGAIN.
DON'T DIM NOW, LITTLE SUN.
DON'T WORRY...

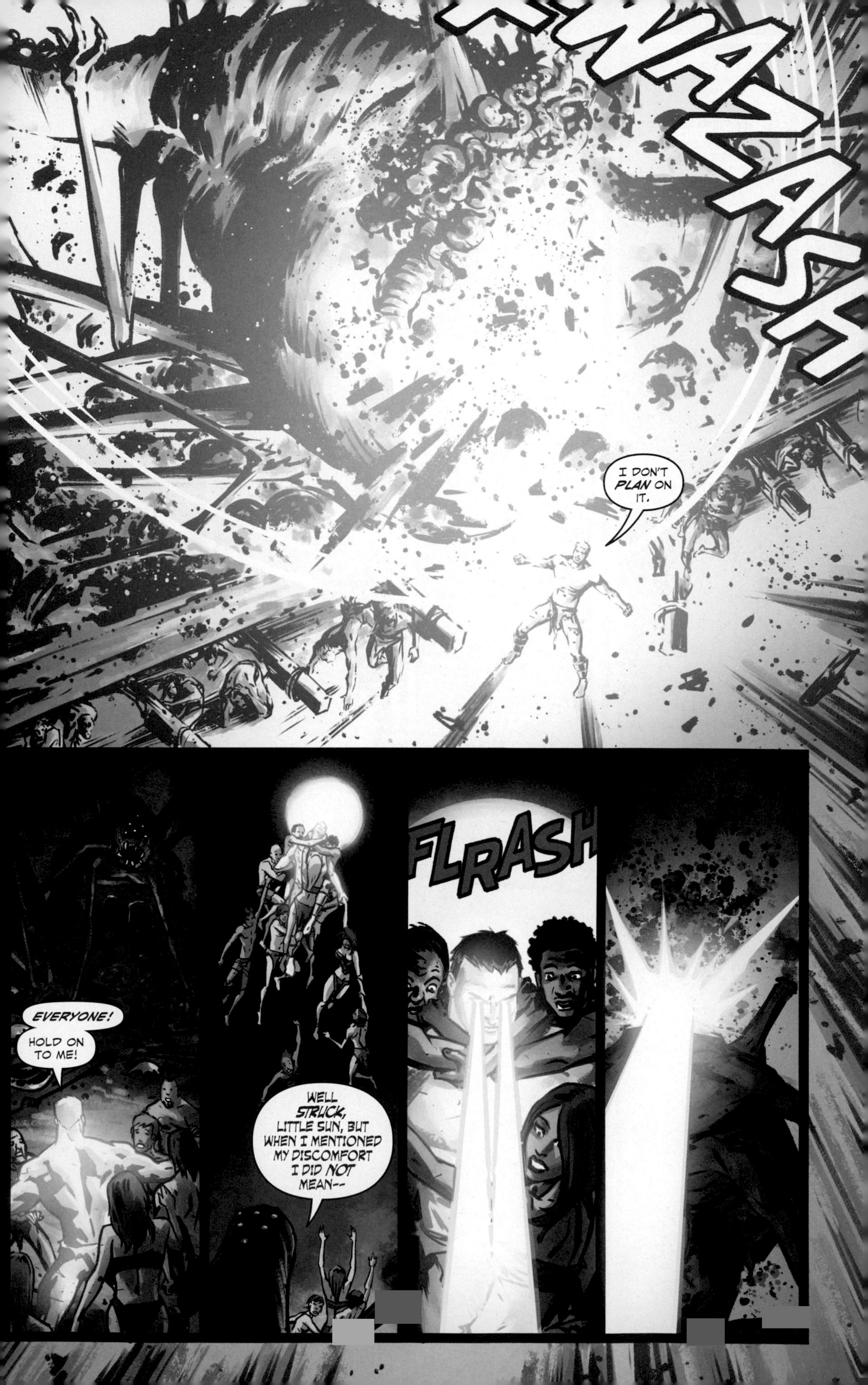
NAZASH
I DON'T *PLAN* ON IT.
EVERYONE!
HOLD ON TO ME!
WELL *STRUCK,* LITTLE SUN, BUT WHEN I MENTIONED MY DISCOMFORT I DID *NOT* MEAN--
FLRASH

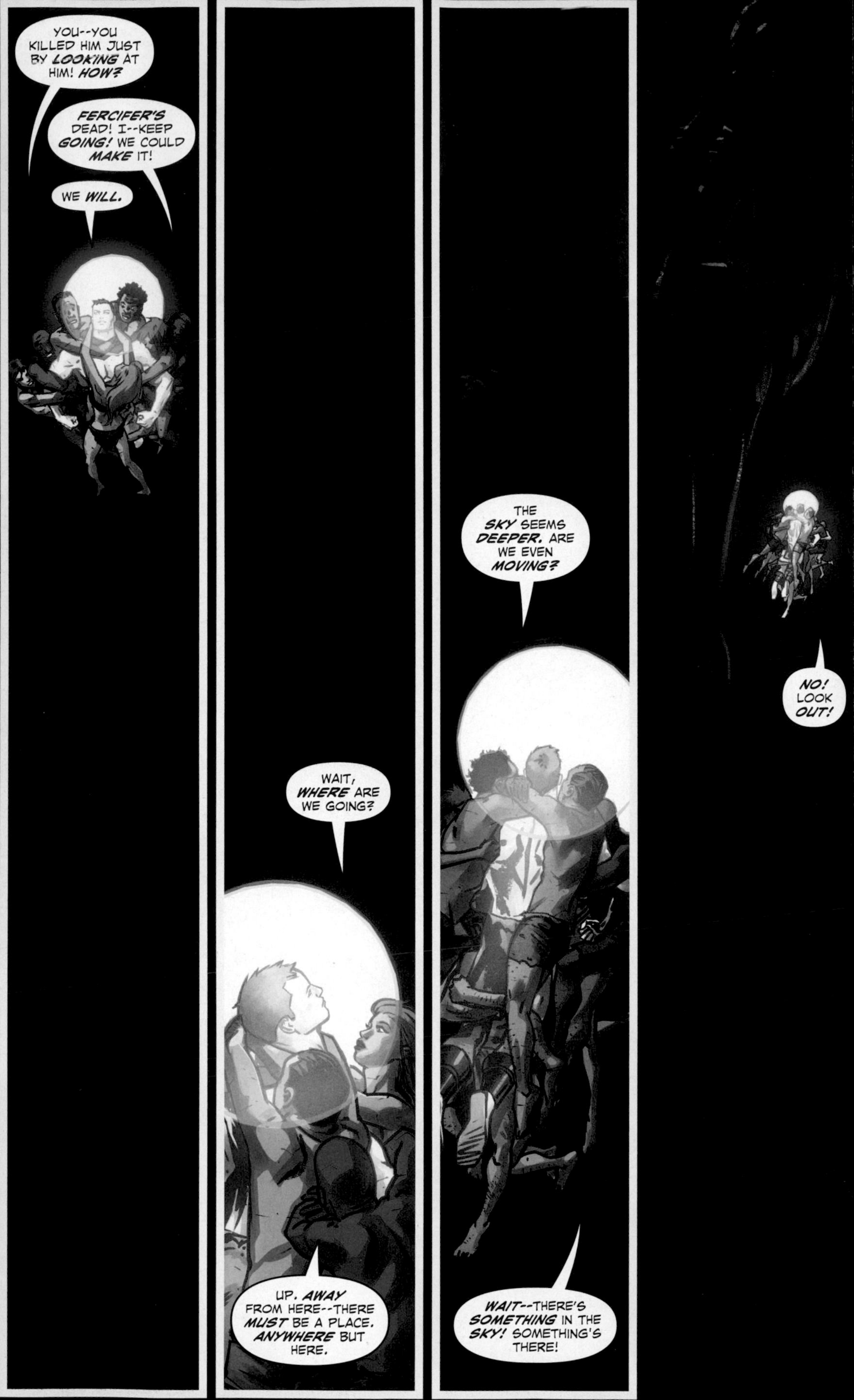
YOU--YOU KILLED HIM JUST BY LOOKING AT HIM! HOW?
FERCIFER'S DEAD! I--KEEP GOING! WE COULD MAKE IT!
WE WILL.
WAIT, WHERE ARE WE GOING?
UP. AWAY FROM HERE--THERE MUST BE A PLACE. ANYWHERE BUT HERE.
THE SKY SEEMS DEEPER. ARE WE EVEN MOVING?
WAIT--THERE'S SOMETHING IN THE SKY! SOMETHING'S THERE!
NO! LOOK OUT!

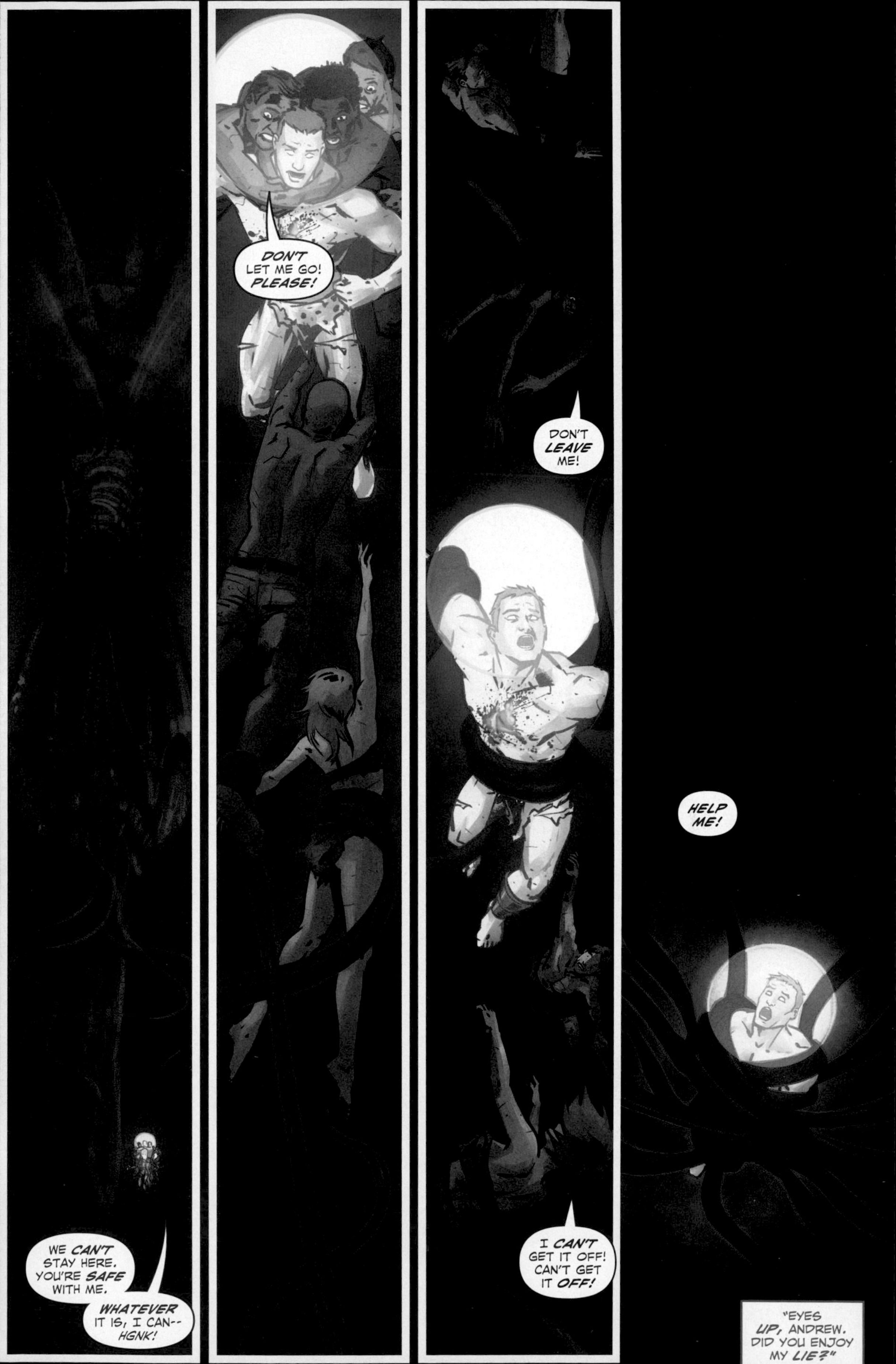
DON'T LET ME GO! PLEASE!
WE CAN'T STAY HERE. YOU'RE SAFE WITH ME.
WHATEVER IT IS, I CAN-- HGNK!
DON'T LEAVE ME!
I CAN'T GET IT OFF! CAN'T GET IT OFF!
HELP ME!
"EYES UP, ANDREW. DID YOU ENJOY MY LIE?"

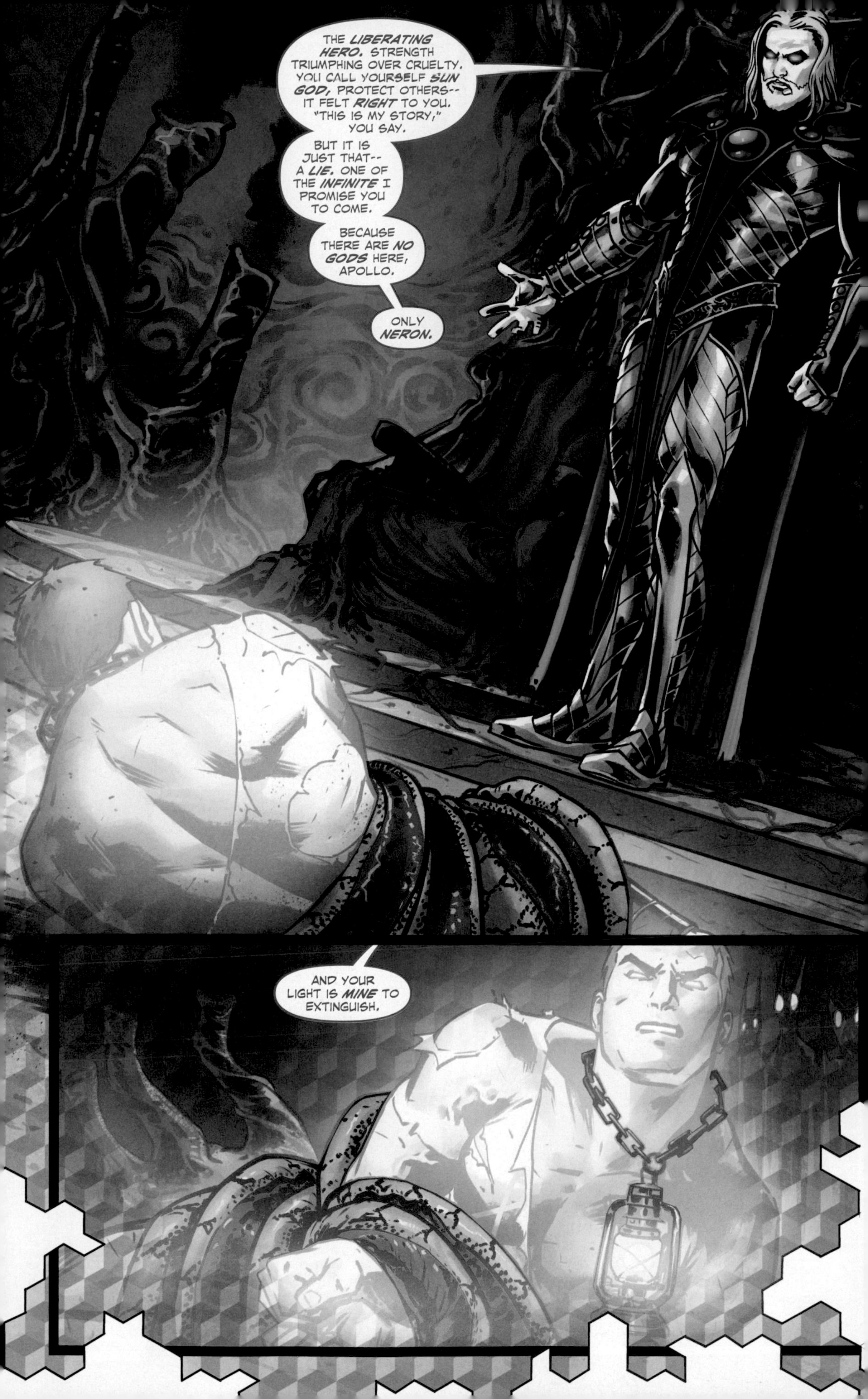
THE LIBERATING HERO. STRENGTH TRIUMPHING OVER CRUELTY. YOU CALL YOURSELF SUN GOD, PROTECT OTHERS-- IT FELT RIGHT TO YOU. "THIS IS MY STORY," YOU SAY.
BUT IT IS JUST THAT-- A LIE. ONE OF THE INFINITE I PROMISE YOU TO COME.
BECAUSE THERE ARE NO GODS HERE, APOLLO.
ONLY NERON.
AND YOUR LIGHT IS MINE TO EXTINGUISH.

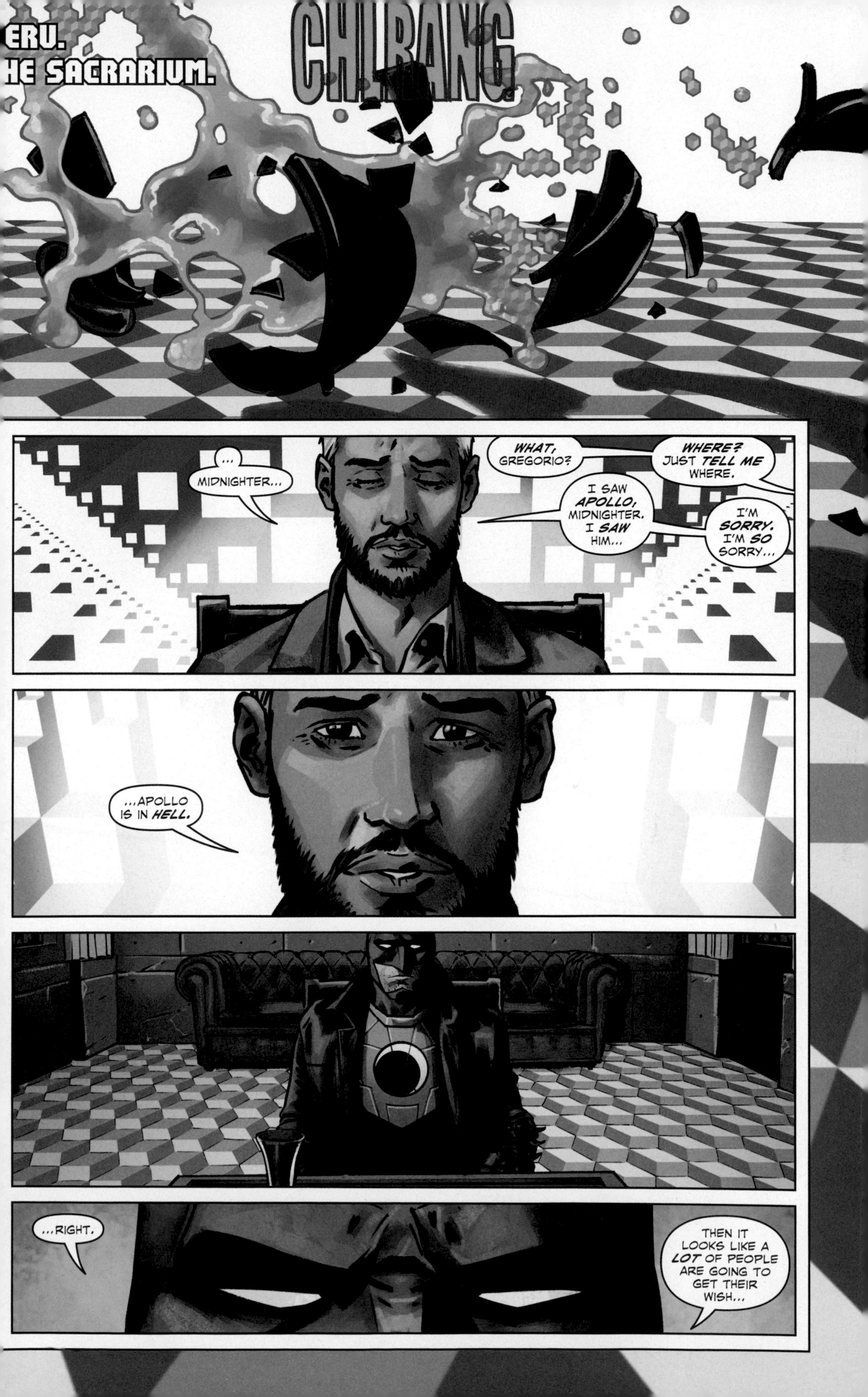
ERU.
HE SACRARIUM.
CHLRANG
...
MIDNIGHTER...
WHAT, GREGORIO?
WHERE? JUST TELL ME WHERE.
I SAW APOLLO, MIDNIGHTER. I SAW HIM...
I'M SORRY. I'M SO SORRY...
...APOLLO IS IN HELL.
...RIGHT.
THEN IT LOOKS LIKE A LOT OF PEOPLE ARE GOING TO GET THEIR WISH...

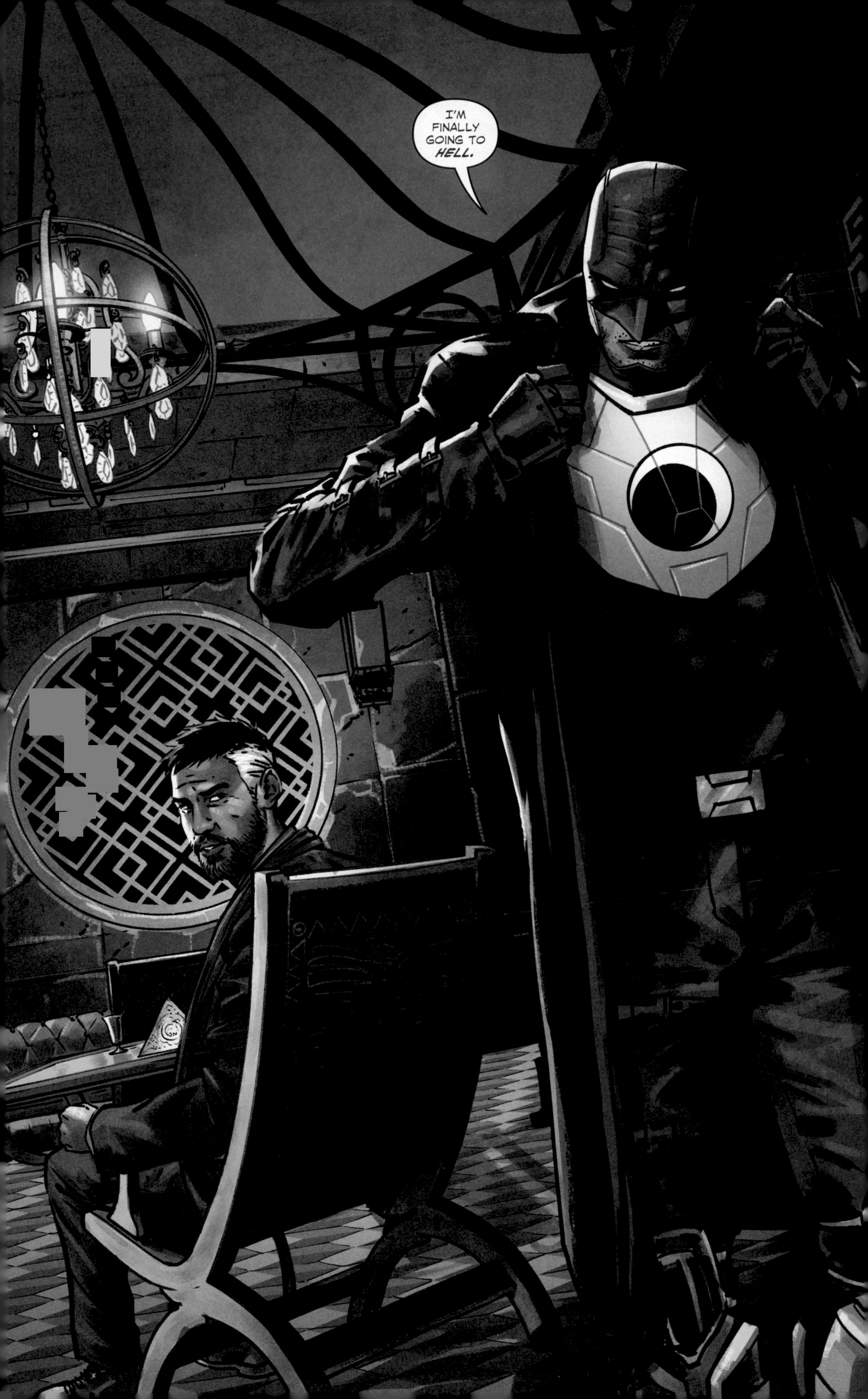
I'M FINALLY GOING TO HELL.

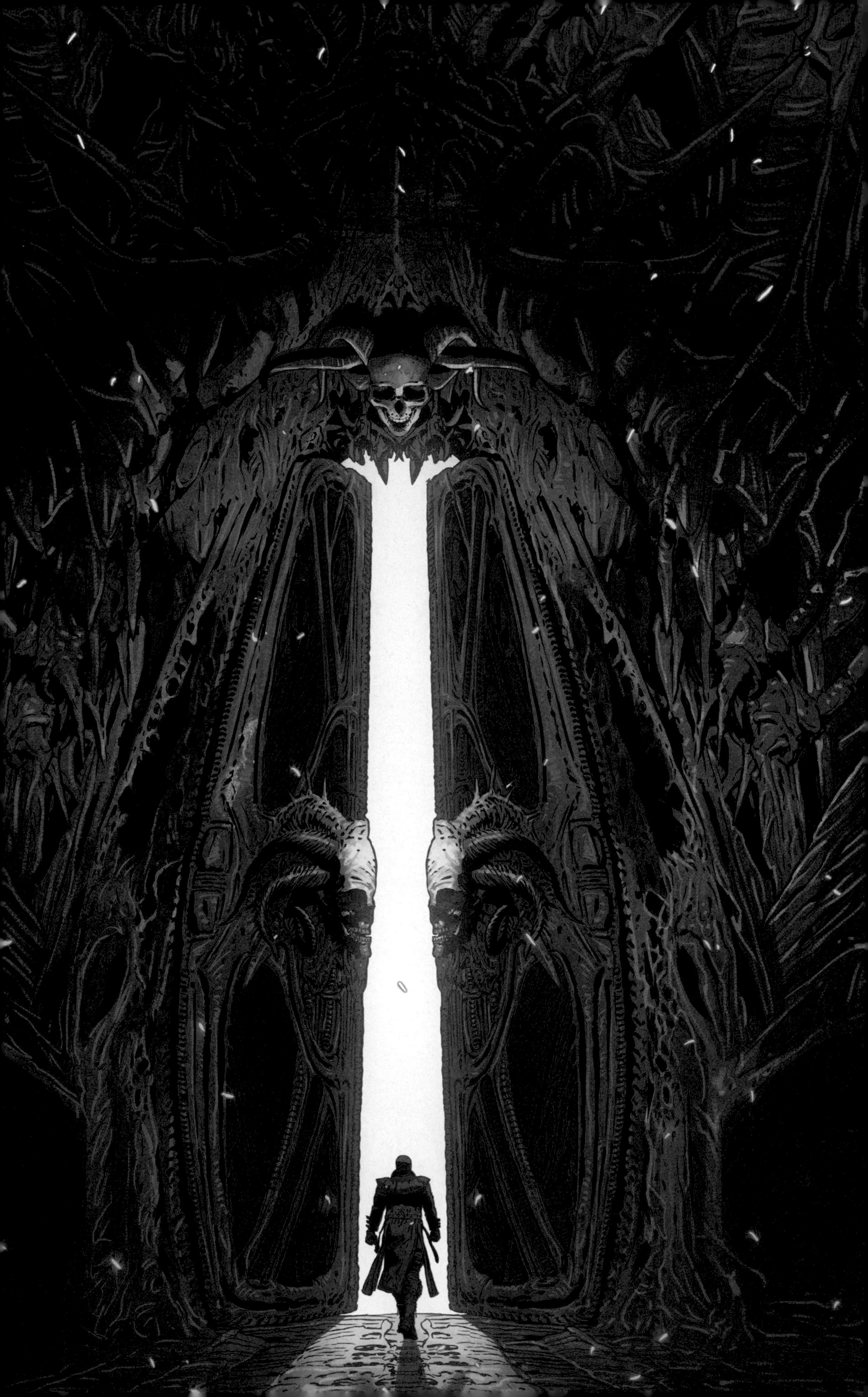

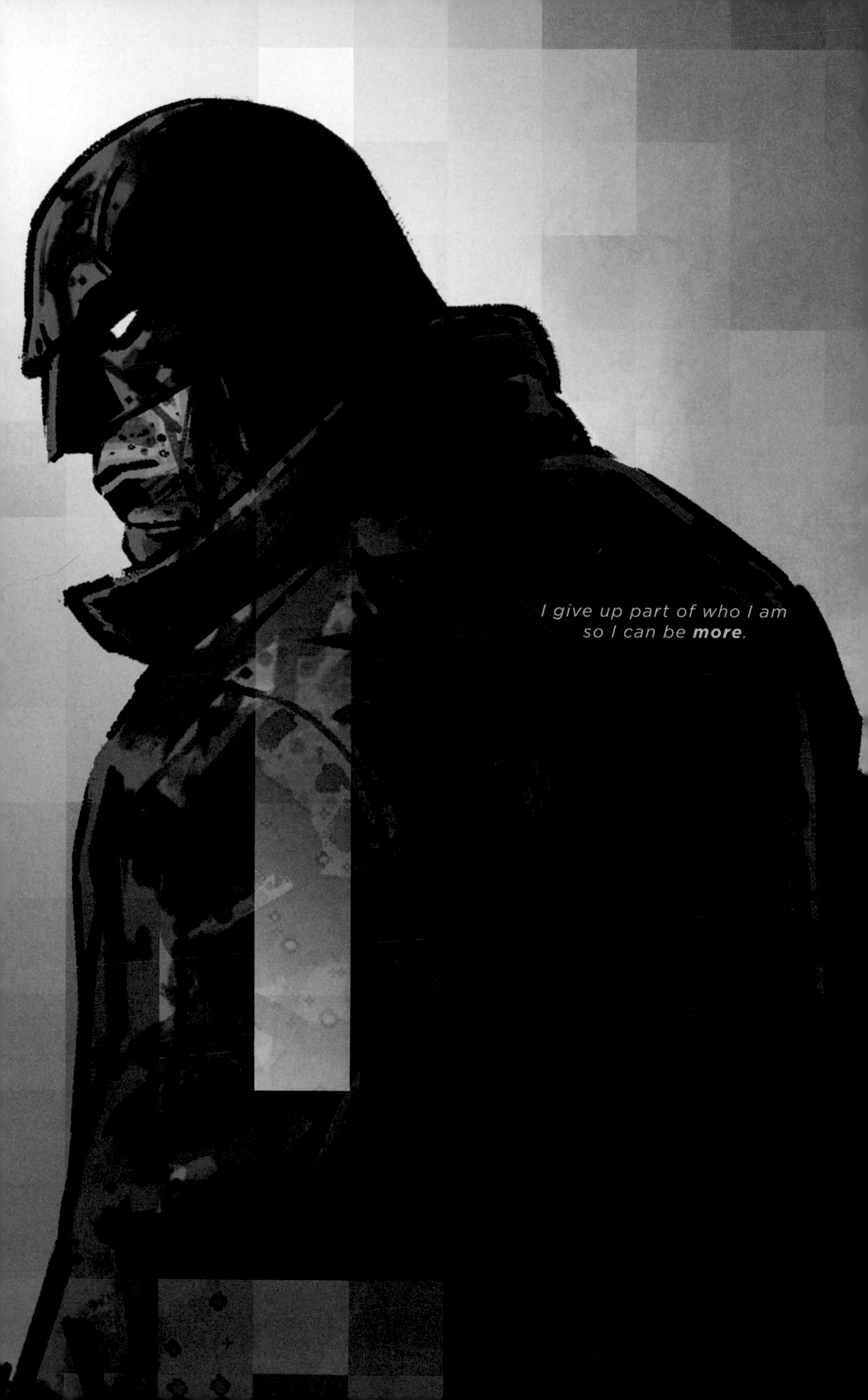
I give up part of who I am
so I can be **more**.

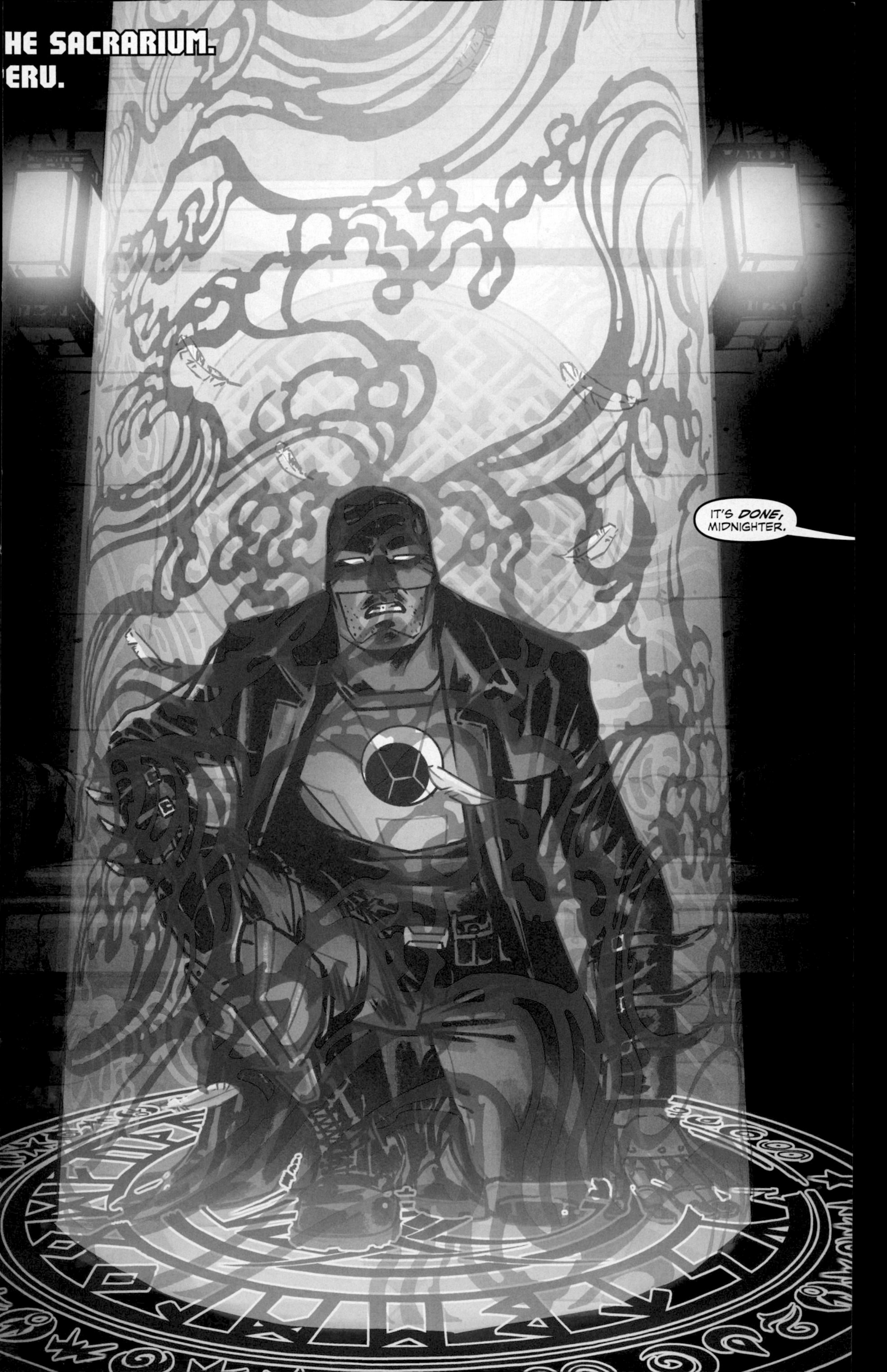
HE SACRARIUM.
ERU.
IT'S DONE, MIDNIGHTER.

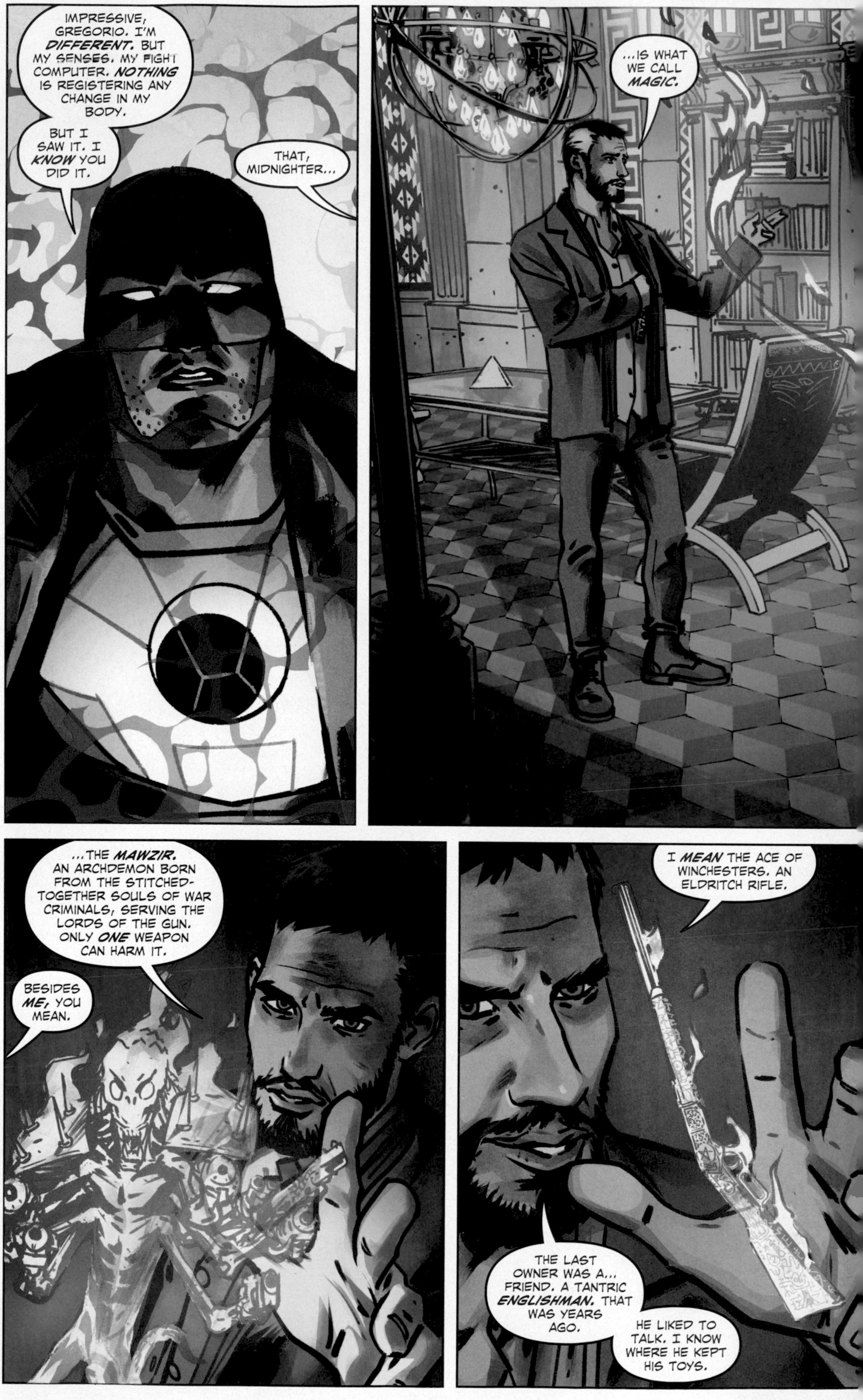
IMPRESSIVE, GREGORIO. I'M DIFFERENT. BUT MY SENSES, MY FIGHT COMPUTER. NOTHING IS REGISTERING ANY CHANGE IN MY BODY.
BUT I SAW IT. I KNOW YOU DID IT.
THAT, MIDNIGHTER...
...IS WHAT WE CALL MAGIC.
...THE MAWZIR. AN ARCHDEMON BORN FROM THE STITCHED-TOGETHER SOULS OF WAR CRIMINALS, SERVING THE LORDS OF THE GUN. ONLY ONE WEAPON CAN HARM IT.
BESIDES ME, YOU MEAN.
I MEAN THE ACE OF WINCHESTERS. AN ELDRITCH RIFLE.
THE LAST OWNER WAS A... FRIEND. A TANTRIC ENGLISHMAN. THAT WAS YEARS AGO.
HE LIKED TO TALK. I KNOW WHERE HE KEPT HIS TOYS.

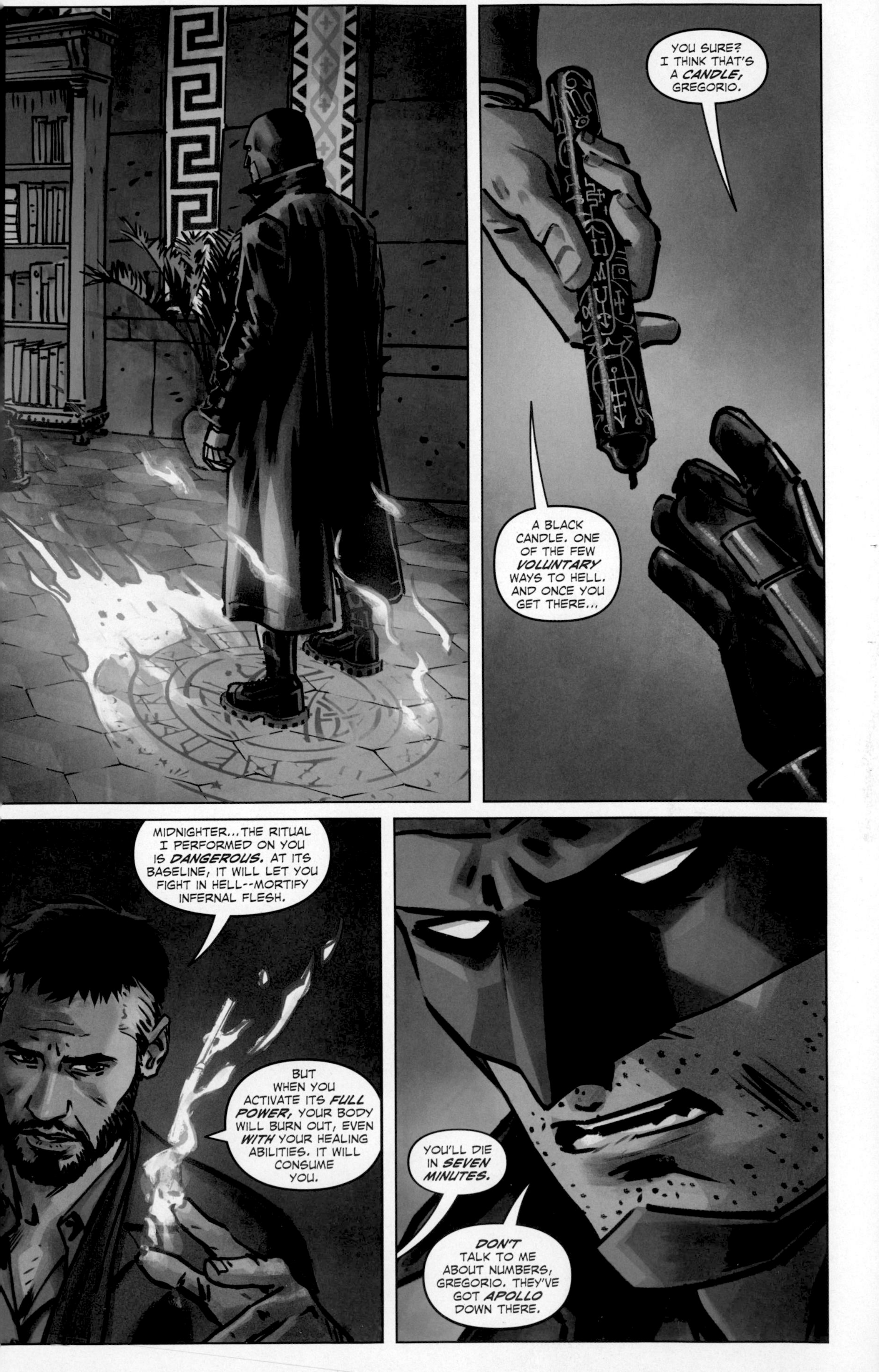
YOU SURE? I THINK THAT'S A *CANDLE,* GREGORIO.
A BLACK CANDLE. ONE OF THE FEW *VOLUNTARY* WAYS TO HELL. AND ONCE YOU GET THERE...
MIDNIGHTER...THE RITUAL I PERFORMED ON YOU IS *DANGEROUS.* AT ITS BASELINE, IT WILL LET YOU FIGHT IN HELL--MORTIFY INFERNAL FLESH.
BUT WHEN YOU ACTIVATE ITS *FULL POWER,* YOUR BODY WILL BURN OUT, EVEN *WITH* YOUR HEALING ABILITIES. IT WILL CONSUME YOU.
YOU'LL DIE IN *SEVEN MINUTES.*
DON'T TALK TO ME ABOUT NUMBERS, GREGORIO. THEY'VE GOT *APOLLO* DOWN THERE.

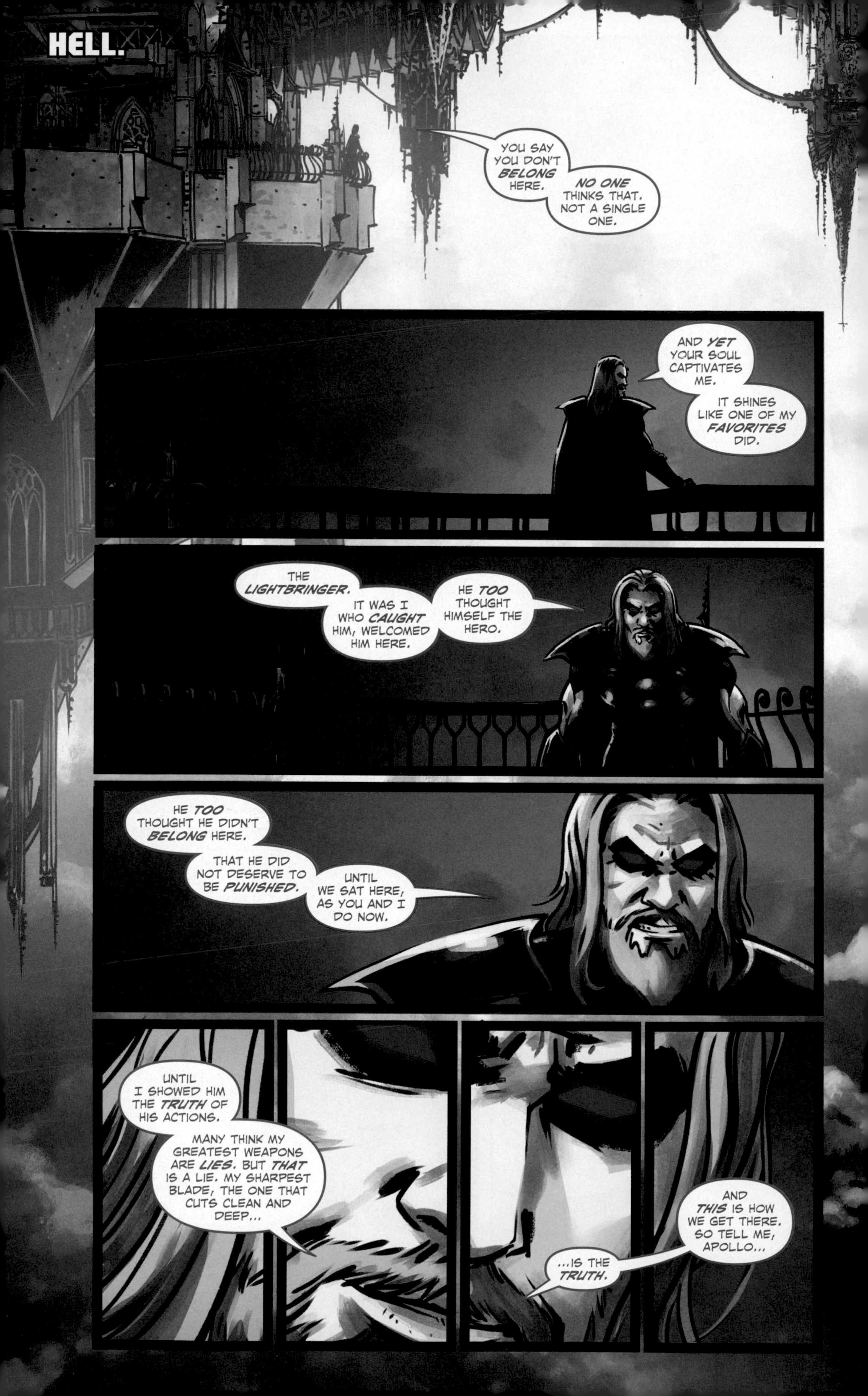
HELL.
YOU SAY YOU DON'T BELONG HERE.
NO ONE THINKS THAT. NOT A SINGLE ONE.
AND YET YOUR SOUL CAPTIVATES ME.
IT SHINES LIKE ONE OF MY FAVORITES DID.
THE LIGHTBRINGER.
IT WAS I WHO CAUGHT HIM, WELCOMED HIM HERE.
HE TOO THOUGHT HIMSELF THE HERO.
HE TOO THOUGHT HE DIDN'T BELONG HERE.
THAT HE DID NOT DESERVE TO BE PUNISHED.
UNTIL WE SAT HERE, AS YOU AND I DO NOW.
UNTIL I SHOWED HIM THE TRUTH OF HIS ACTIONS.
MANY THINK MY GREATEST WEAPONS ARE LIES. BUT THAT IS A LIE. MY SHARPEST BLADE, THE ONE THAT CUTS CLEAN AND DEEP...
...IS THE TRUTH.
AND THIS IS HOW WE GET THERE. SO TELL ME, APOLLO...

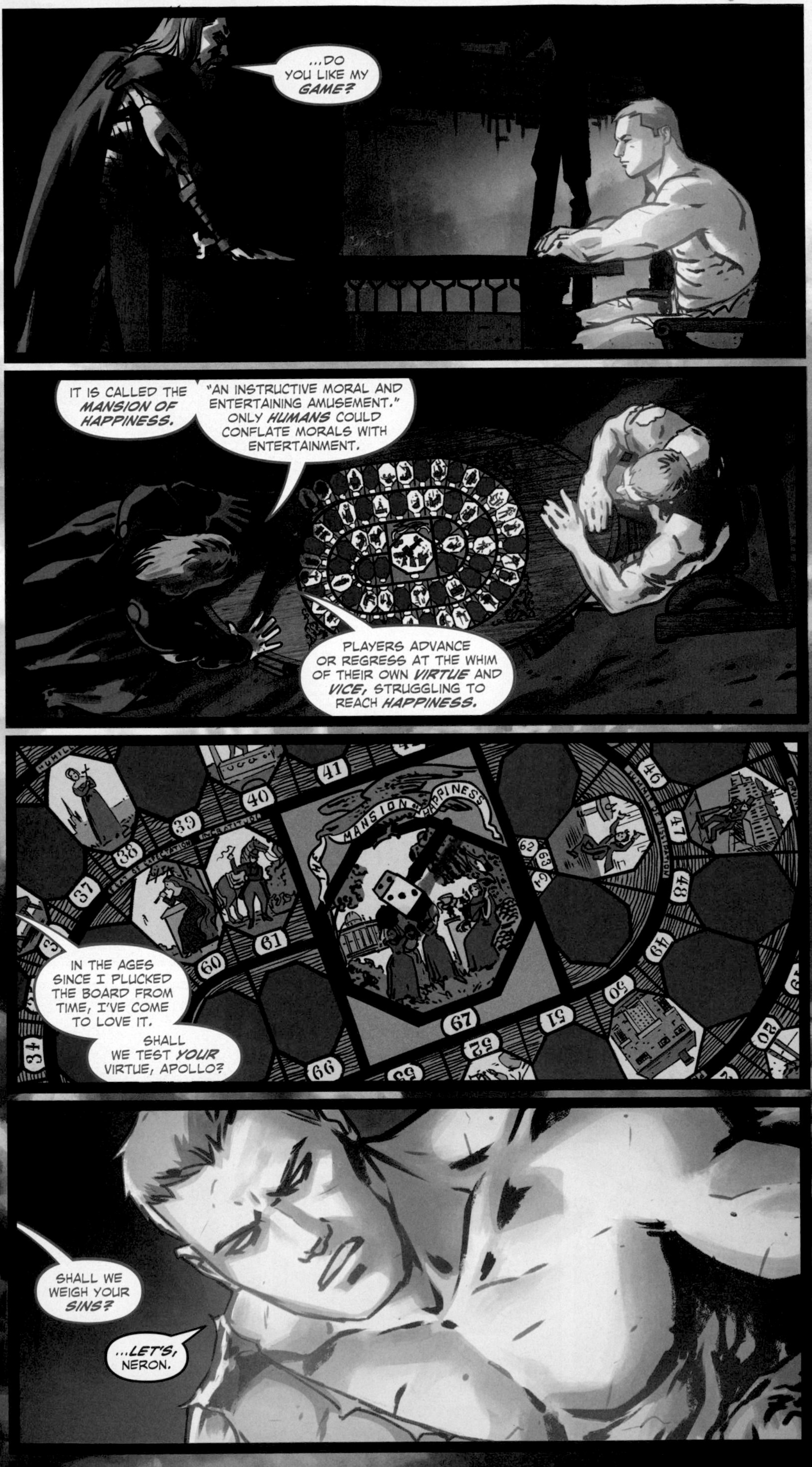
...DO YOU LIKE MY GAME?
IT IS CALLED THE MANSION OF HAPPINESS.
"AN INSTRUCTIVE MORAL AND ENTERTAINING AMUSEMENT." ONLY HUMANS COULD CONFLATE MORALS WITH ENTERTAINMENT.
PLAYERS ADVANCE OR REGRESS AT THE WHIM OF THEIR OWN VIRTUE AND VICE, STRUGGLING TO REACH HAPPINESS.
MANSION OF HAPPINESS
IN THE AGES SINCE I PLUCKED THE BOARD FROM TIME, I'VE COME TO LOVE IT.
SHALL WE TEST YOUR VIRTUE, APOLLO?
SHALL WE WEIGH YOUR SINS?
...LET'S, NERON.

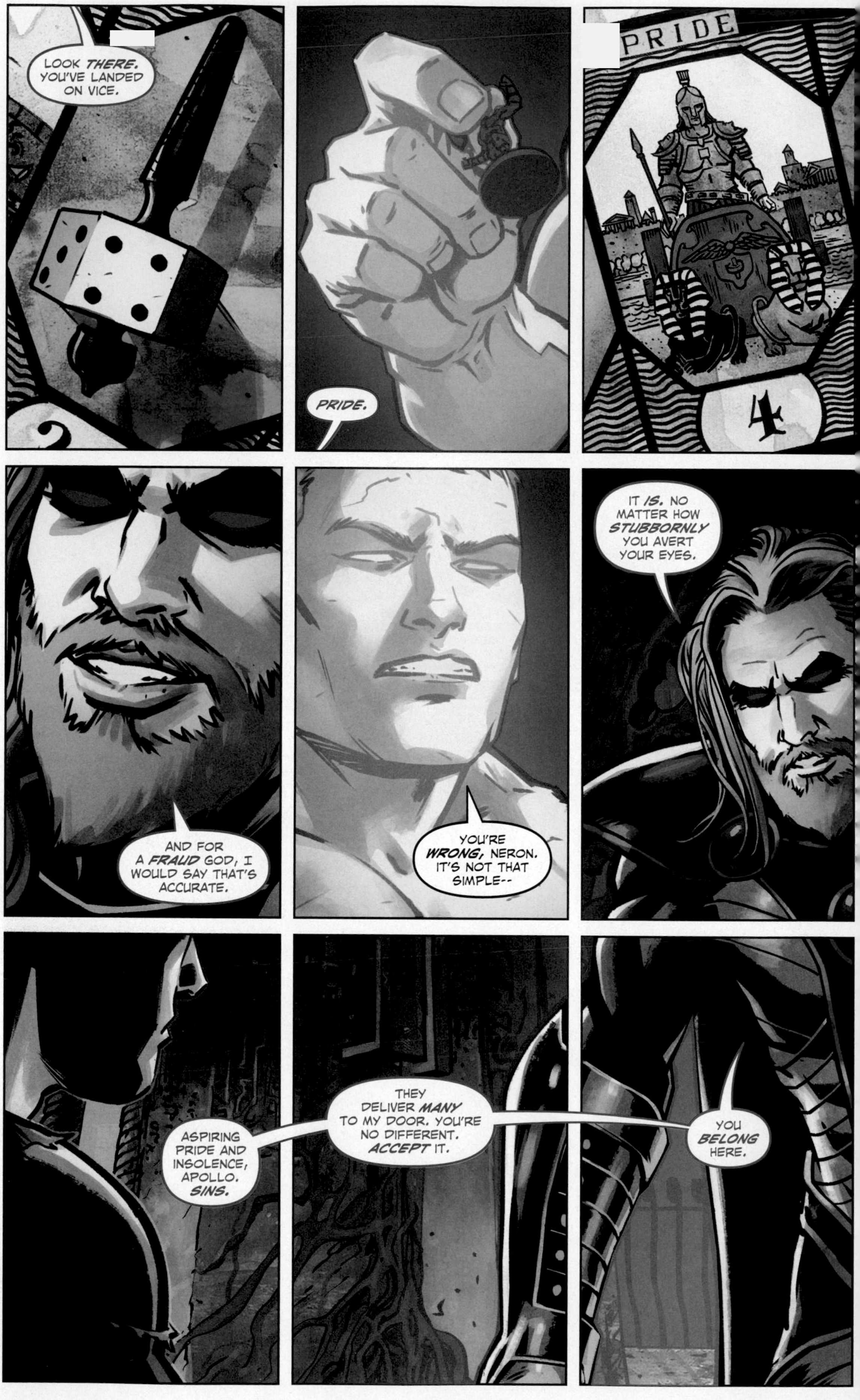
LOOK THERE. YOU'VE LANDED ON VICE.
PRIDE.
PRIDE
4
AND FOR A FRAUD GOD, I WOULD SAY THAT'S ACCURATE.
YOU'RE WRONG, NERON. IT'S NOT THAT SIMPLE--
IT IS. NO MATTER HOW STUBBORNLY YOU AVERT YOUR EYES.
ASPIRING PRIDE AND INSOLENCE, APOLLO. SINS.
THEY DELIVER MANY TO MY DOOR. YOU'RE NO DIFFERENT. ACCEPT IT.
YOU BELONG HERE.

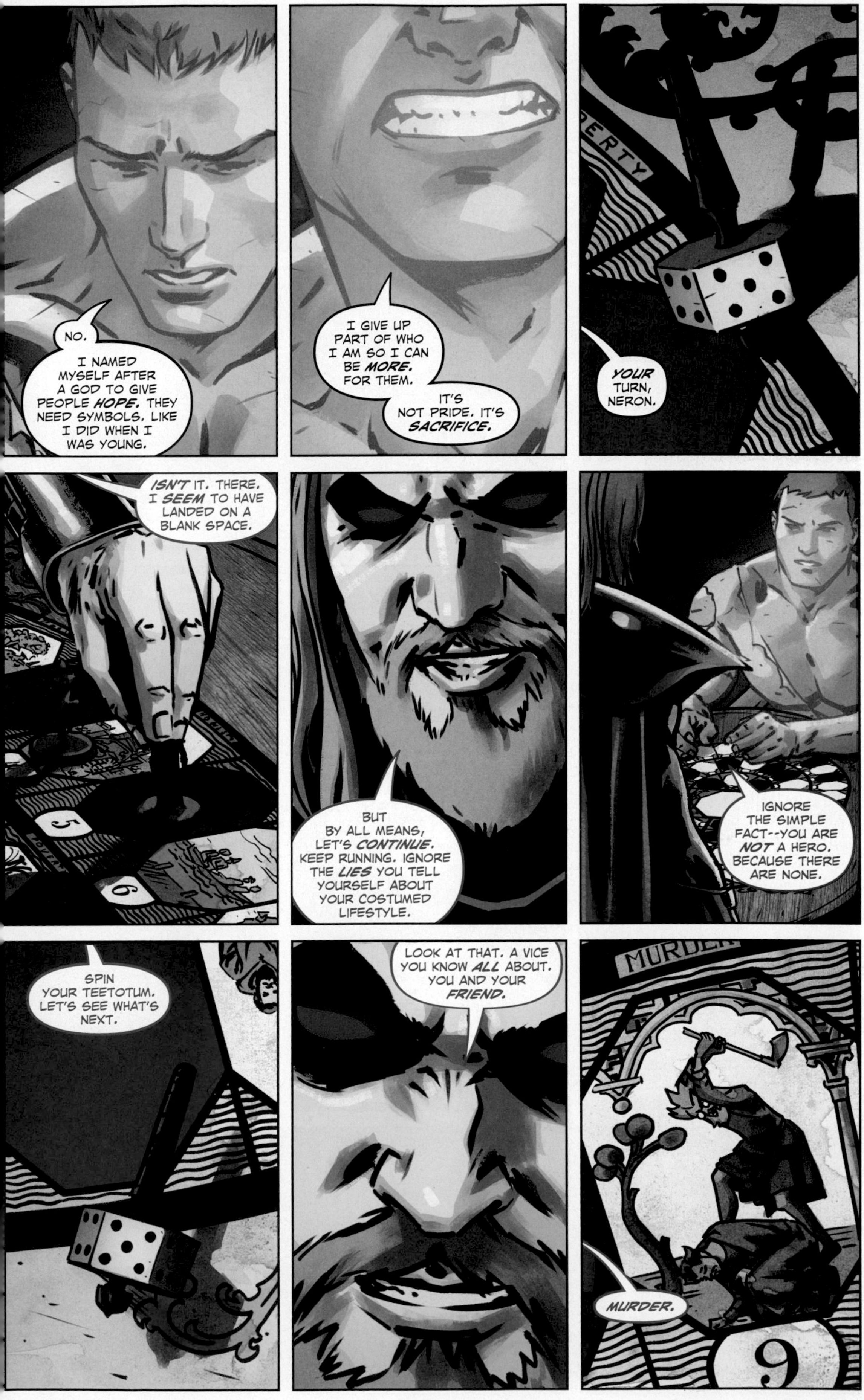
NO.
I NAMED MYSELF AFTER A GOD TO GIVE PEOPLE HOPE. THEY NEED SYMBOLS. LIKE I DID WHEN I WAS YOUNG.
I GIVE UP PART OF WHO I AM SO I CAN BE MORE. FOR THEM.
IT'S NOT PRIDE. IT'S SACRIFICE.
ERTY
YOUR TURN, NERON.
ISN'T IT. THERE. I SEEM TO HAVE LANDED ON A BLANK SPACE.
5
6
BUT BY ALL MEANS, LET'S CONTINUE. KEEP RUNNING. IGNORE THE LIES YOU TELL YOURSELF ABOUT YOUR COSTUMED LIFESTYLE.
IGNORE THE SIMPLE FACT--YOU ARE NOT A HERO. BECAUSE THERE ARE NONE.
SPIN YOUR TEETOTUM. LET'S SEE WHAT'S NEXT.
LOOK AT THAT. A VICE YOU KNOW ALL ABOUT. YOU AND YOUR FRIEND.
MURDER.
9

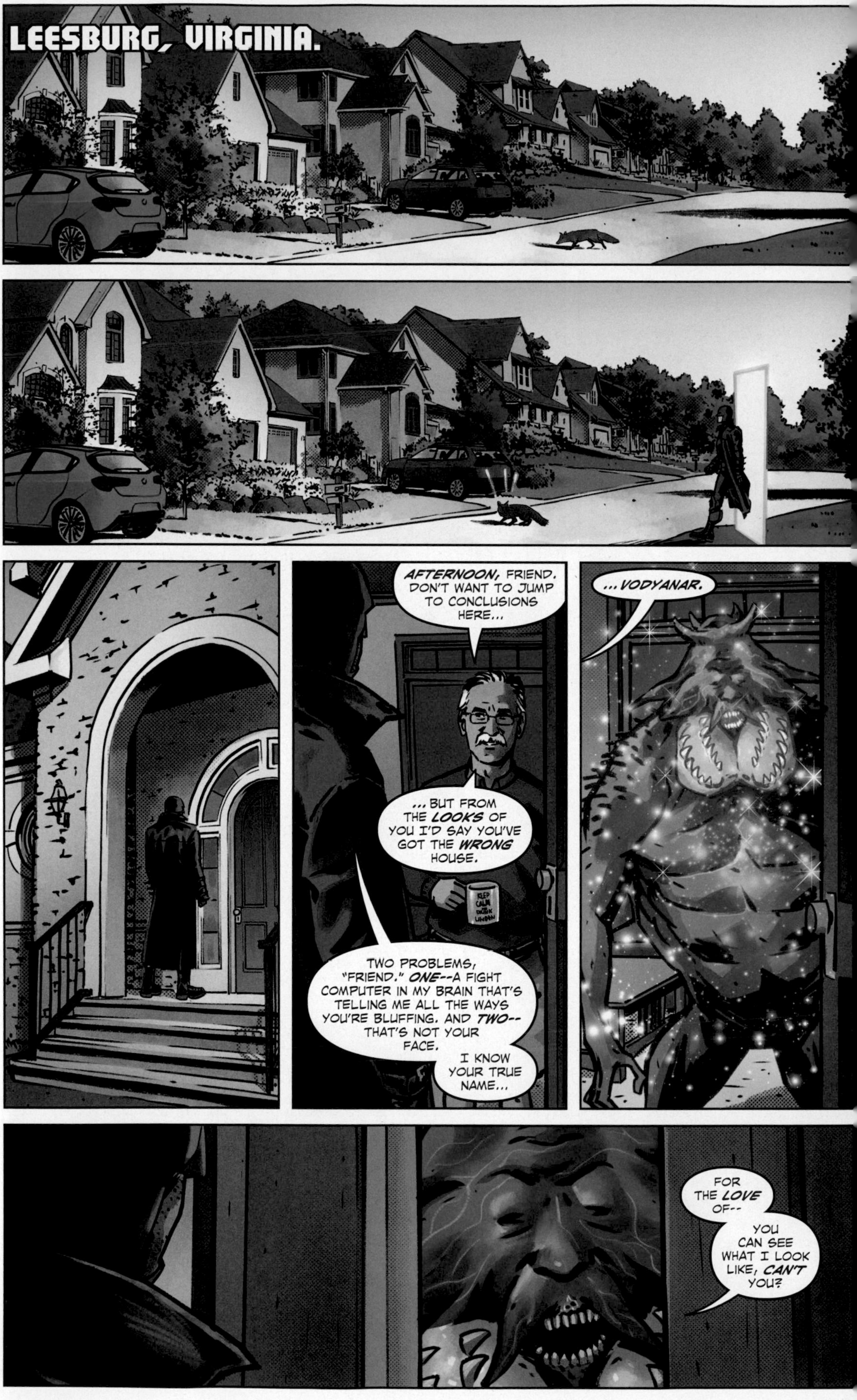
LEESBURG, VIRGINIA.
AFTERNOON, FRIEND. DON'T WANT TO JUMP TO CONCLUSIONS HERE...
...BUT FROM THE LOOKS OF YOU I'D SAY YOU'VE GOT THE WRONG HOUSE.
TWO PROBLEMS, "FRIEND." ONE--A FIGHT COMPUTER IN MY BRAIN THAT'S TELLING ME ALL THE WAYS YOU'RE BLUFFING. AND TWO--THAT'S NOT YOUR FACE.
I KNOW YOUR TRUE NAME...
...VODYANAR.
FOR THE LOVE OF--
YOU CAN SEE WHAT I LOOK LIKE, CAN'T YOU?

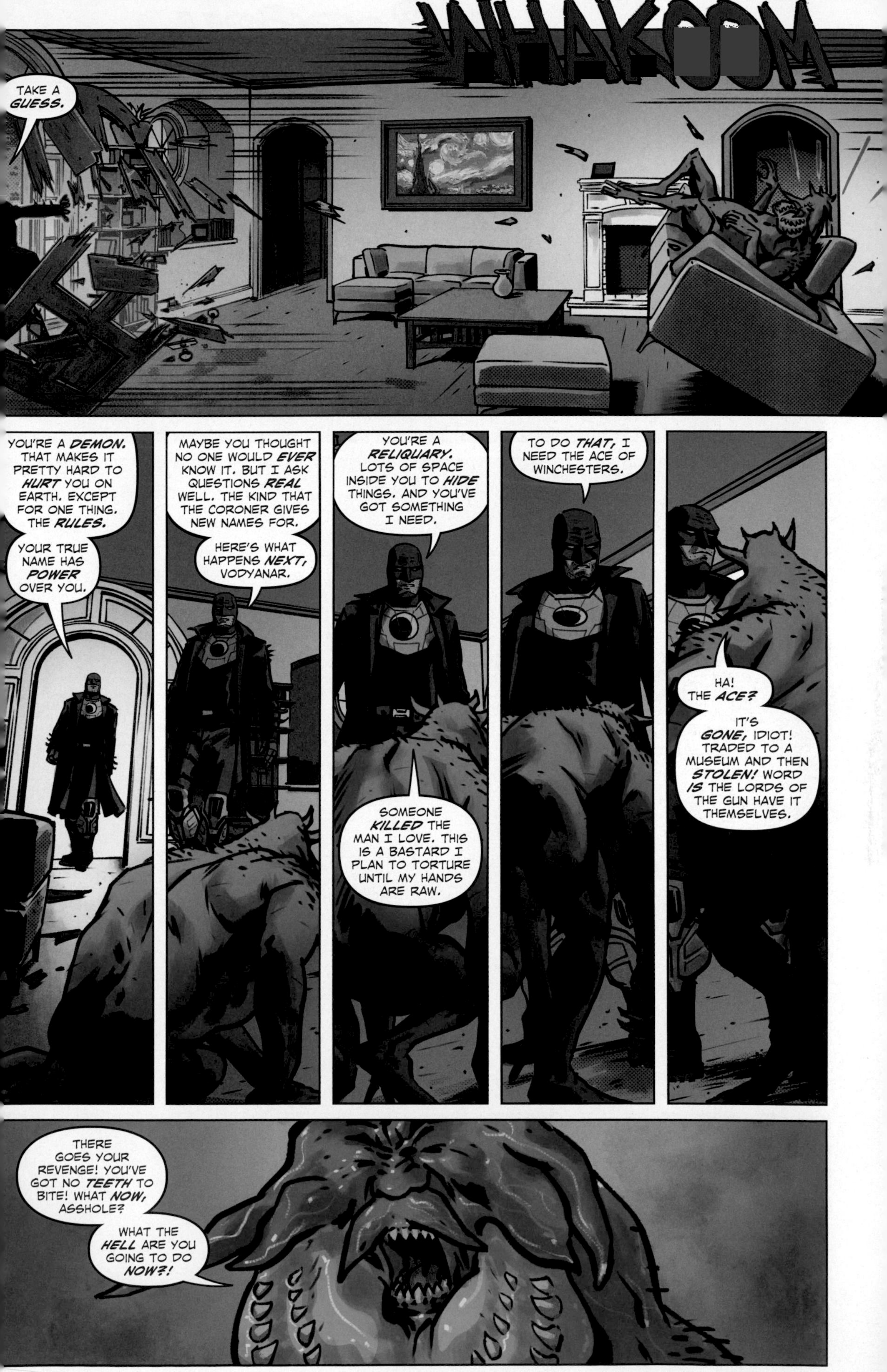

WHAKOOM
TAKE A GUESS.
YOU'RE A DEMON. THAT MAKES IT PRETTY HARD TO HURT YOU ON EARTH. EXCEPT FOR ONE THING. THE RULES.
YOUR TRUE NAME HAS POWER OVER YOU.
MAYBE YOU THOUGHT NO ONE WOULD EVER KNOW IT. BUT I ASK QUESTIONS REAL WELL. THE KIND THAT THE CORONER GIVES NEW NAMES FOR.
HERE'S WHAT HAPPENS NEXT, VODYANAR.
YOU'RE A RELIQUARY. LOTS OF SPACE INSIDE YOU TO HIDE THINGS. AND YOU'VE GOT SOMETHING I NEED.
SOMEONE KILLED THE MAN I LOVE. THIS IS A BASTARD I PLAN TO TORTURE UNTIL MY HANDS ARE RAW.
TO DO THAT, I NEED THE ACE OF WINCHESTERS.
HA! THE ACE?
IT'S GONE, IDIOT! TRADED TO A MUSEUM AND THEN STOLEN! WORD IS THE LORDS OF THE GUN HAVE IT THEMSELVES.
THERE GOES YOUR REVENGE! YOU'VE GOT NO TEETH TO BITE! WHAT NOW, ASSHOLE?
WHAT THE HELL ARE YOU GOING TO DO NOW?!

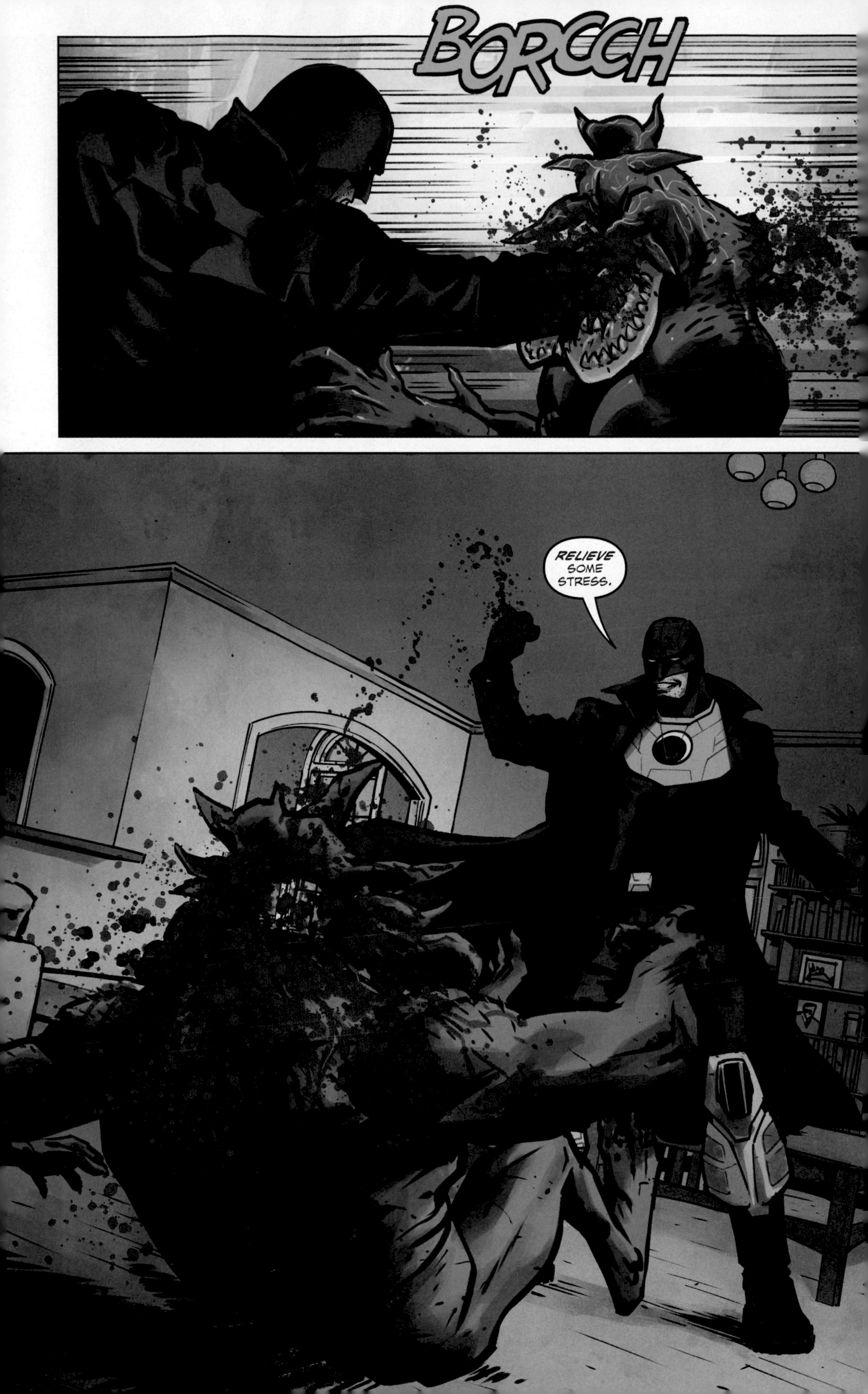
BORCCH
RELIEVE SOME STRESS.

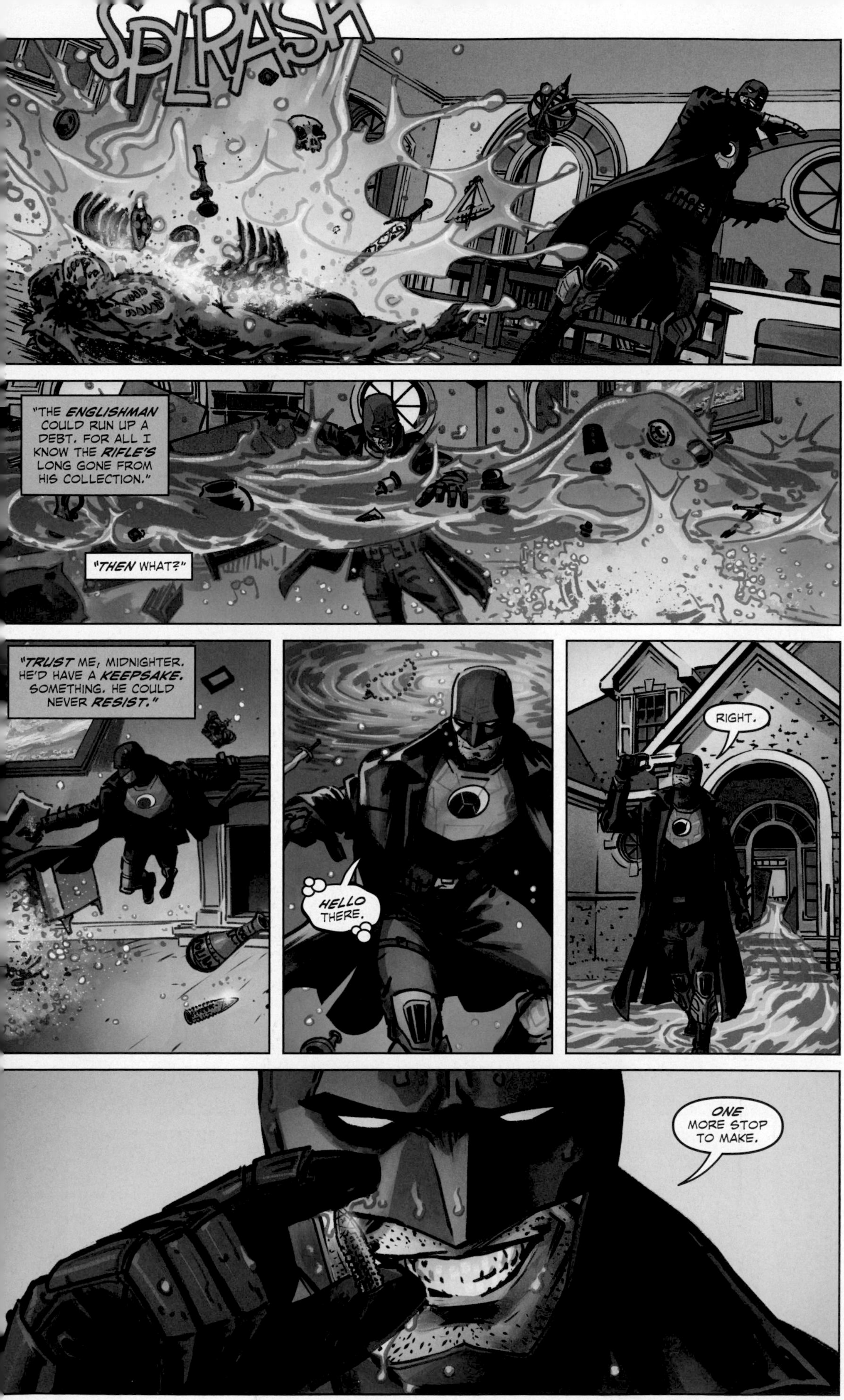
SPLRASH
"THE ENGLISHMAN COULD RUN UP A DEBT. FOR ALL I KNOW THE RIFLE'S LONG GONE FROM HIS COLLECTION."
"THEN WHAT?"
"TRUST ME, MIDNIGHTER. HE'D HAVE A KEEPSAKE. SOMETHING. HE COULD NEVER RESIST."
HELLO THERE.
RIGHT.
ONE MORE STOP TO MAKE.

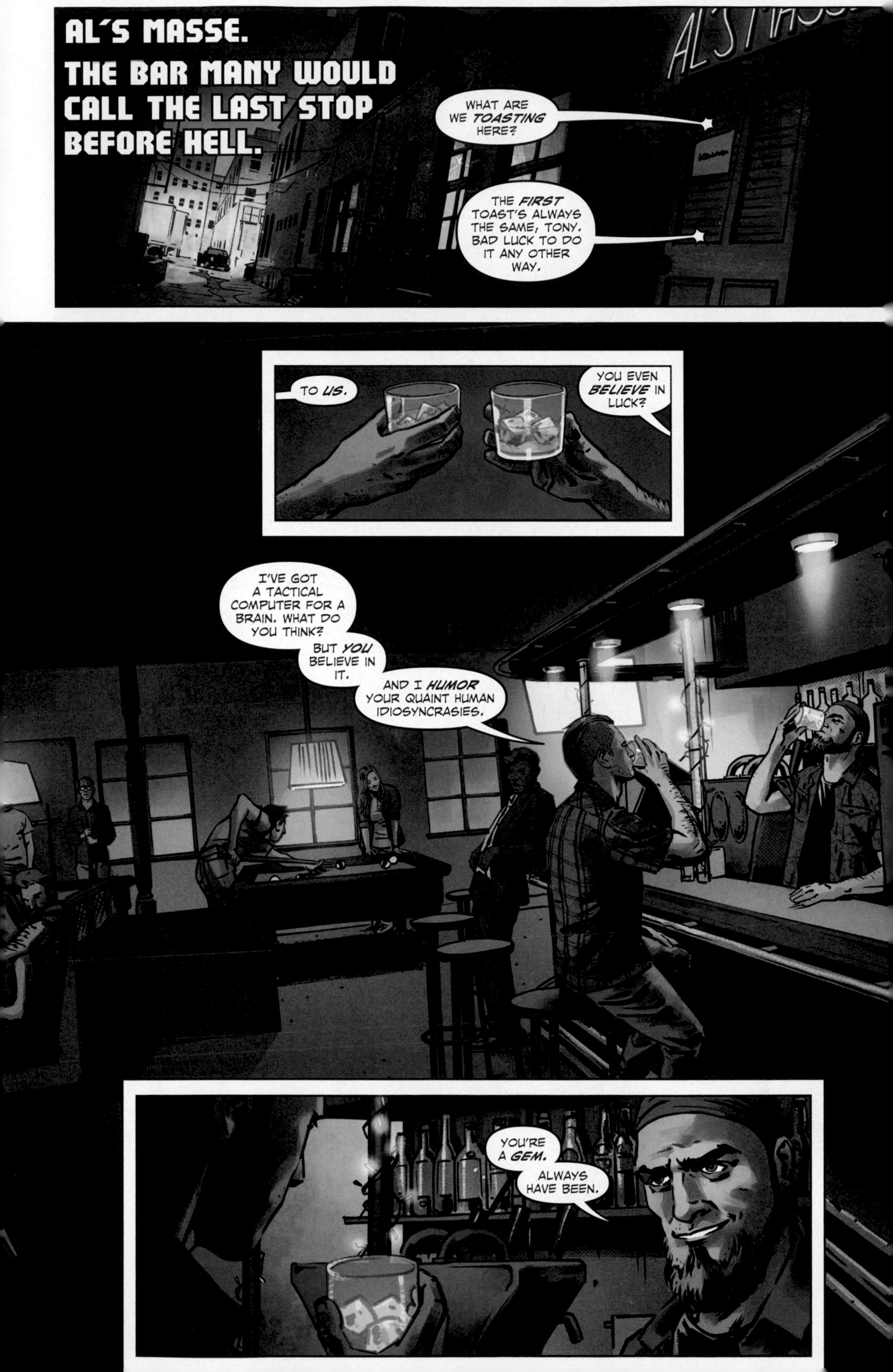
AL'S MASSE.
THE BAR MANY WOULD CALL THE LAST STOP BEFORE HELL.
WHAT ARE WE TOASTING HERE?
THE FIRST TOAST'S ALWAYS THE SAME, TONY. BAD LUCK TO DO IT ANY OTHER WAY.
TO US.
YOU EVEN BELIEVE IN LUCK?
I'VE GOT A TACTICAL COMPUTER FOR A BRAIN. WHAT DO YOU THINK?
BUT YOU BELIEVE IN IT.
AND I HUMOR YOUR QUAINT HUMAN IDIOSYNCRASIES.
YOU'RE A GEM.
ALWAYS HAVE BEEN.

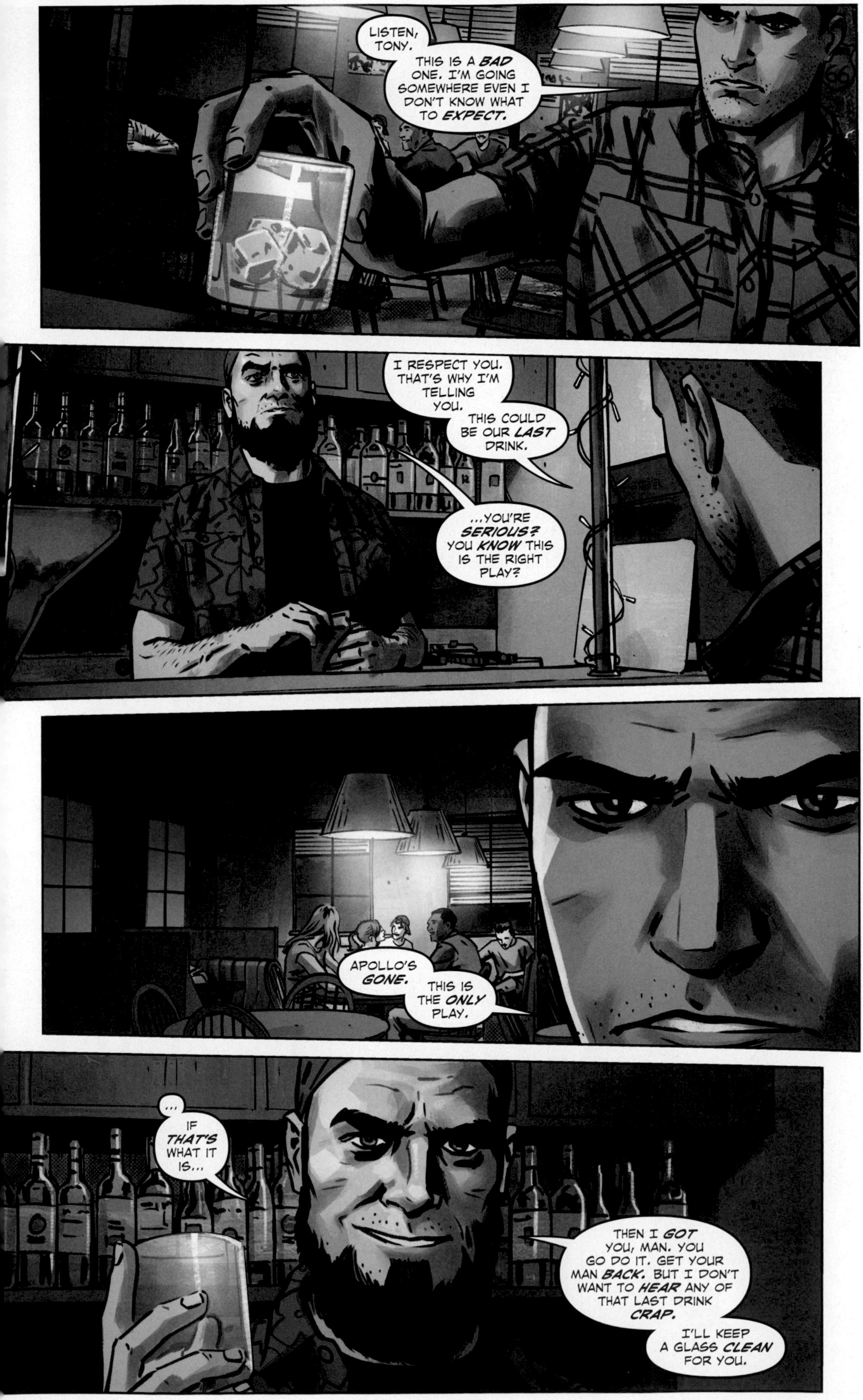
LISTEN, TONY.
THIS IS A BAD ONE. I'M GOING SOMEWHERE EVEN I DON'T KNOW WHAT TO EXPECT.
I RESPECT YOU. THAT'S WHY I'M TELLING YOU.
THIS COULD BE OUR LAST DRINK.
...YOU'RE SERIOUS? YOU KNOW THIS IS THE RIGHT PLAY?
APOLLO'S GONE.
THIS IS THE ONLY PLAY.
...
IF THAT'S WHAT IT IS...
THEN I GOT YOU, MAN. YOU GO DO IT. GET YOUR MAN BACK. BUT I DON'T WANT TO HEAR ANY OF THAT LAST DRINK CRAP.
I'LL KEEP A GLASS CLEAN FOR YOU.

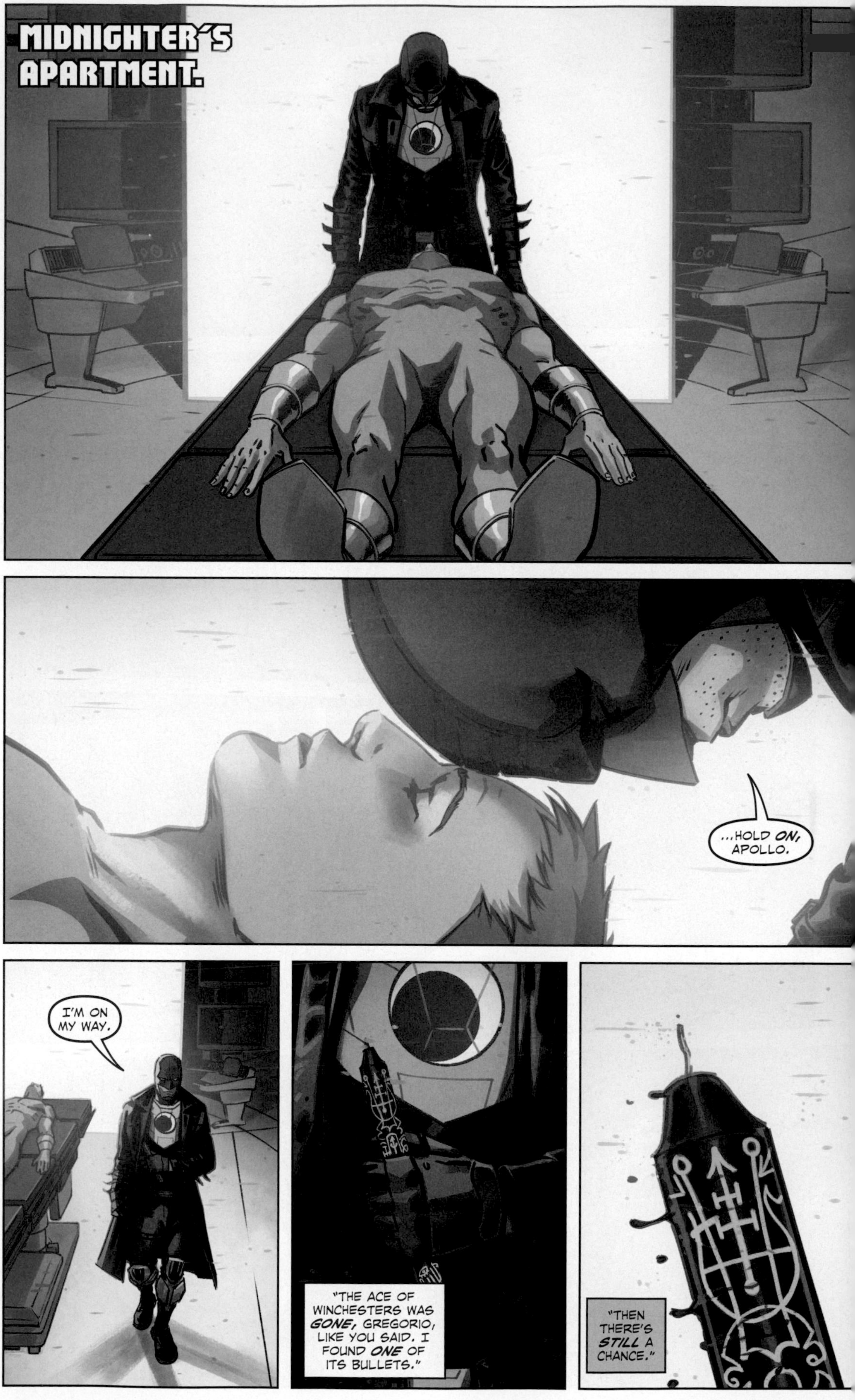
MIDNIGHTER'S APARTMENT.
...HOLD ON, APOLLO.
I'M ON MY WAY.
"THE ACE OF WINCHESTERS WAS GONE, GREGORIO, LIKE YOU SAID. I FOUND ONE OF ITS BULLETS."
"THEN THERE'S STILL A CHANCE."

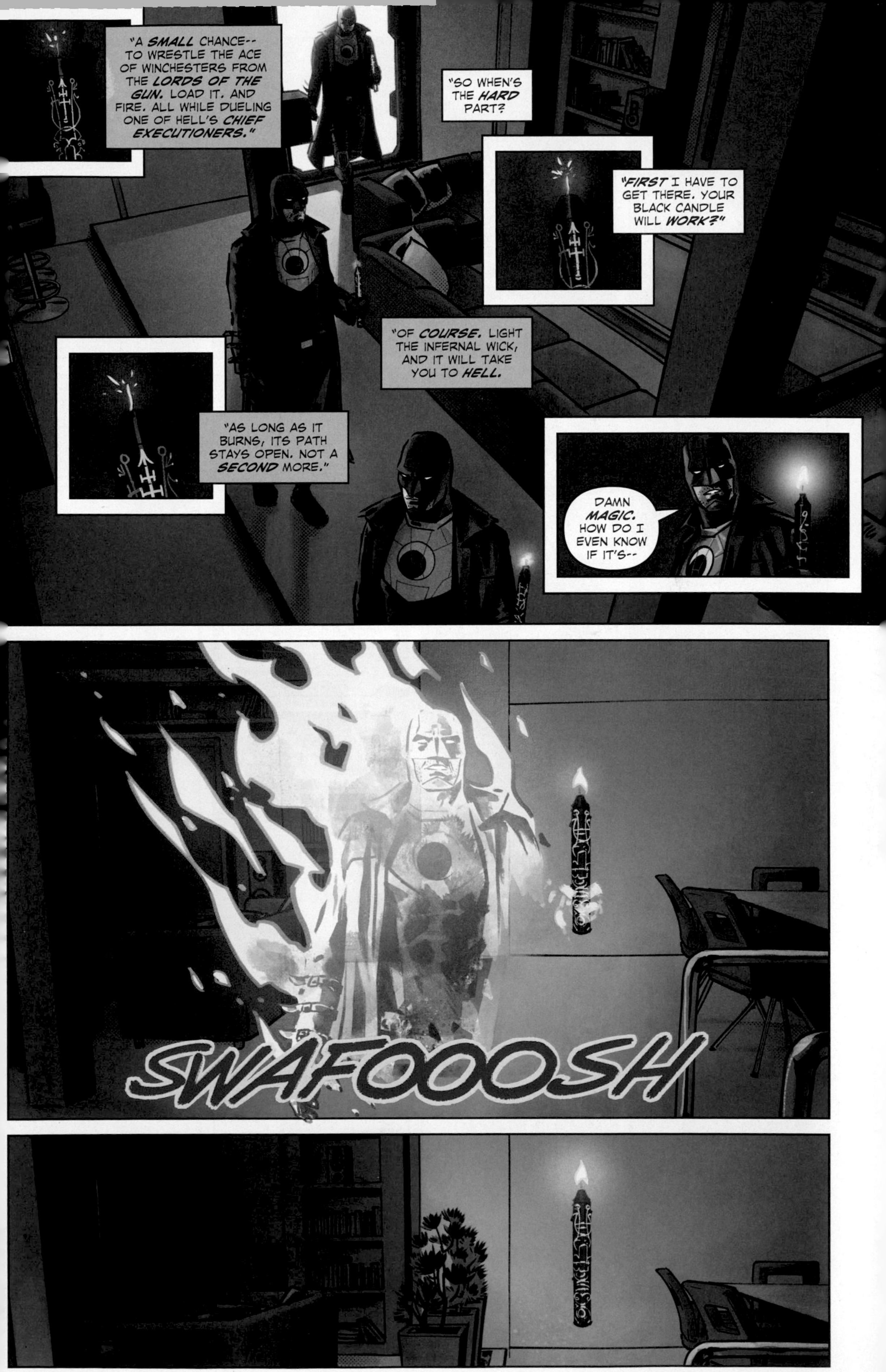
"A SMALL CHANCE-- TO WRESTLE THE ACE OF WINCHESTERS FROM THE LORDS OF THE GUN. LOAD IT. AND FIRE. ALL WHILE DUELING ONE OF HELL'S CHIEF EXECUTIONERS."
"SO WHEN'S THE HARD PART?
"FIRST I HAVE TO GET THERE. YOUR BLACK CANDLE WILL WORK?"
"OF COURSE. LIGHT THE INFERNAL WICK, AND IT WILL TAKE YOU TO HELL.
"AS LONG AS IT BURNS, ITS PATH STAYS OPEN. NOT A SECOND MORE."
DAMN MAGIC. HOW DO I EVEN KNOW IF IT'S--
SWAFOOOSH

HELL.

YOUR *MOVE*, APOLLO.

AND *AGAIN* YOU LAND ON *MURDER*.

TAKE THE *HINT*. YOU *STILL* SAY YOU DON'T BELONG HERE? YOU KILL. AND *KILL*.

YOU THINK I DON'T UNDERSTAND *KILLING*, NERON?

I KNOW ALL TOO WELL WHAT IT MEANS. AND I *ACCEPT* IT.

IT'S A BAD WORLD. IT HURT *ME*. IT HURT *MIDNIGHTER*. PEOPLE DESERVE WHAT *WE* NEVER HAD. THEY DESERVE TO KNOW THE BAD THINGS ARE GONE FOR *GOOD*.

THEY *DESERVE* THAT.

MURDER DIDN'T BRING ME HERE, NERON. AND EVEN IF IT *DID?*

I WOULD *GLADLY* GO TO HELL IF IT MEANT SOMEONE ELSE DIDN'T HAVE TO.

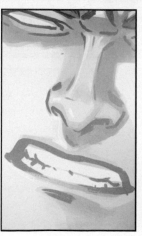

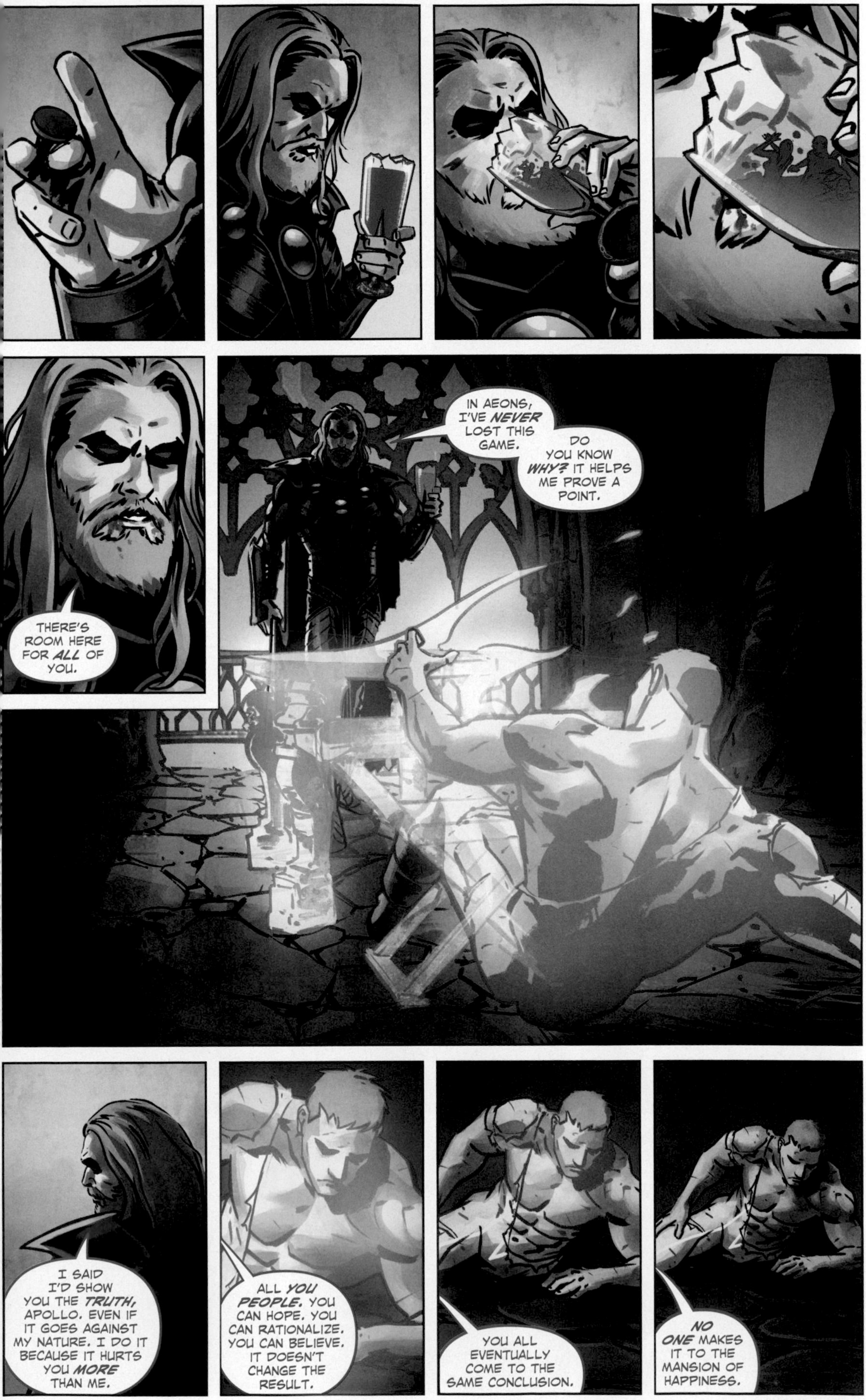
THERE'S ROOM HERE FOR ALL OF YOU.
IN AEONS, I'VE NEVER LOST THIS GAME.
DO YOU KNOW WHY? IT HELPS ME PROVE A POINT.
I SAID I'D SHOW YOU THE TRUTH, APOLLO. EVEN IF IT GOES AGAINST MY NATURE. I DO IT BECAUSE IT HURTS YOU MORE THAN ME.
ALL YOU PEOPLE. YOU CAN HOPE. YOU CAN RATIONALIZE. YOU CAN BELIEVE. IT DOESN'T CHANGE THE RESULT.
YOU ALL EVENTUALLY COME TO THE SAME CONCLUSION.
NO ONE MAKES IT TO THE MANSION OF HAPPINESS.

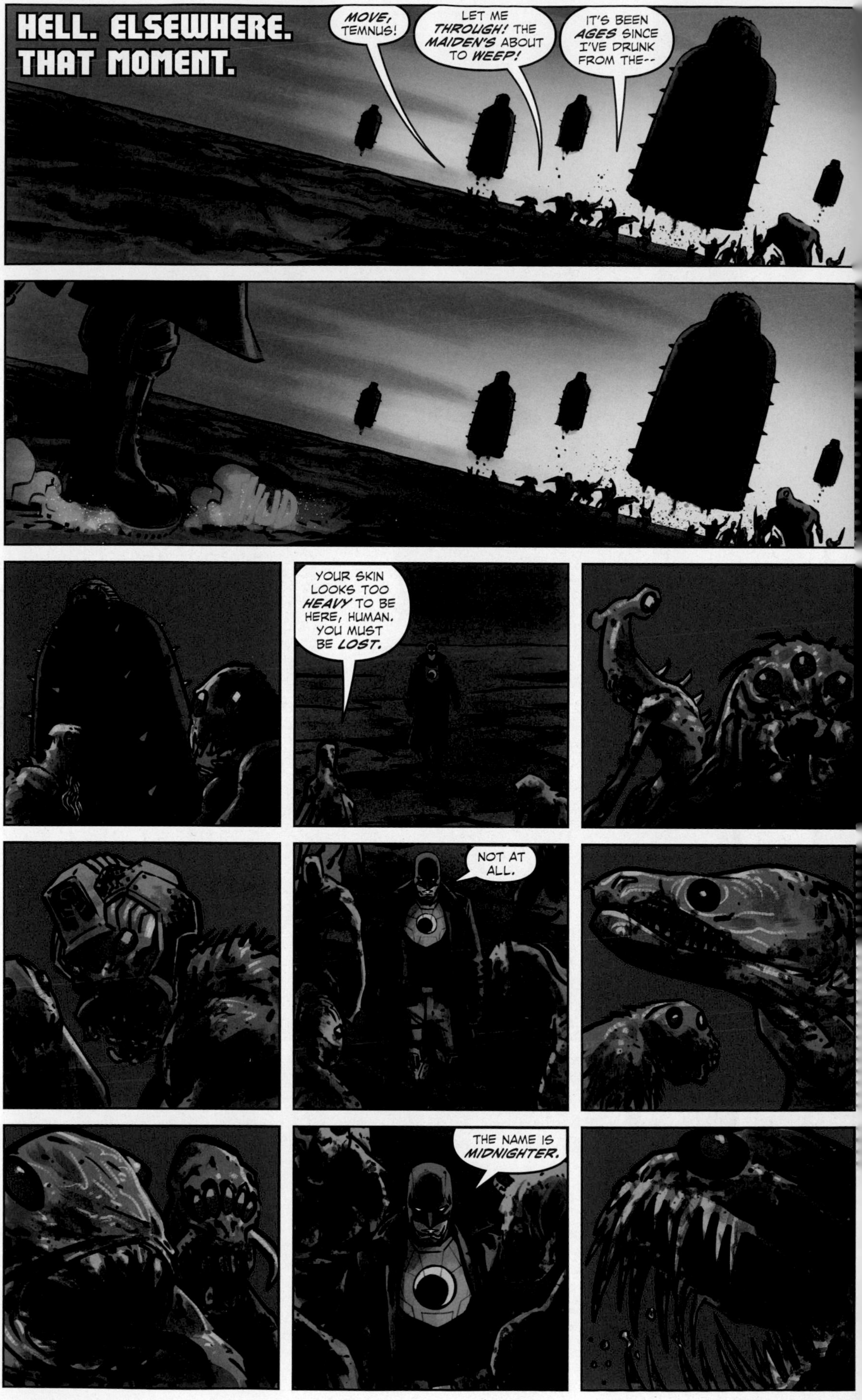
HELL. ELSEWHERE. THAT MOMENT.
MOVE, TEMNUS!
LET ME THROUGH! THE MAIDEN'S ABOUT TO WEEP!
IT'S BEEN AGES SINCE I'VE DRUNK FROM THE--
THUD
YOUR SKIN LOOKS TOO HEAVY TO BE HERE, HUMAN. YOU MUST BE LOST.
NOT AT ALL.
THE NAME IS MIDNIGHTER.

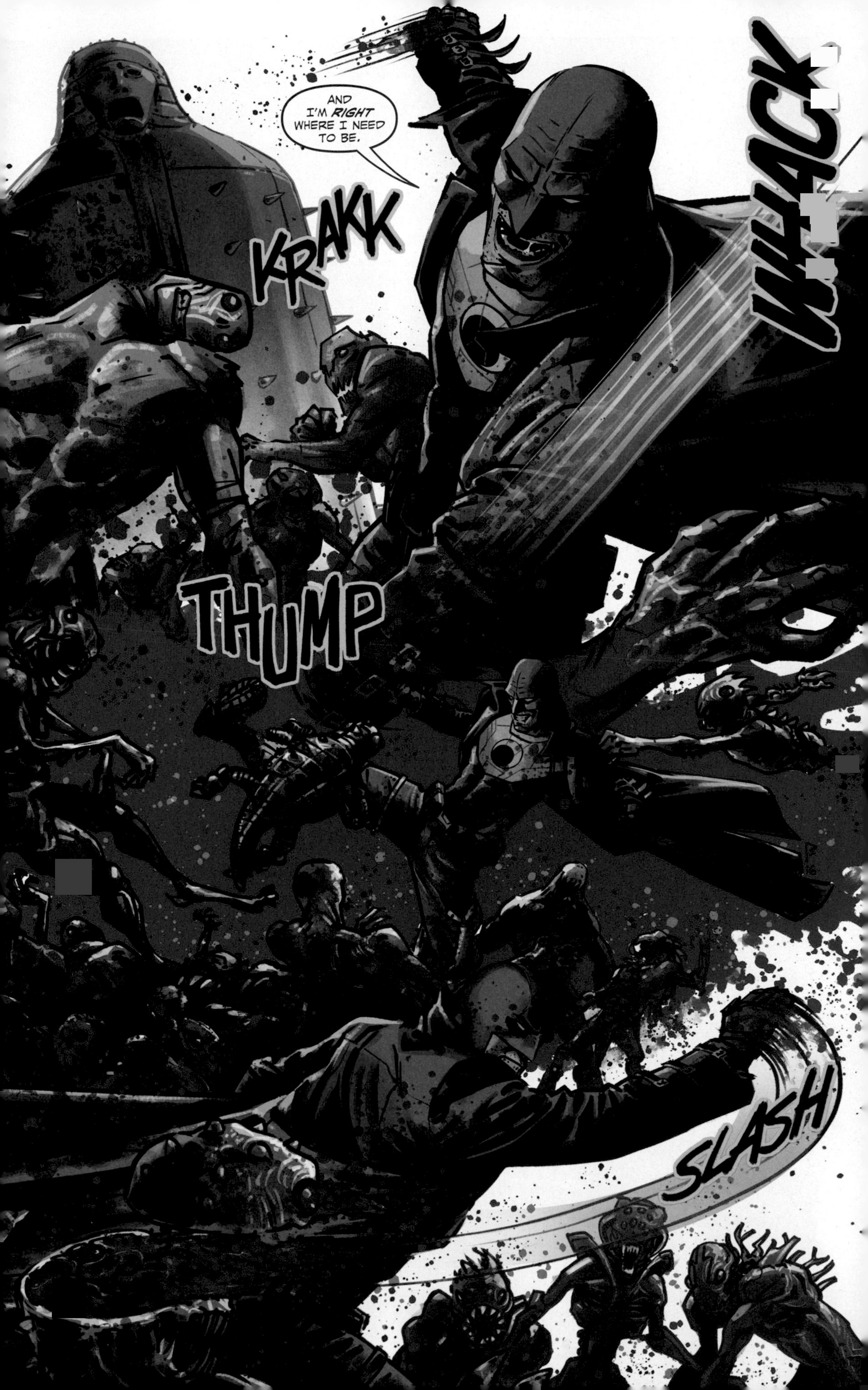
AND I'M *RIGHT* WHERE I NEED TO BE.
KRAKK
WHACK
THUMP
SLASH

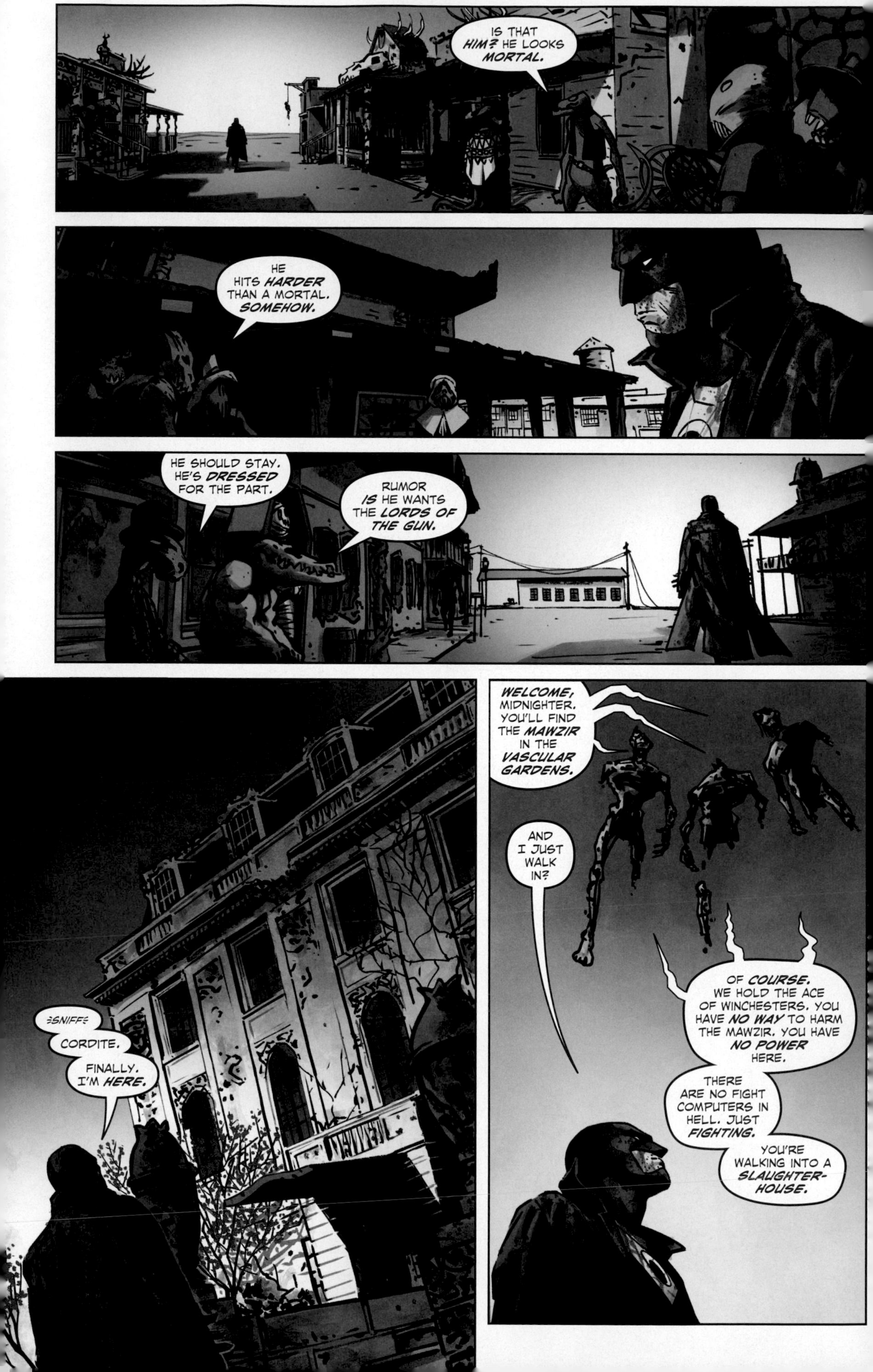
IS THAT HIM? HE LOOKS MORTAL.
HE HITS HARDER THAN A MORTAL. SOMEHOW.
HE SHOULD STAY. HE'S DRESSED FOR THE PART.
RUMOR IS HE WANTS THE LORDS OF THE GUN.
SNIFF
CORDITE.
FINALLY. I'M HERE.
WELCOME, MIDNIGHTER. YOU'LL FIND THE MAWZIR IN THE VASCULAR GARDENS.
AND I JUST WALK IN?
OF COURSE. WE HOLD THE ACE OF WINCHESTERS. YOU HAVE NO WAY TO HARM THE MAWZIR. YOU HAVE NO POWER HERE.
THERE ARE NO FIGHT COMPUTERS IN HELL. JUST FIGHTING.
YOU'RE WALKING INTO A SLAUGHTER-HOUSE.

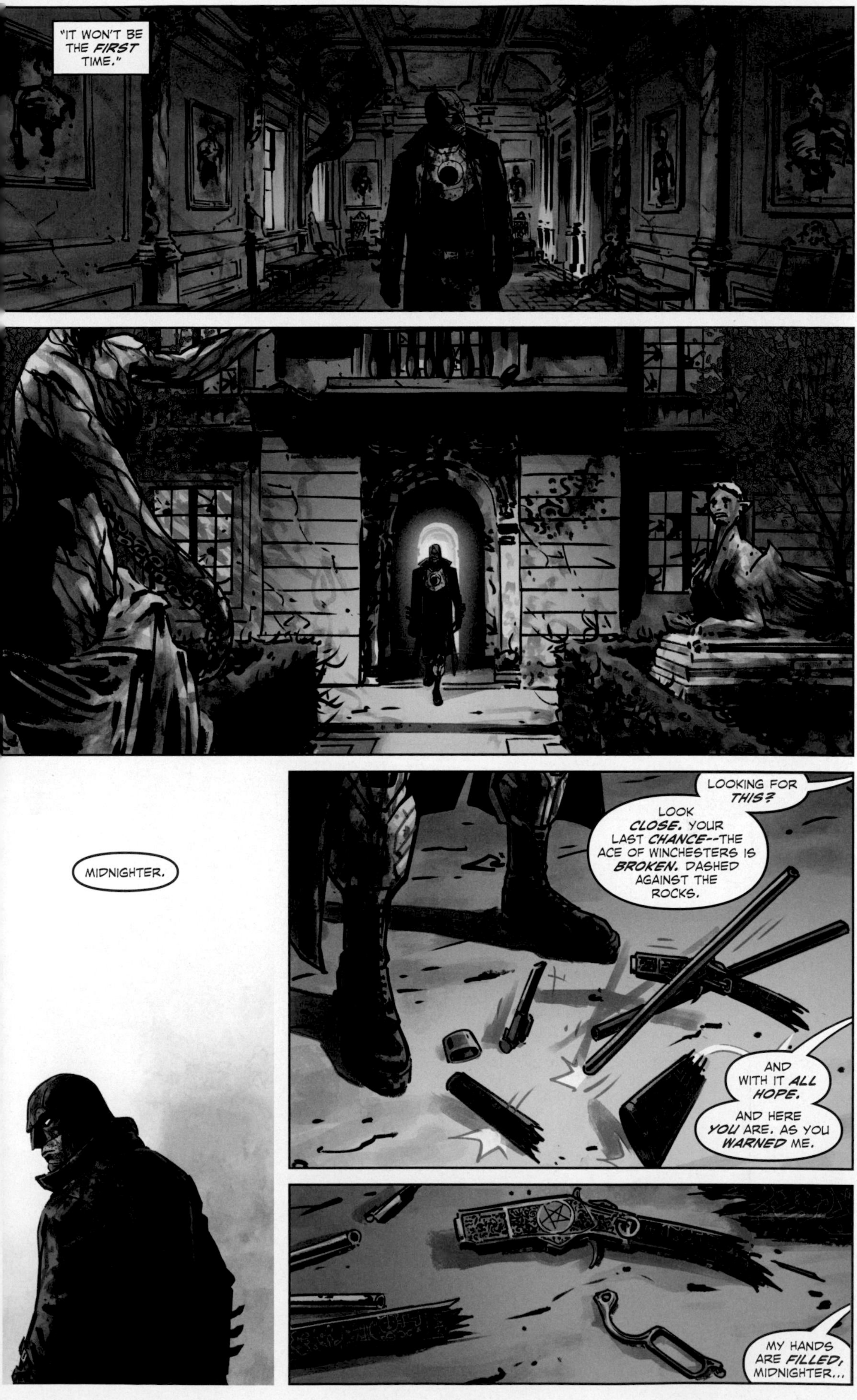
"IT WON'T BE THE *FIRST* TIME."
MIDNIGHTER.
LOOKING FOR *THIS?*
LOOK *CLOSE.* YOUR LAST *CHANCE*--THE ACE OF WINCHESTERS IS *BROKEN.* DASHED AGAINST THE ROCKS.
AND WITH IT *ALL HOPE.*
AND HERE *YOU* ARE. AS YOU *WARNED* ME.
MY HANDS ARE *FILLED,* MIDNIGHTER...

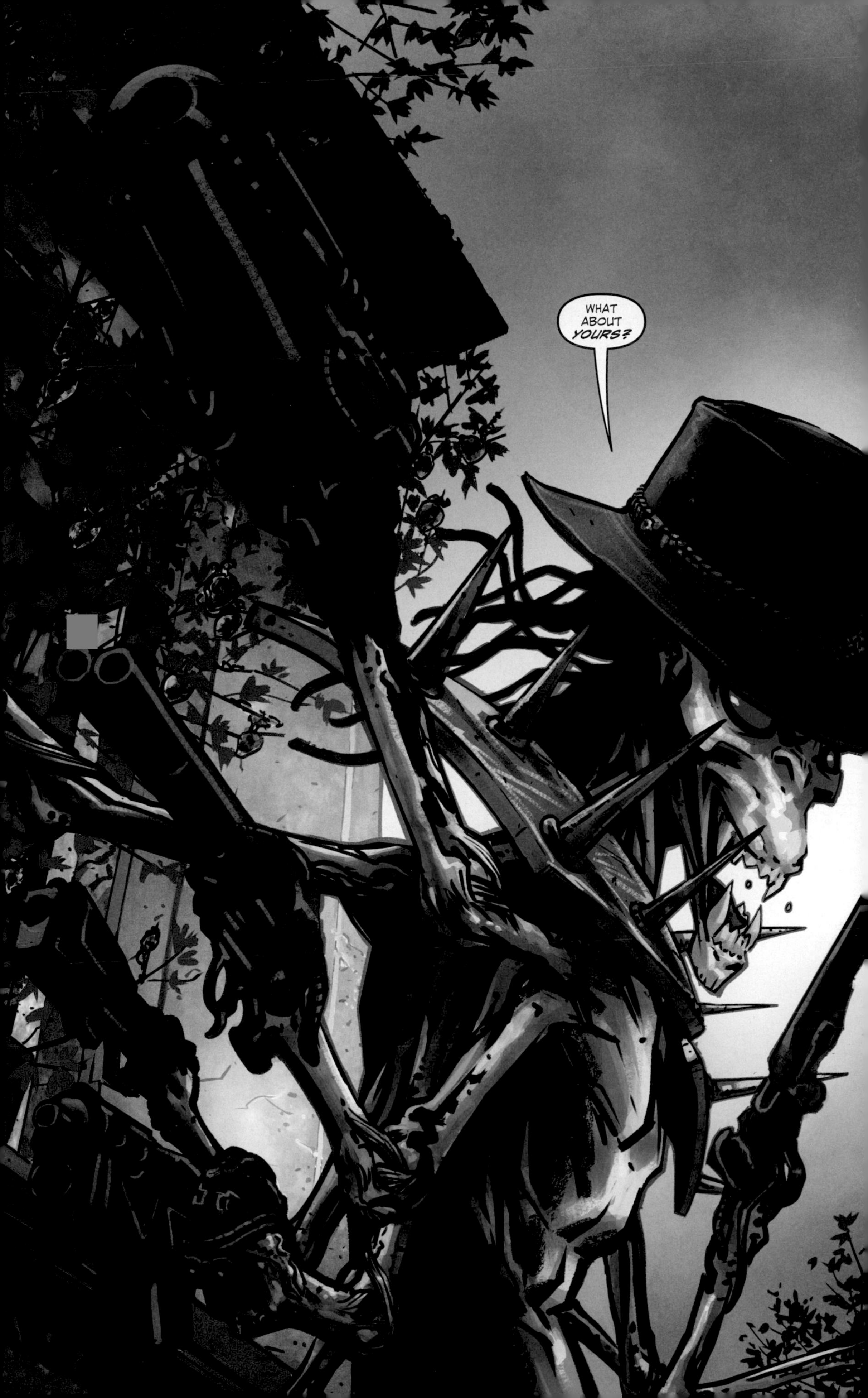
WHAT ABOUT YOURS?

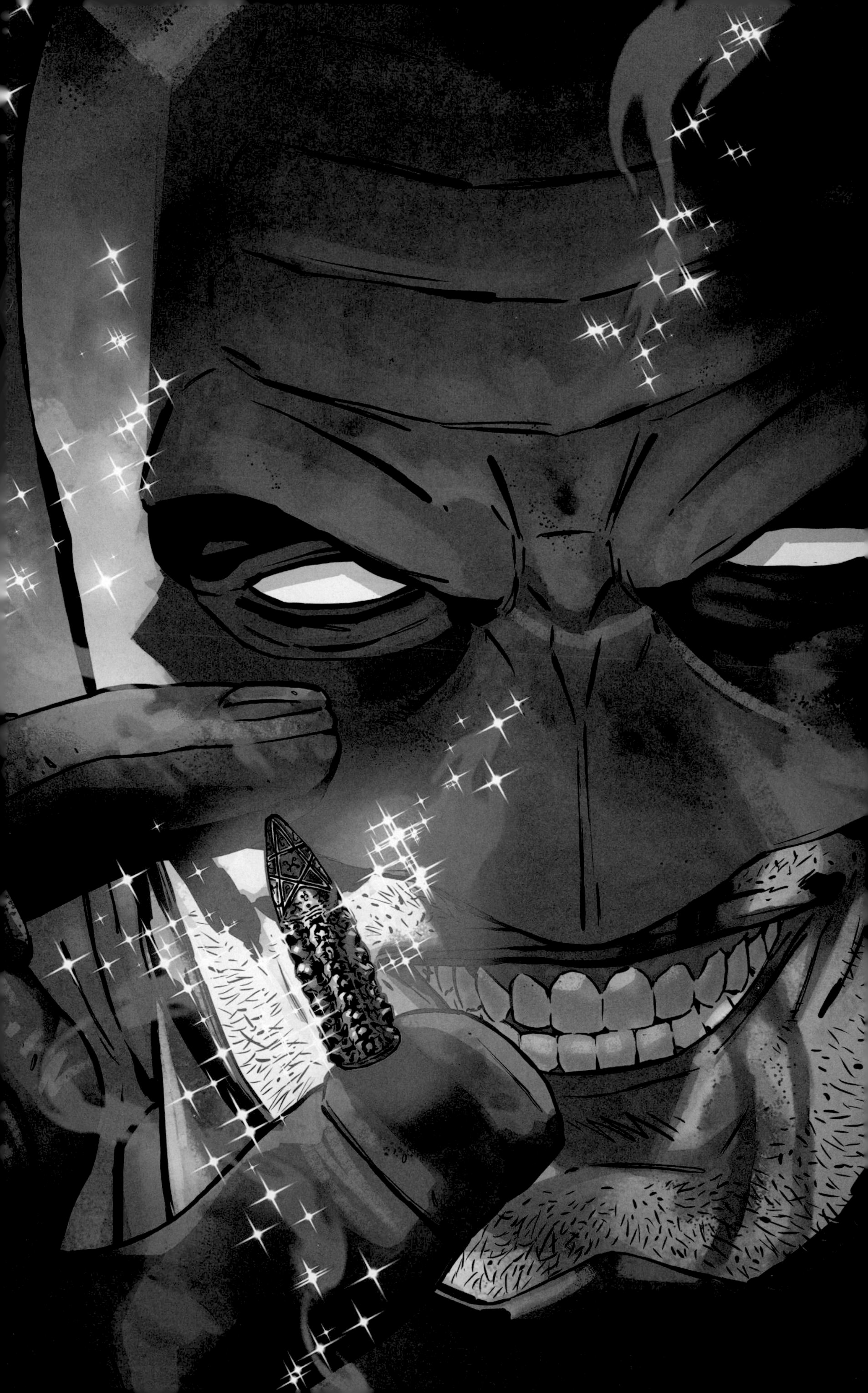

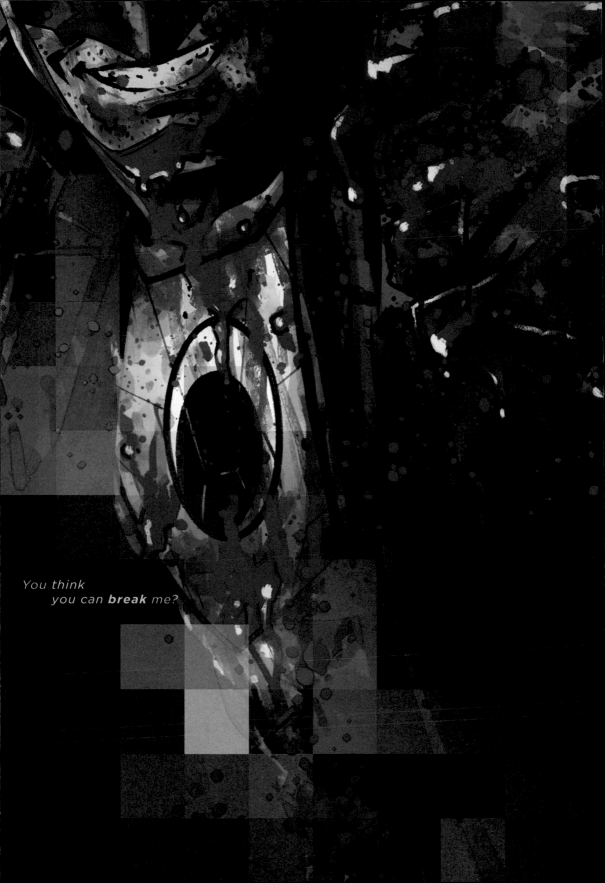

You think
   you can **break** me?

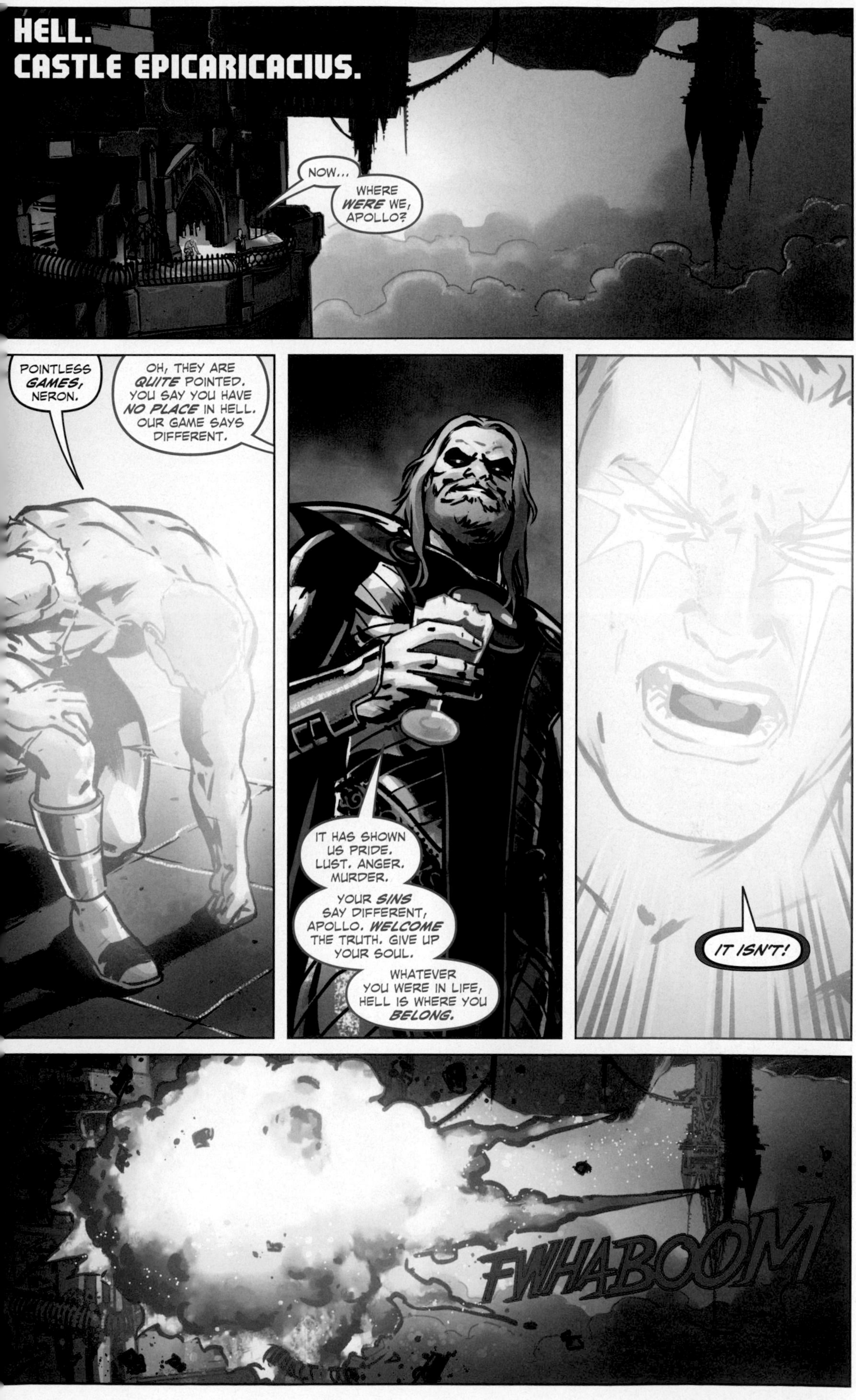

HELL.
CASTLE EPICARICACIUS.
NOW...
WHERE WERE WE, APOLLO?
POINTLESS GAMES, NERON.
OH, THEY ARE QUITE POINTED. YOU SAY YOU HAVE NO PLACE IN HELL. OUR GAME SAYS DIFFERENT.
IT HAS SHOWN US PRIDE. LUST. ANGER. MURDER.
YOUR SINS SAY DIFFERENT, APOLLO. WELCOME THE TRUTH. GIVE UP YOUR SOUL.
WHATEVER YOU WERE IN LIFE, HELL IS WHERE YOU BELONG.
IT ISN'T!
FWHABOOM

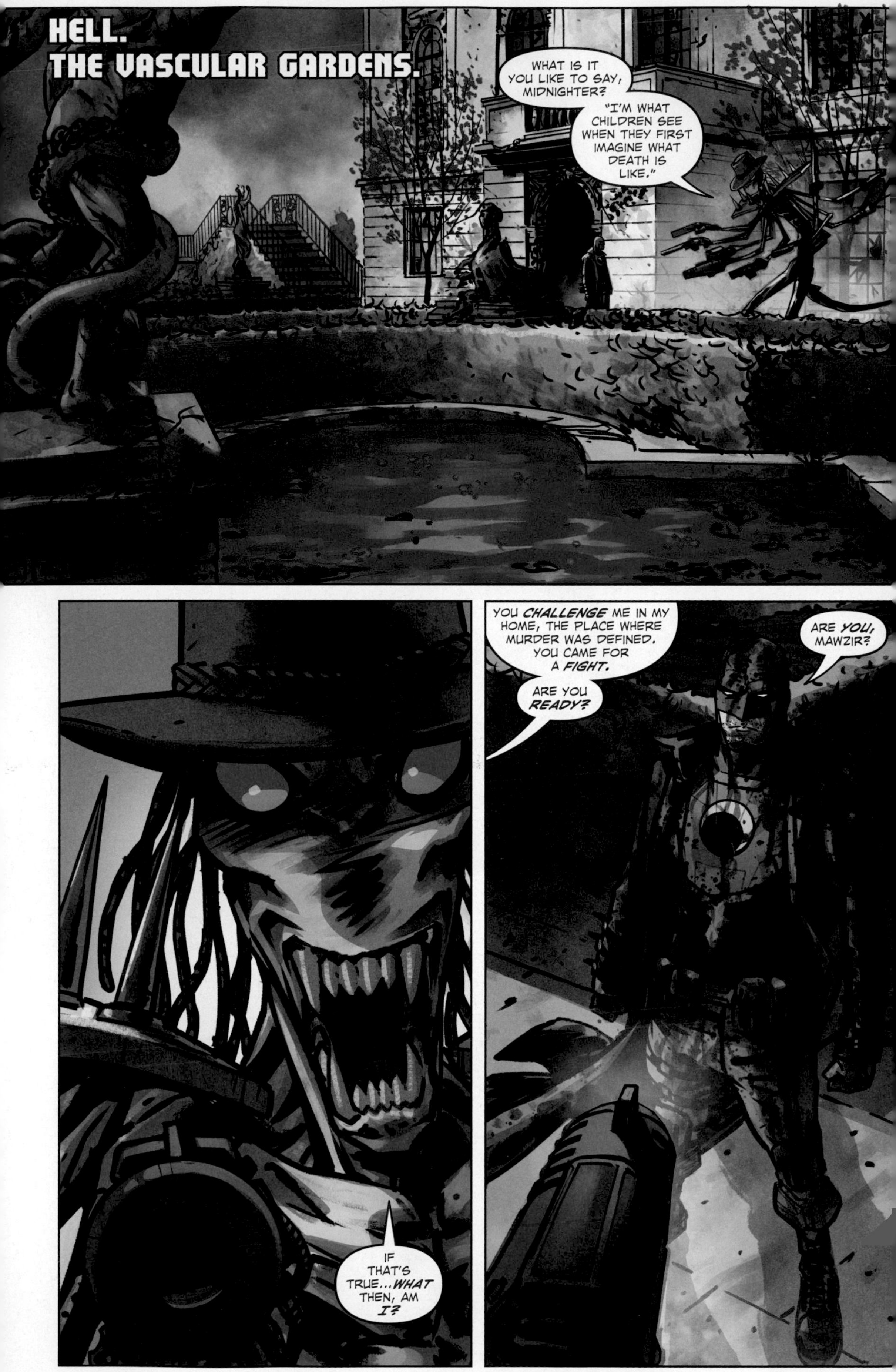
HELL.
THE VASCULAR GARDENS.
WHAT IS IT YOU LIKE TO SAY, MIDNIGHTER?
"I'M WHAT CHILDREN SEE WHEN THEY FIRST IMAGINE WHAT DEATH IS LIKE."
IF THAT'S TRUE...WHAT THEN, AM I?
YOU CHALLENGE ME IN MY HOME, THE PLACE WHERE MURDER WAS DEFINED. YOU CAME FOR A FIGHT.
ARE YOU READY?
ARE YOU, MAWZIR?

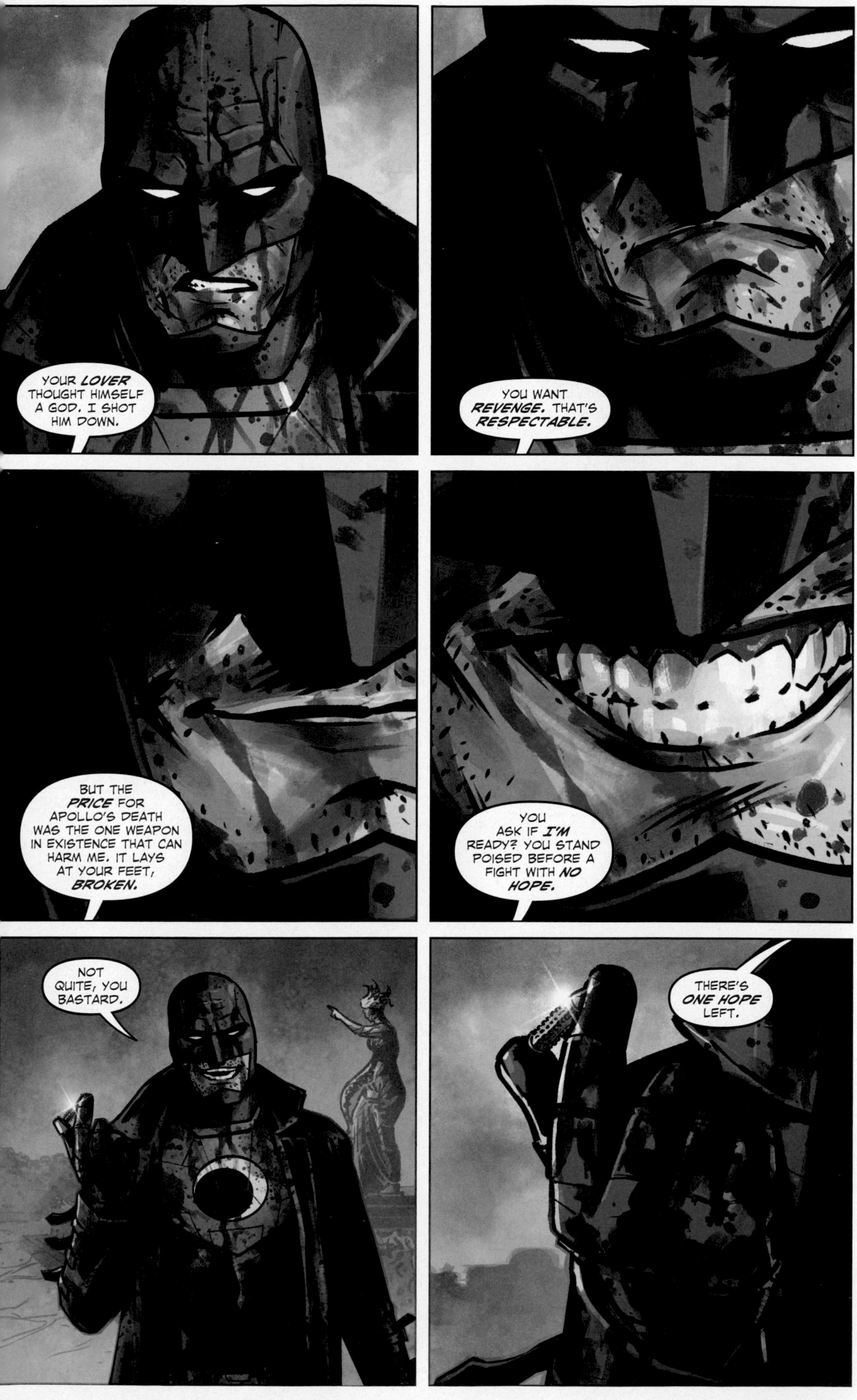
YOUR LOVER THOUGHT HIMSELF A GOD. I SHOT HIM DOWN.
YOU WANT REVENGE. THAT'S RESPECTABLE.
BUT THE PRICE FOR APOLLO'S DEATH WAS THE ONE WEAPON IN EXISTENCE THAT CAN HARM ME. IT LAYS AT YOUR FEET, BROKEN.
YOU ASK IF I'M READY? YOU STAND POISED BEFORE A FIGHT WITH NO HOPE.
NOT QUITE, YOU BASTARD.
THERE'S ONE HOPE LEFT.

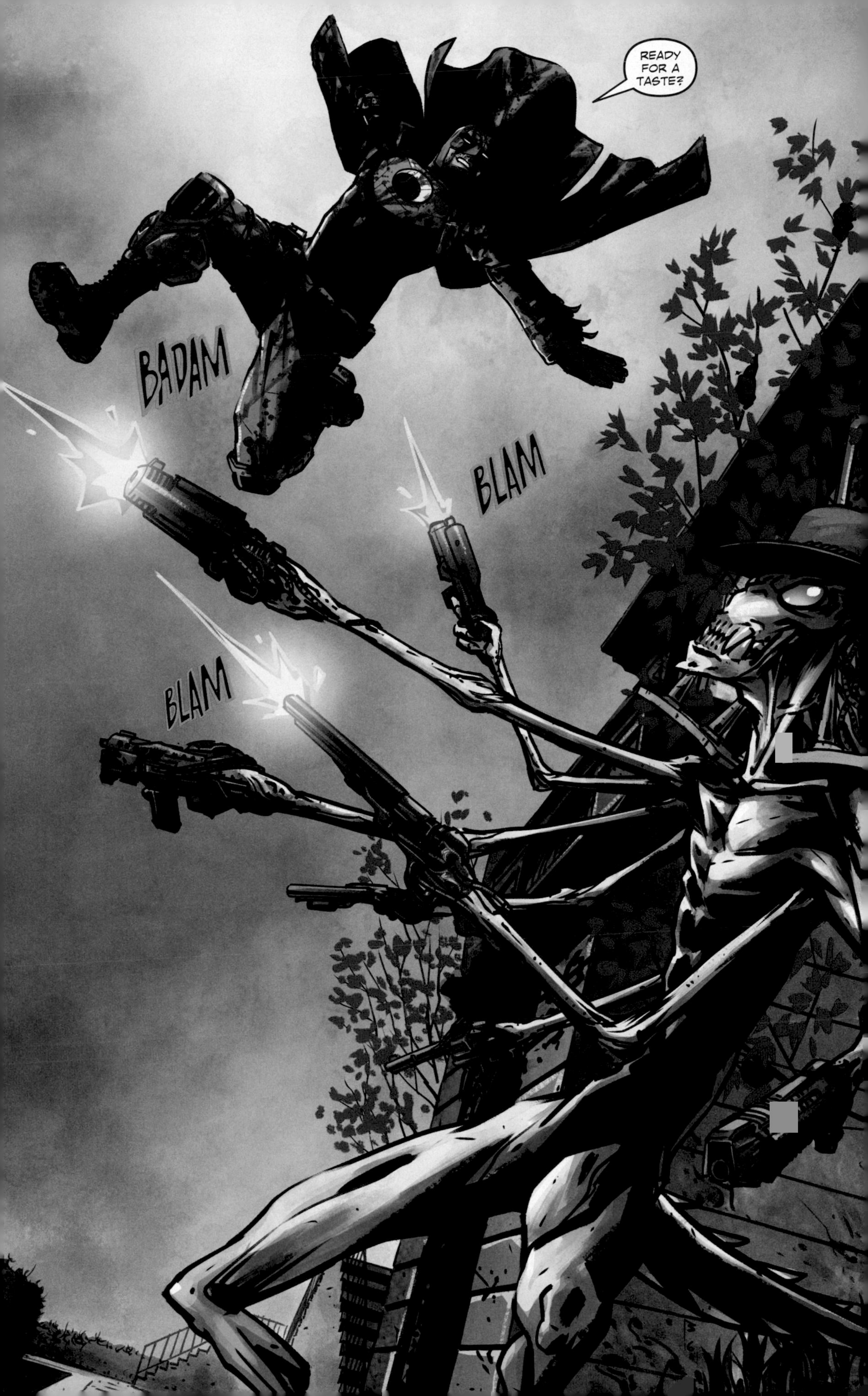
READY FOR A TASTE?
BADAM
BLAM
BLAM

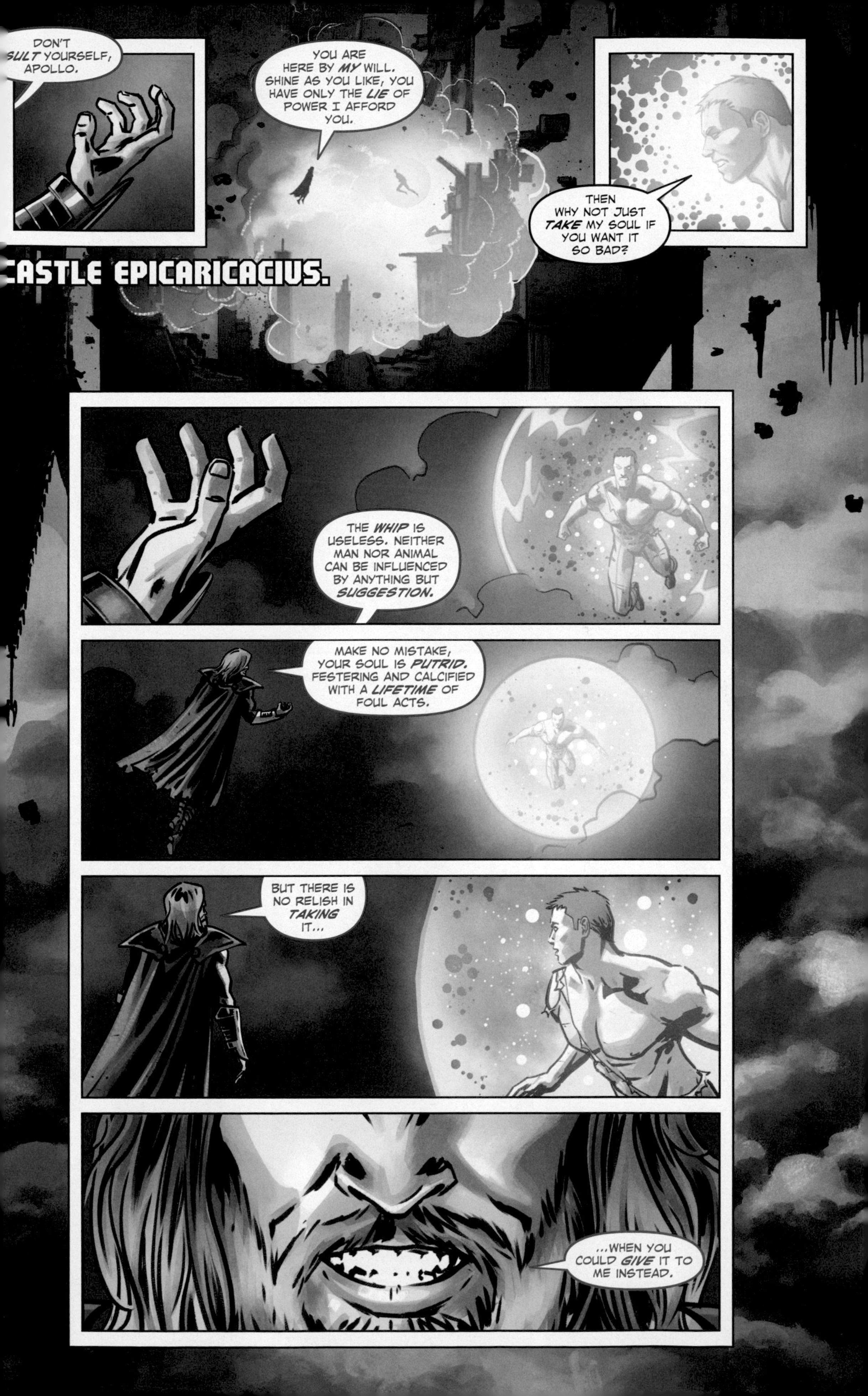
DON'T ...SULT YOURSELF, APOLLO.
YOU ARE HERE BY MY WILL. SHINE AS YOU LIKE, YOU HAVE ONLY THE LIE OF POWER I AFFORD YOU.
THEN WHY NOT JUST TAKE MY SOUL IF YOU WANT IT SO BAD?
CASTLE EPICARICACIUS.
THE WHIP IS USELESS. NEITHER MAN NOR ANIMAL CAN BE INFLUENCED BY ANYTHING BUT SUGGESTION.
MAKE NO MISTAKE, YOUR SOUL IS PUTRID. FESTERING AND CALCIFIED WITH A LIFETIME OF FOUL ACTS.
BUT THERE IS NO RELISH IN TAKING IT...
...WHEN YOU COULD GIVE IT TO ME INSTEAD.

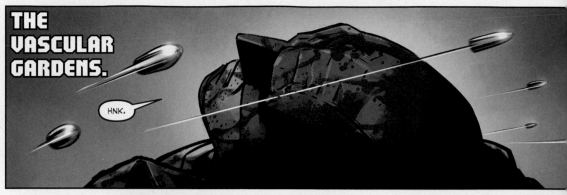

THE VASCULAR GARDENS.

HNK.

LOOK AT YOU GO.

WITHOUT YOUR *EARTHLY* TRAPPINGS, YOUR FIGHT COMPUTER, ENHANCED SENSES-- YOU *STILL* FIGHT.

BADAM

BADAM

WHACK

ADMIRABLE. DIVERTING.

USELESS.

BLAM

WHAM

...I'LL KILL YOU.

CARE TO TRY IT WITH A *ROUND* IN YOUR HEAD, HUMAN?

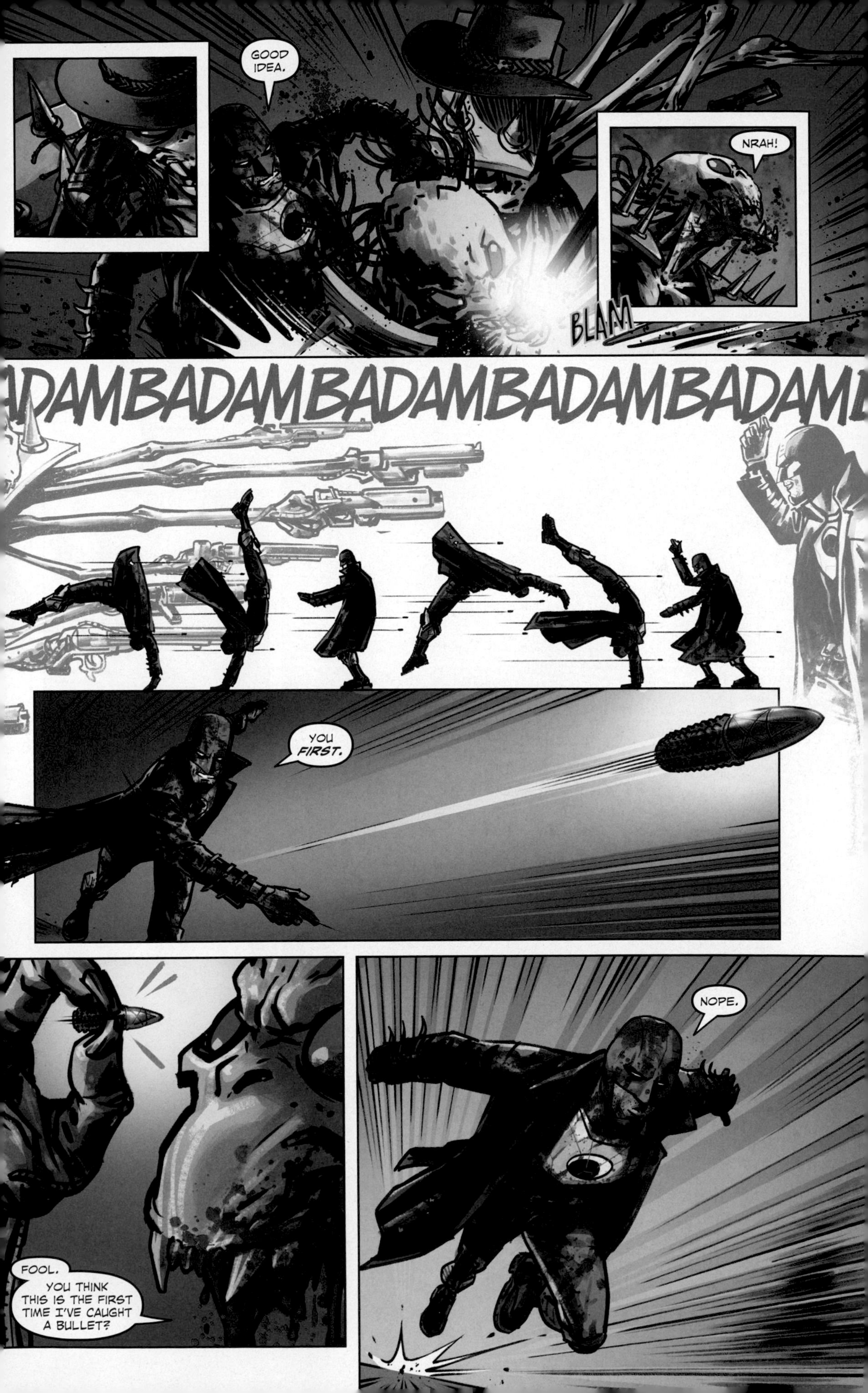
GOOD IDEA.
NRAH!
BLAM
BADAMBADAMBADAMBADAM
YOU FIRST.
FOOL. YOU THINK THIS IS THE FIRST TIME I'VE CAUGHT A BULLET?
NOPE.

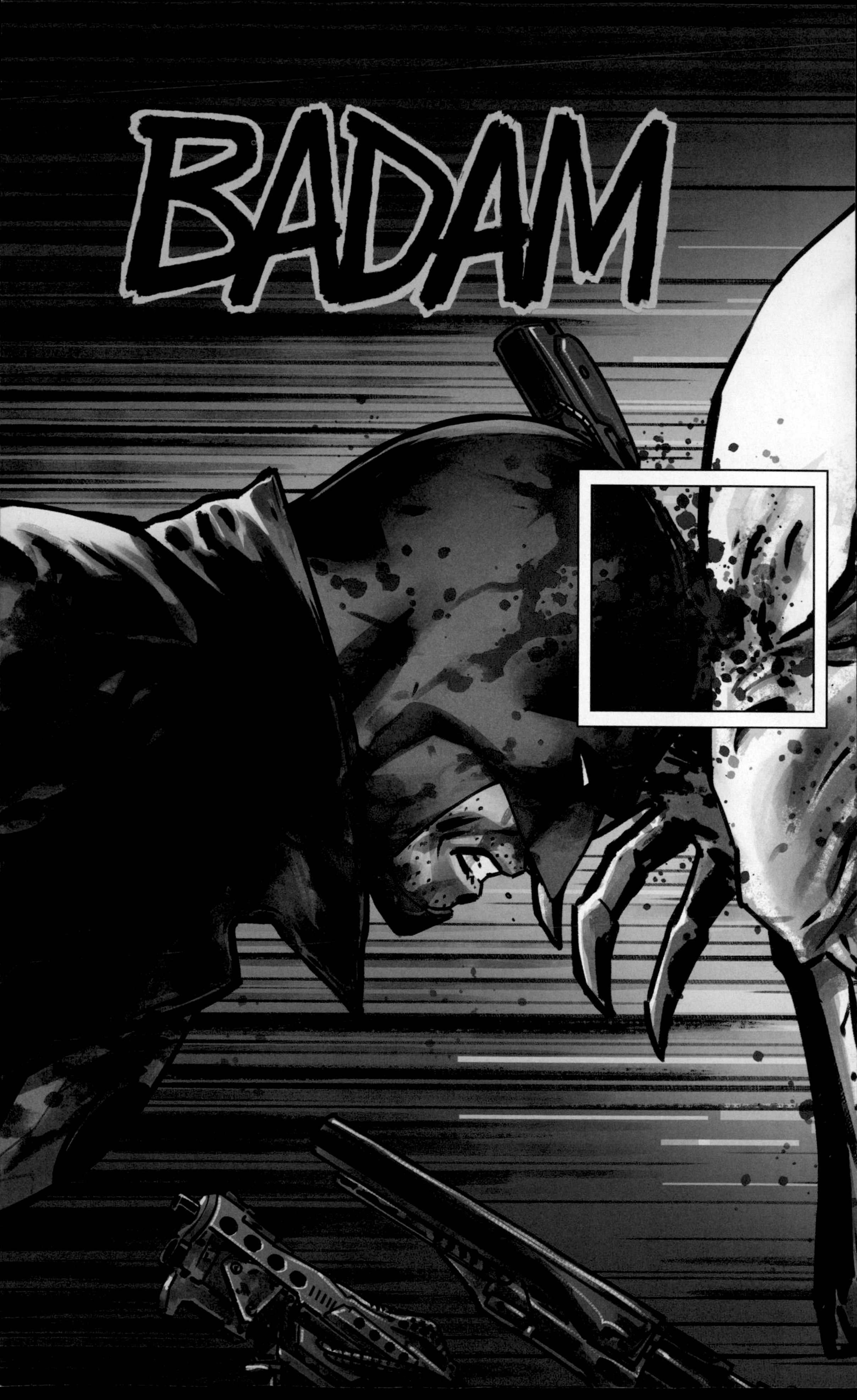
BADAM

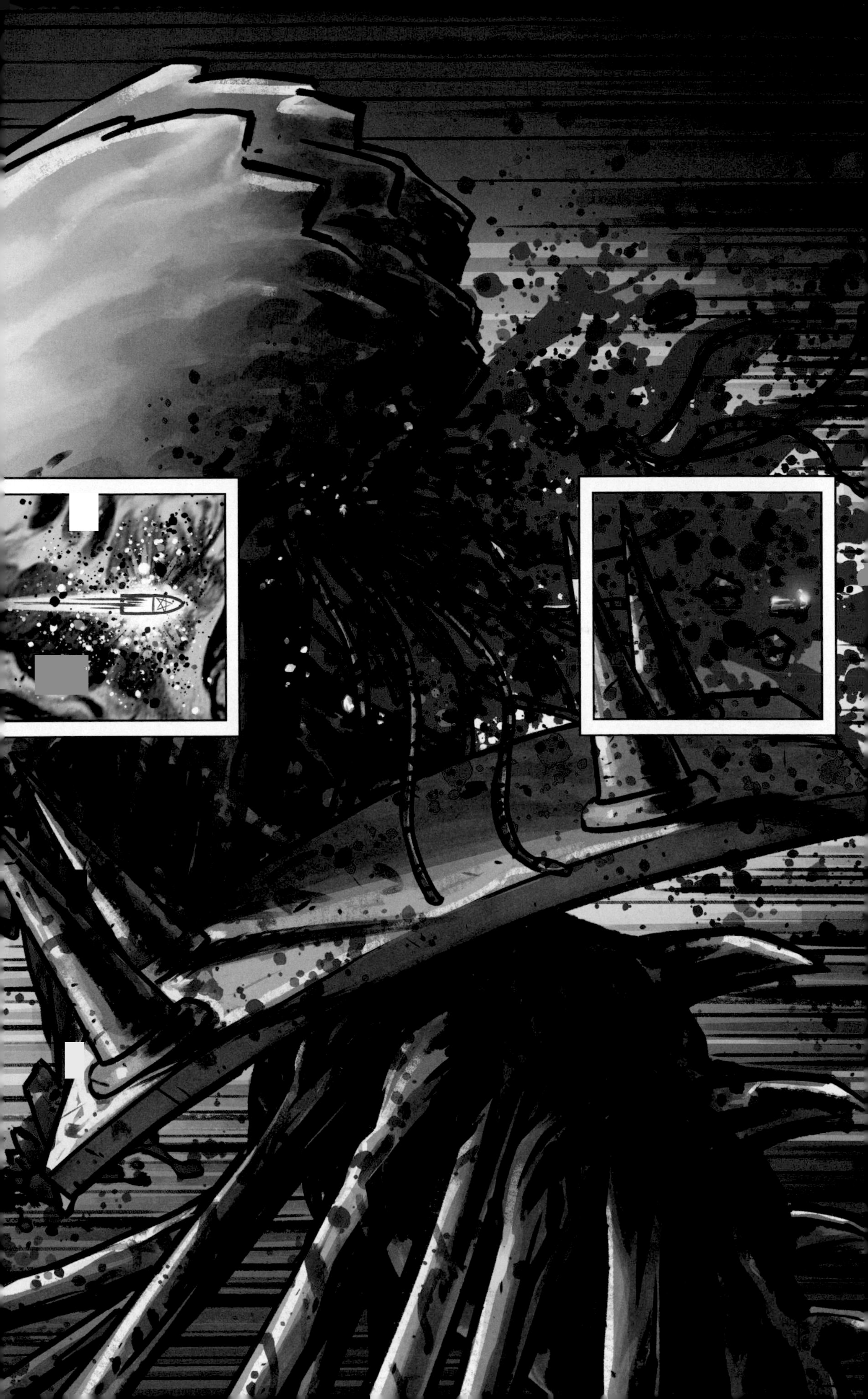

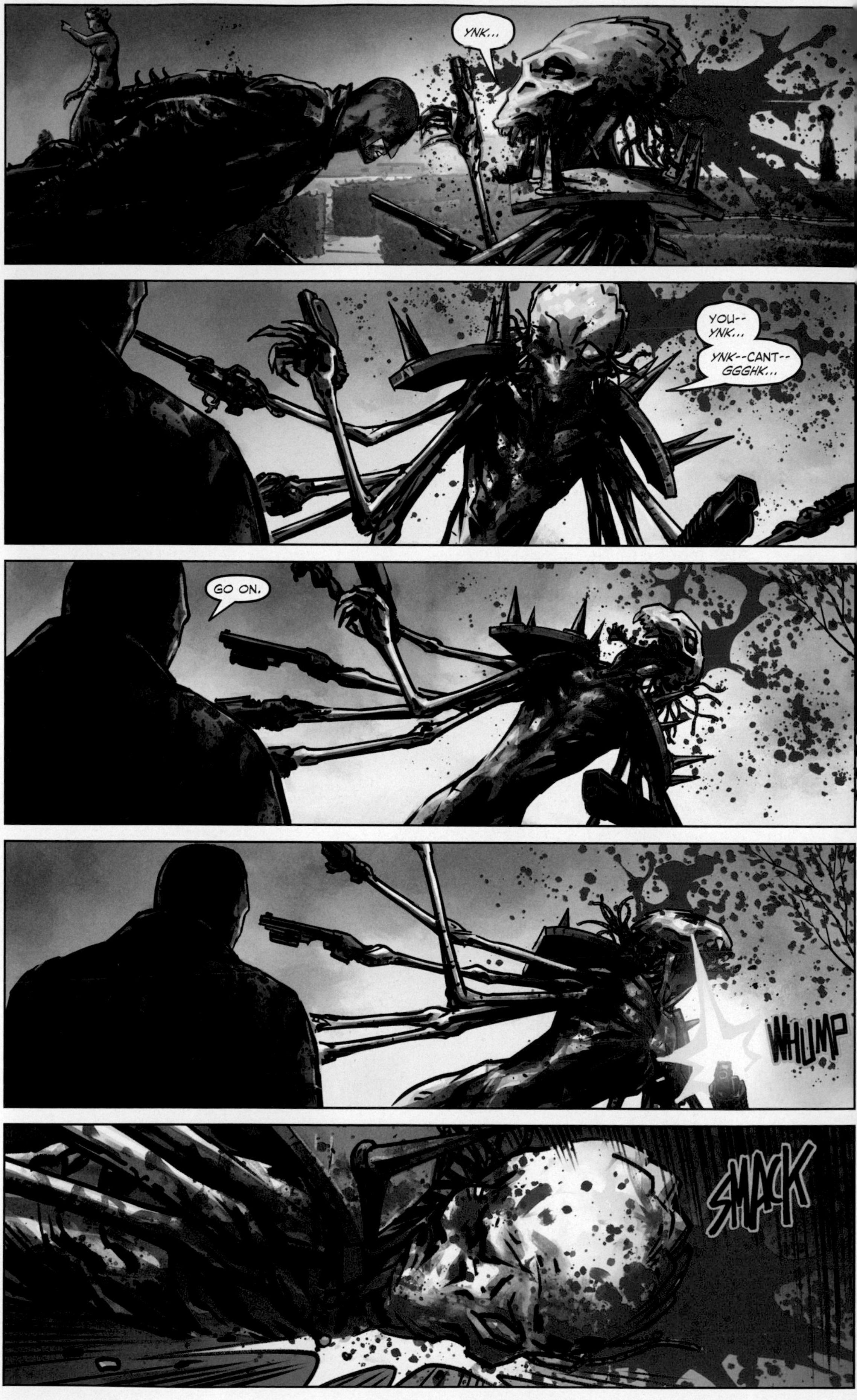
YNK...
YOU-- YNK...
YNK--CANT-- GGGHK...
GO ON.
WHUMP
SMACK

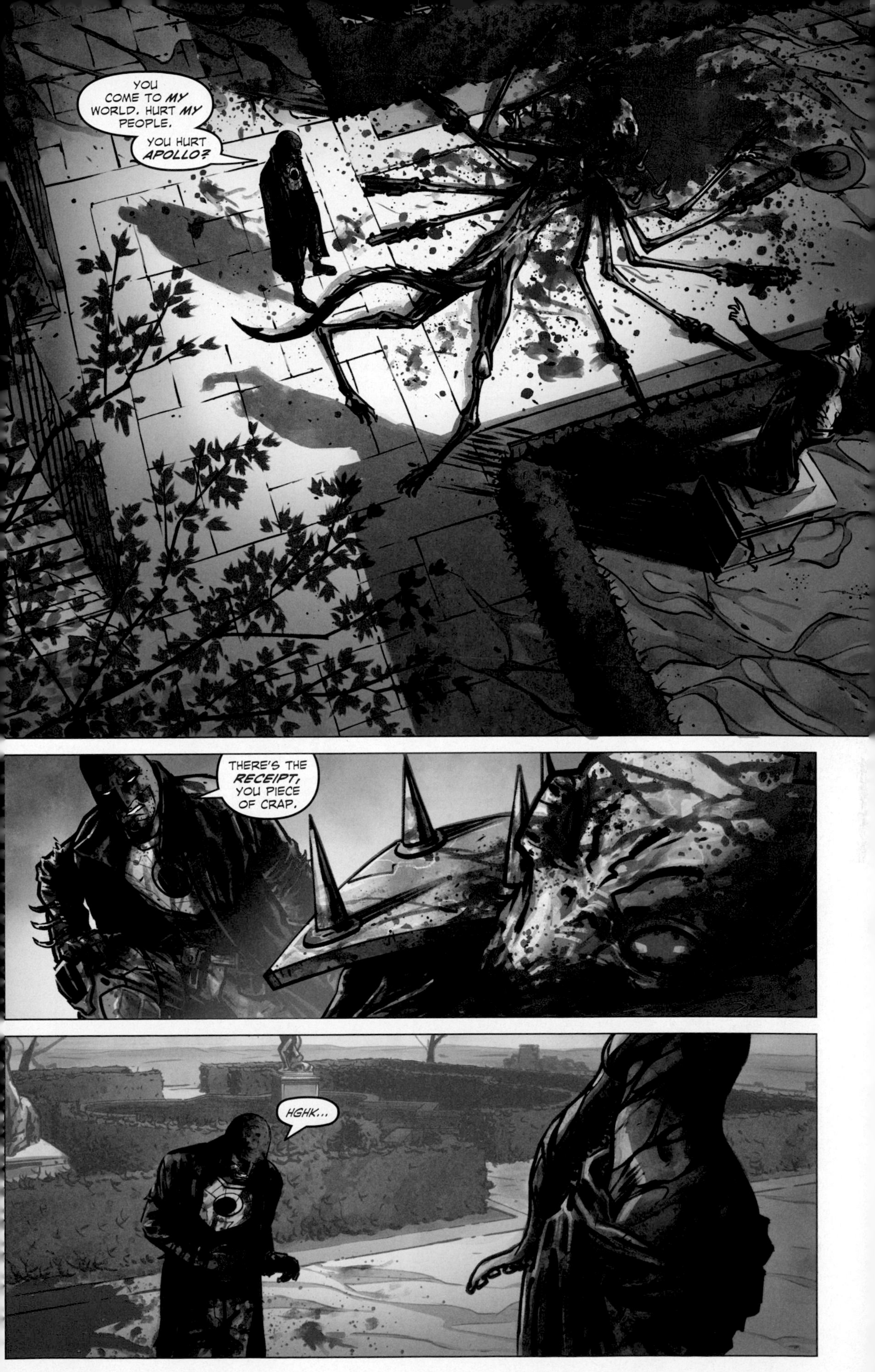
YOU COME TO *MY* WORLD. HURT *MY* PEOPLE.
YOU HURT *APOLLO?*
THERE'S THE *RECEIPT,* YOU PIECE OF CRAP.
HGHK...

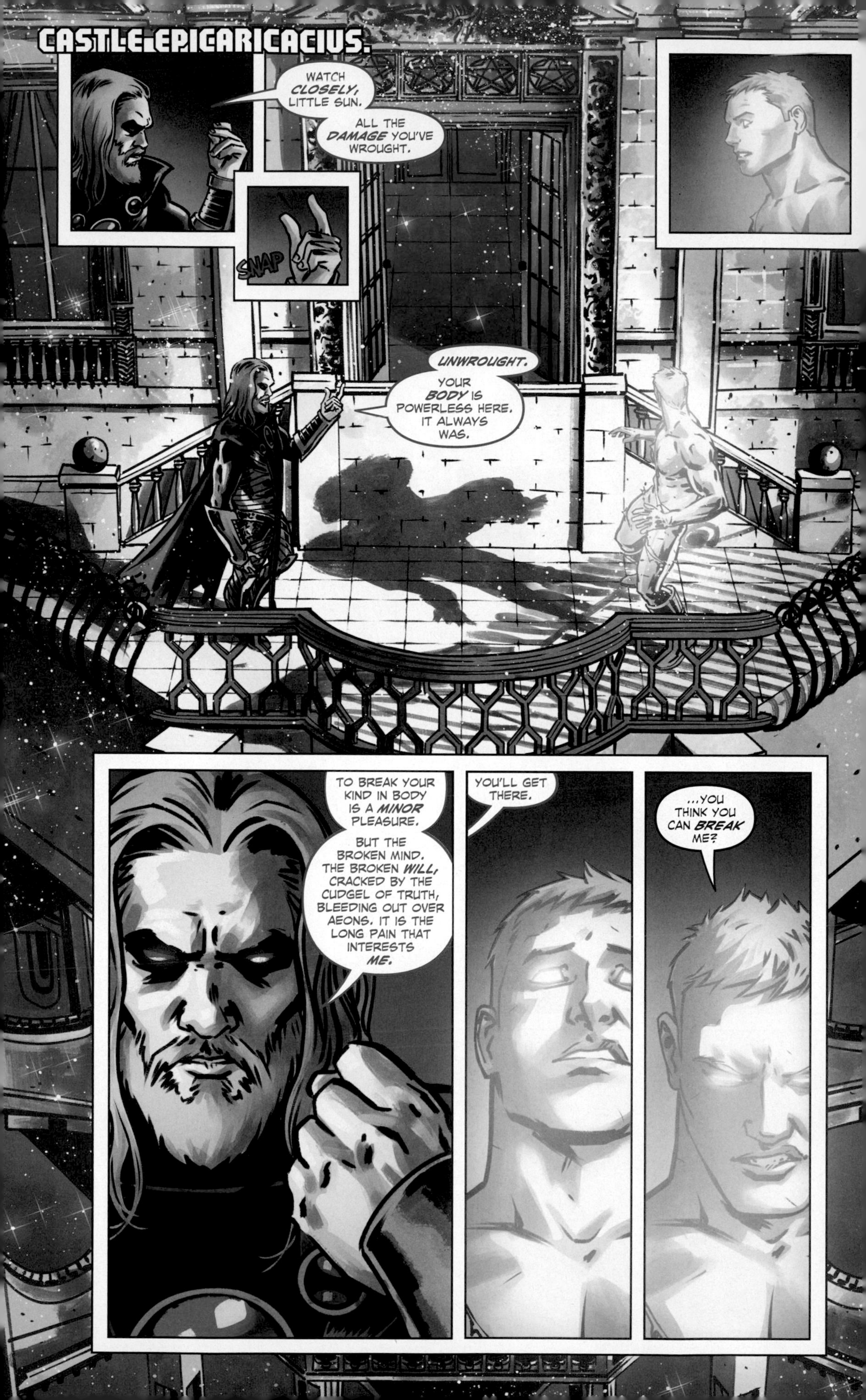
CASTLE EPICARICACIUS.
WATCH CLOSELY, LITTLE SUN.
ALL THE DAMAGE YOU'VE WROUGHT.
SNAP
UNWROUGHT.
YOUR BODY IS POWERLESS HERE. IT ALWAYS WAS.
TO BREAK YOUR KIND IN BODY IS A MINOR PLEASURE.
BUT THE BROKEN MIND. THE BROKEN WILL, CRACKED BY THE CUDGEL OF TRUTH, BLEEDING OUT OVER AEONS. IT IS THE LONG PAIN THAT INTERESTS ME.
YOU'LL GET THERE.
...YOU THINK YOU CAN BREAK ME?

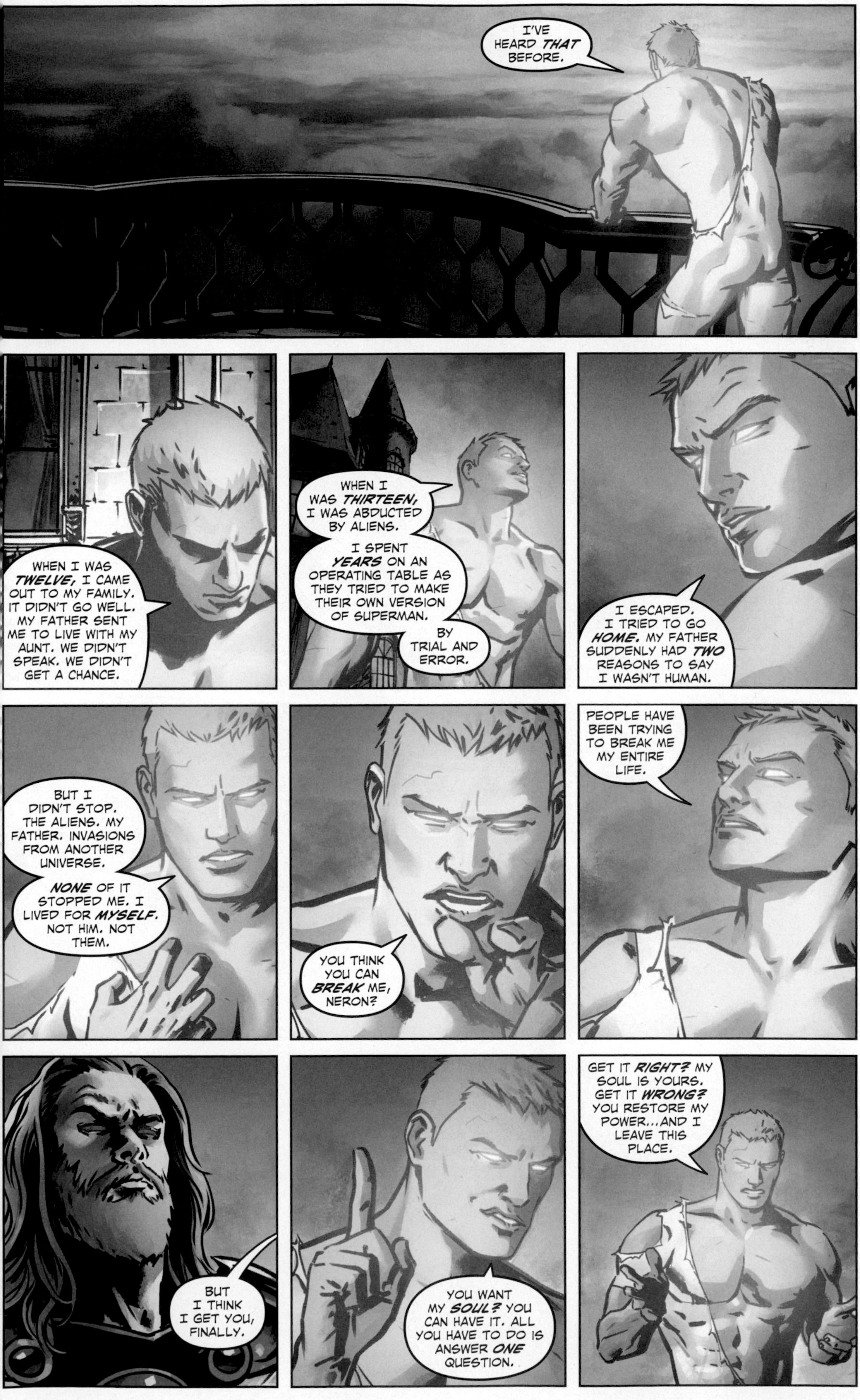
I'VE HEARD THAT BEFORE.
WHEN I WAS TWELVE, I CAME OUT TO MY FAMILY. IT DIDN'T GO WELL. MY FATHER SENT ME TO LIVE WITH MY AUNT. WE DIDN'T SPEAK. WE DIDN'T GET A CHANCE.
WHEN I WAS THIRTEEN, I WAS ABDUCTED BY ALIENS.
I SPENT YEARS ON AN OPERATING TABLE AS THEY TRIED TO MAKE THEIR OWN VERSION OF SUPERMAN.
BY TRIAL AND ERROR.
I ESCAPED. I TRIED TO GO HOME. MY FATHER SUDDENLY HAD TWO REASONS TO SAY I WASN'T HUMAN.
BUT I DIDN'T STOP. THE ALIENS. MY FATHER. INVASIONS FROM ANOTHER UNIVERSE.
NONE OF IT STOPPED ME. I LIVED FOR MYSELF. NOT HIM. NOT THEM.
YOU THINK YOU CAN BREAK ME, NERON?
PEOPLE HAVE BEEN TRYING TO BREAK ME MY ENTIRE LIFE.
BUT I THINK I GET YOU, FINALLY.
YOU WANT MY SOUL? YOU CAN HAVE IT. ALL YOU HAVE TO DO IS ANSWER ONE QUESTION.
GET IT RIGHT? MY SOUL IS YOURS. GET IT WRONG? YOU RESTORE MY POWER...AND I LEAVE THIS PLACE.

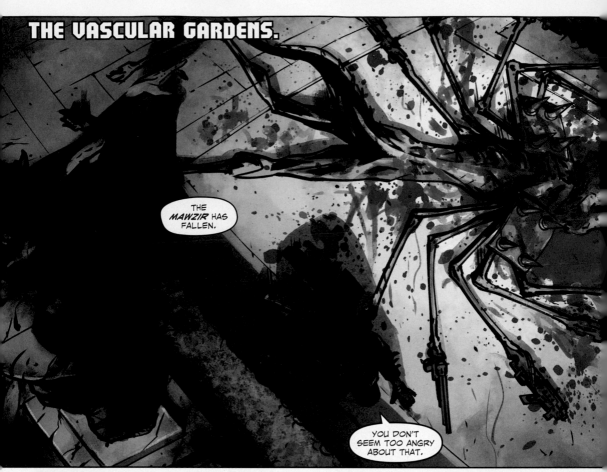

THE *MAWZIR* HAS FALLEN.

YOU DON'T SEEM TOO ANGRY ABOUT THAT.

ANGRY?

THE LORDS OF THE GUN STAND *IMPRESSED.*

YOU KILLED OUR ELITE AGENT. AS HE KILLED THE ONE BEFORE HIM. WE THUS LOOM HERE WITH AN *OFFER.*

YOU'VE ACHIEVED YOUR REVENGE, MIDNIGHTER. GIVE UP YOUR *PAINFULLY* HUMAN QUEST FOR YOUR *LOVER.* LET HIM *GO* AND JOIN US IN OUR GUN-SLINGING FOLD.

WE CAN *PERFECT* YOUR KILLING TACT.

THERE IS A *KERNEL* OF STRANGE POWER IN YOU, UNBLOSSOMED--

WANT A CLOSER LOOK?

NO WORLD EXISTS WHERE SOMEONE COULD HURT APOLLO AND ESCAPE ME. DO YOU UNDERSTAND?

I WANTED THE MAWZIR'S HEAD. I TOOK IT. NOW I WANT APOLLO BACK.

...BARTERED HIS...SOUL...IN DEBT TO--

I KNOW YOU DON'T HAVE HIM. AND YEAH--I'VE GOT SOMETHING SPECIAL IN ME. I KNOW YOU CAN SENSE IT.

IF YOU DON'T WANT TO SEE WHAT IT IS...

...YOU'LL TELL ME WHERE TO FIND APOLLO. AND THE ONE WHO HAS HIM.

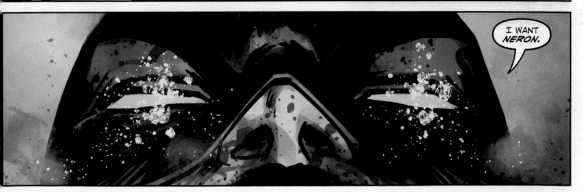

I WANT NERON.

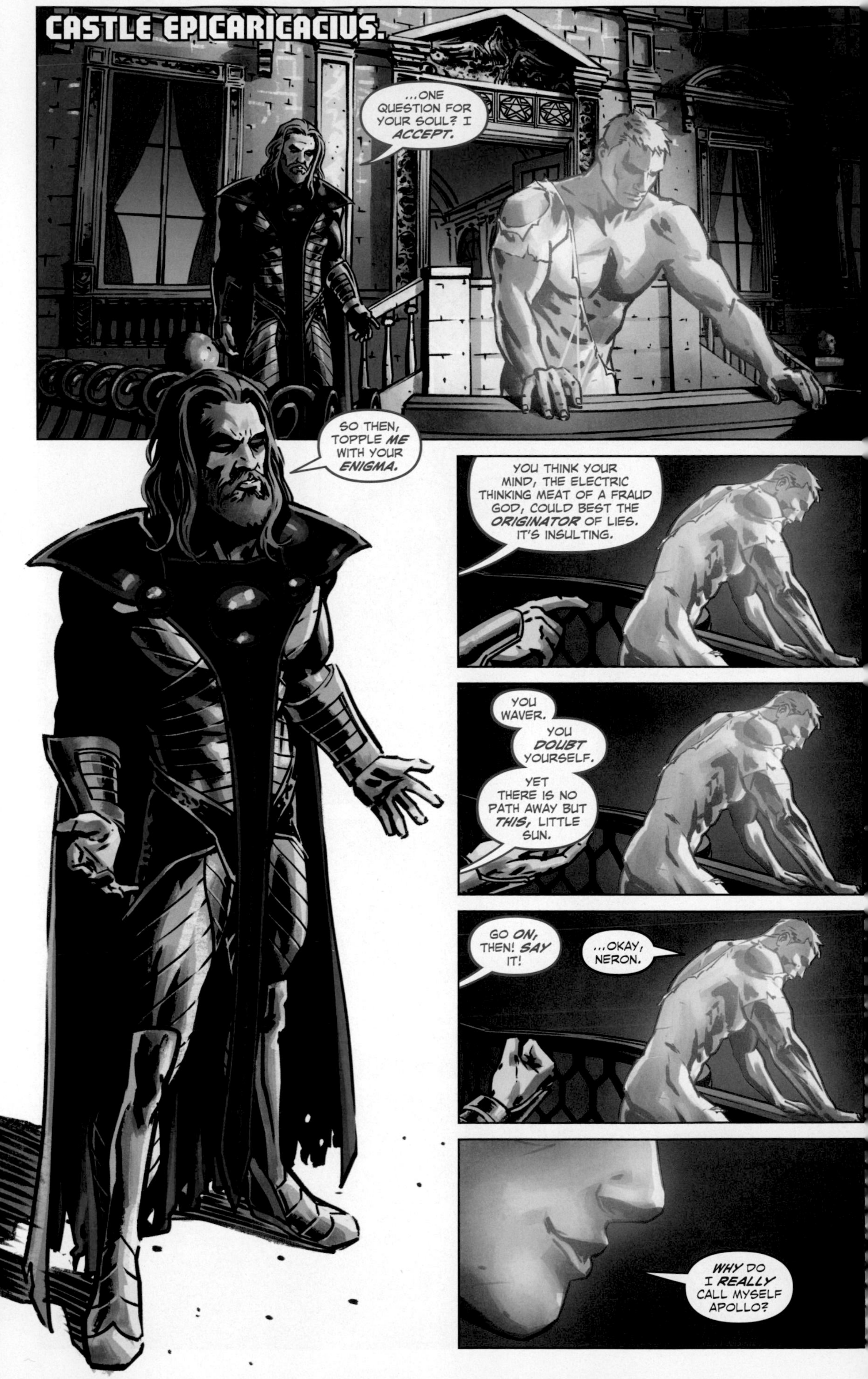
CASTLE EPICARICACIUS.
...ONE QUESTION FOR YOUR SOUL? I ACCEPT.
SO THEN, TOPPLE ME WITH YOUR ENIGMA.
YOU THINK YOUR MIND, THE ELECTRIC THINKING MEAT OF A FRAUD GOD, COULD BEST THE ORIGINATOR OF LIES. IT'S INSULTING.
YOU WAVER.
YOU DOUBT YOURSELF.
YET THERE IS NO PATH AWAY BUT THIS, LITTLE SUN.
GO ON, THEN! SAY IT!
...OKAY, NERON.
WHY DO I REALLY CALL MYSELF APOLLO?

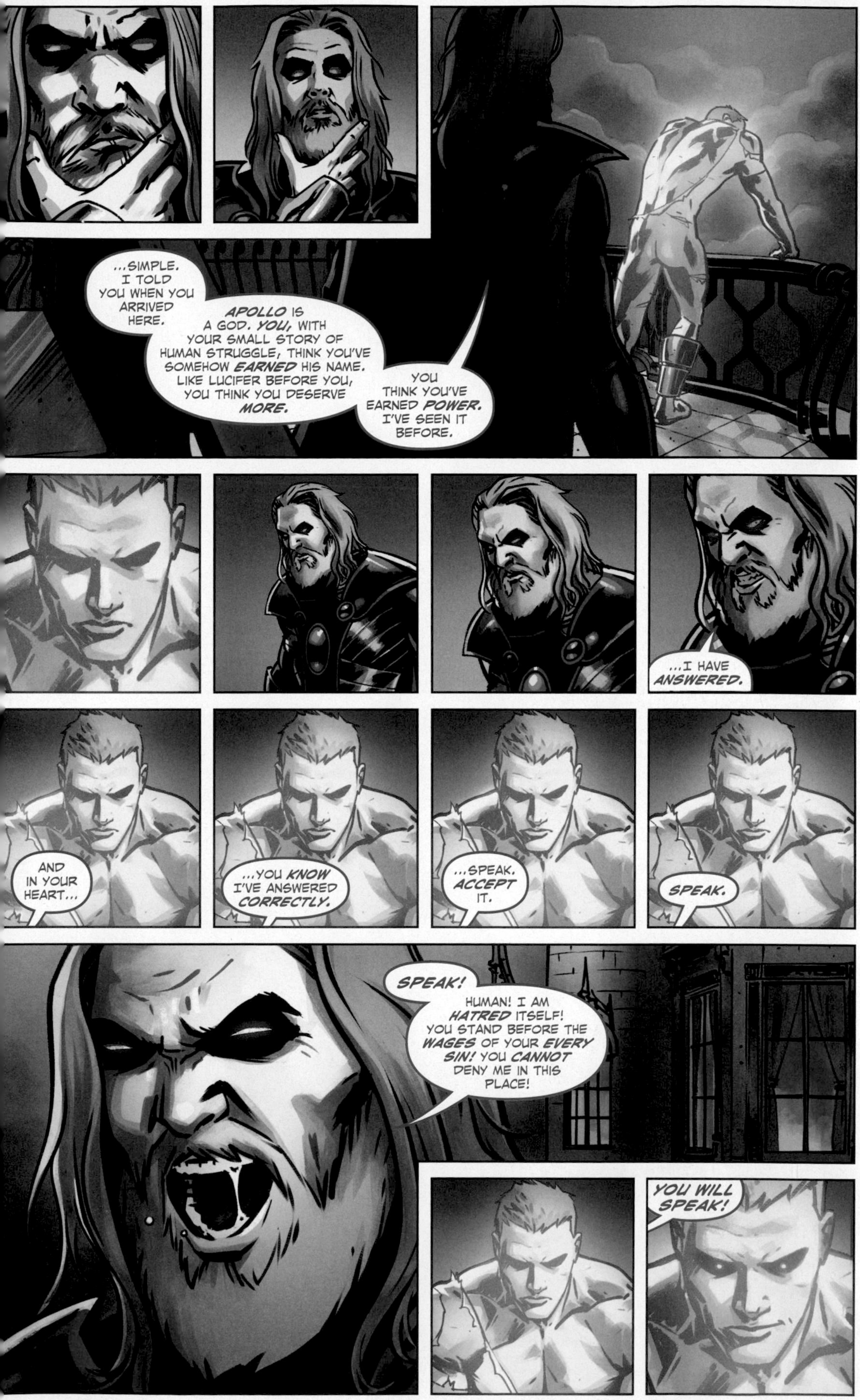
...SIMPLE. I TOLD YOU WHEN YOU ARRIVED HERE.
APOLLO IS A GOD. YOU, WITH YOUR SMALL STORY OF HUMAN STRUGGLE, THINK YOU'VE SOMEHOW EARNED HIS NAME. LIKE LUCIFER BEFORE YOU, YOU THINK YOU DESERVE MORE.
YOU THINK YOU'VE EARNED POWER. I'VE SEEN IT BEFORE.
...I HAVE ANSWERED.
AND IN YOUR HEART...
...YOU KNOW I'VE ANSWERED CORRECTLY.
...SPEAK. ACCEPT IT.
SPEAK.
SPEAK!
HUMAN! I AM HATRED ITSELF! YOU STAND BEFORE THE WAGES OF YOUR EVERY SIN! YOU CANNOT DENY ME IN THIS PLACE!
YOU WILL SPEAK!

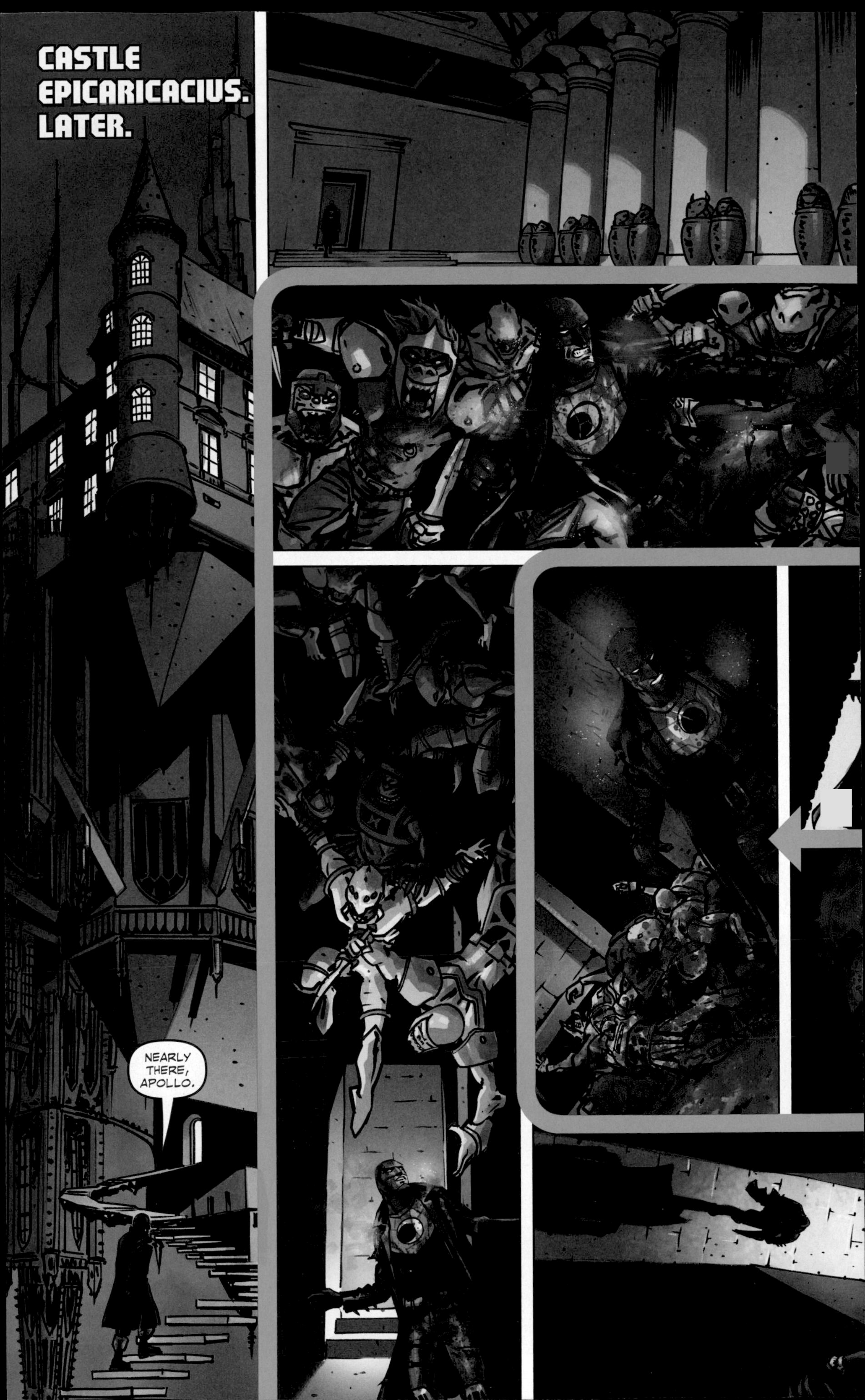
CASTLE EPICARICACIUS. LATER.
NEARLY THERE, APOLLO.

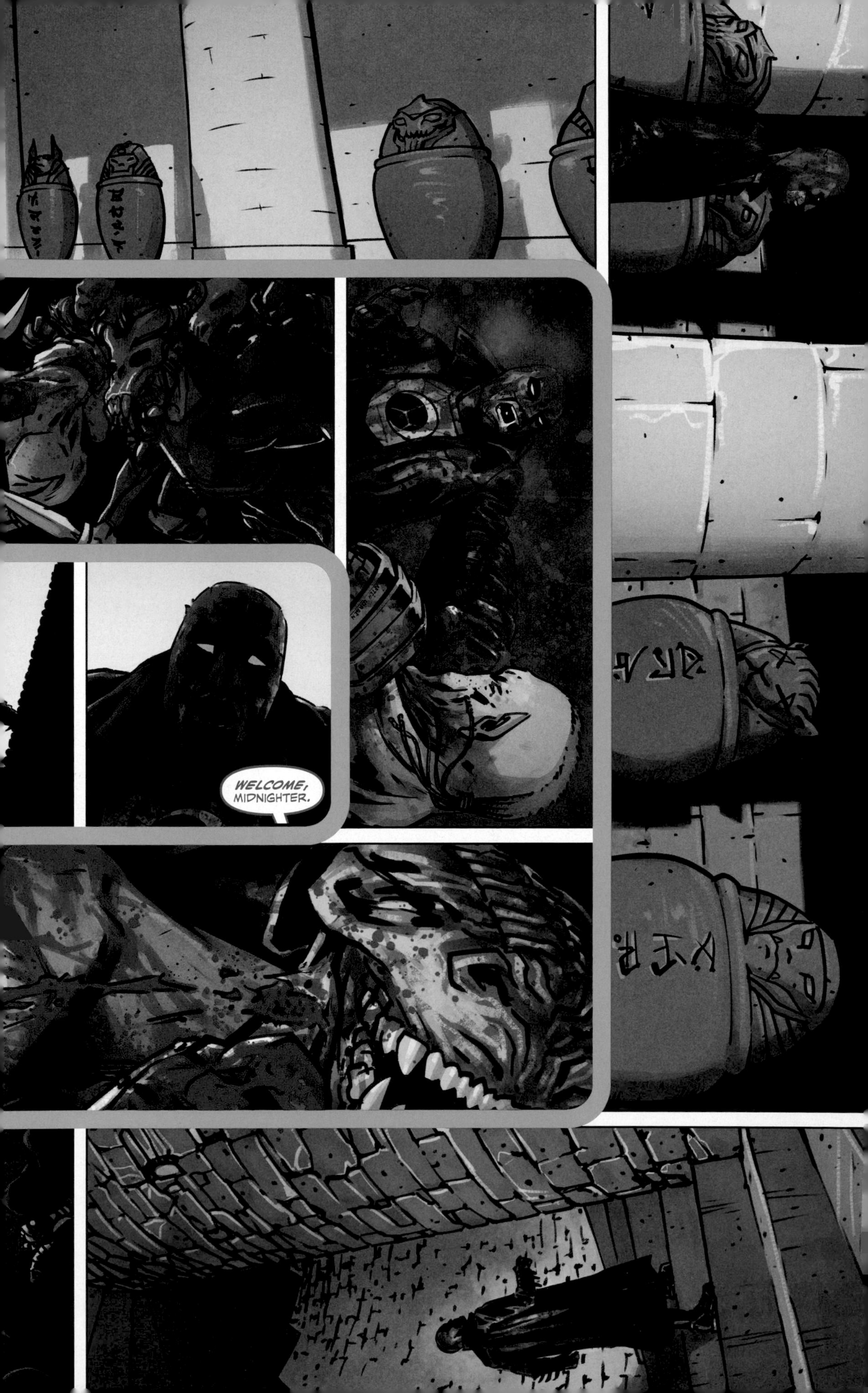
WELCOME, MIDNIGHTER.

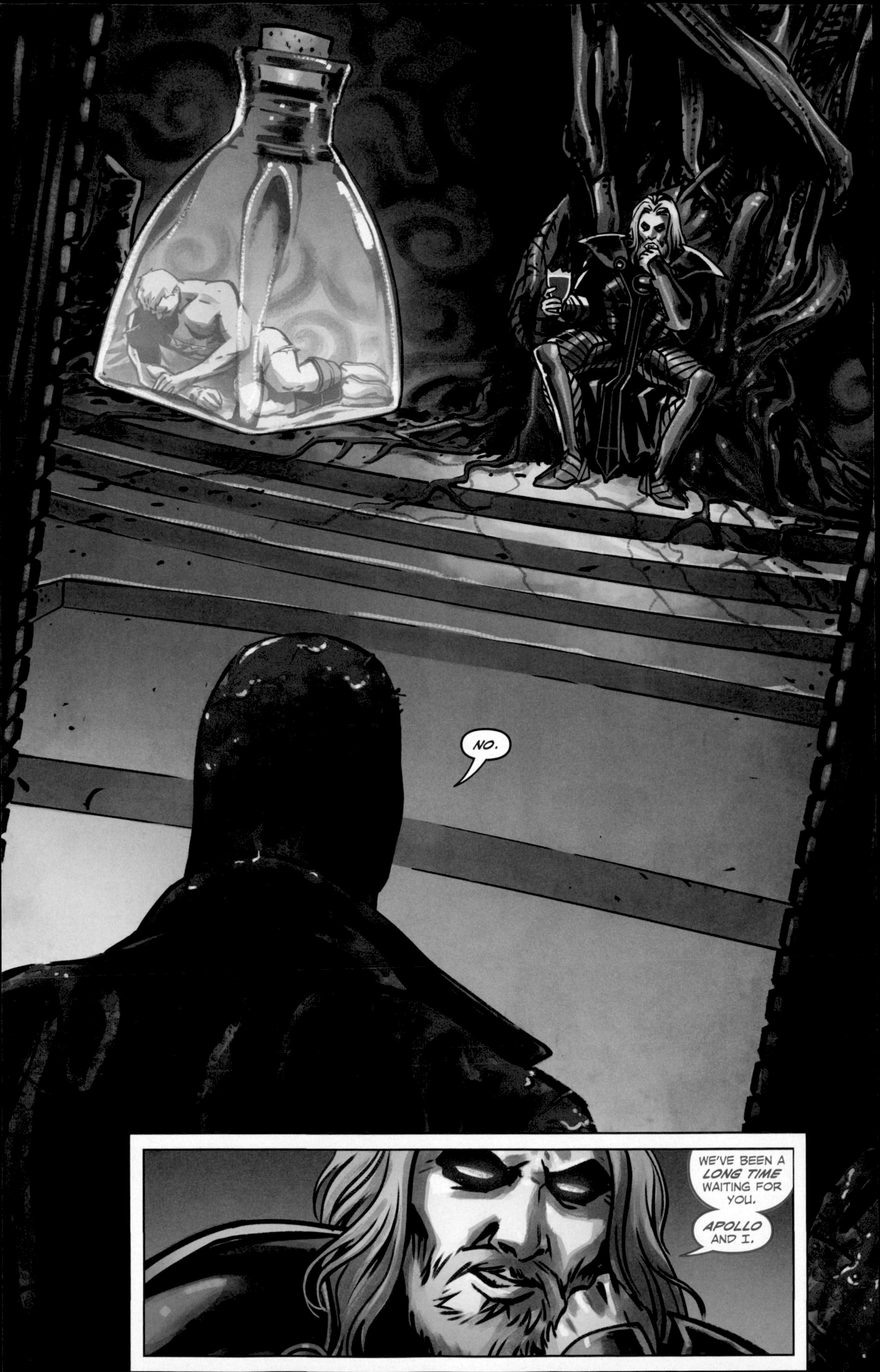
NO.
WE'VE BEEN A LONG TIME WAITING FOR YOU.
APOLLO AND I.

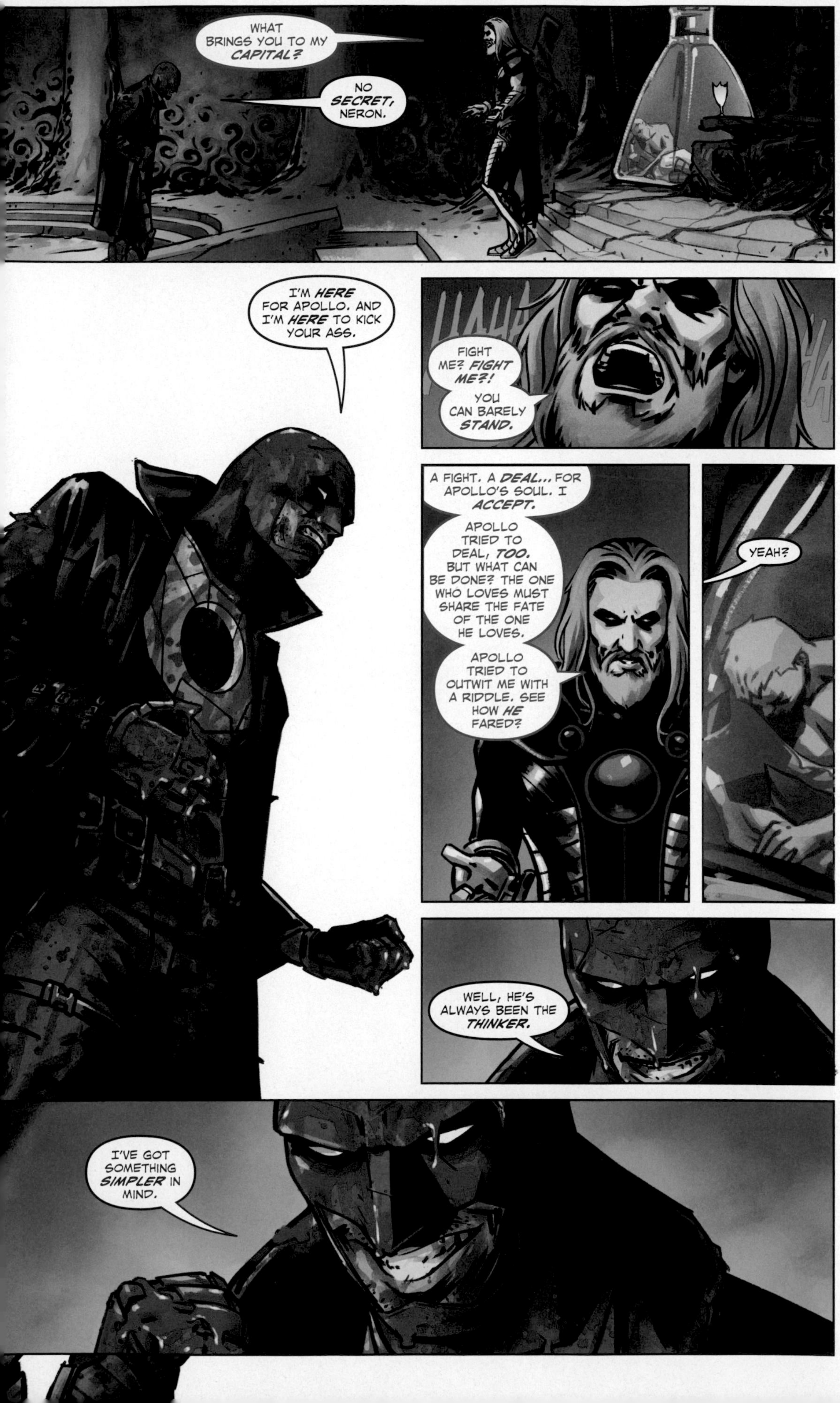

WHAT BRINGS YOU TO MY CAPITAL?
NO SECRET, NERON.
I'M HERE FOR APOLLO. AND I'M HERE TO KICK YOUR ASS.
FIGHT ME? FIGHT ME?!
YOU CAN BARELY STAND.
A FIGHT. A DEAL... FOR APOLLO'S SOUL. I ACCEPT.
APOLLO TRIED TO DEAL, TOO. BUT WHAT CAN BE DONE? THE ONE WHO LOVES MUST SHARE THE FATE OF THE ONE HE LOVES.
APOLLO TRIED TO OUTWIT ME WITH A RIDDLE. SEE HOW HE FARED?
YEAH?
WELL, HE'S ALWAYS BEEN THE THINKER.
I'VE GOT SOMETHING SIMPLER IN MIND.

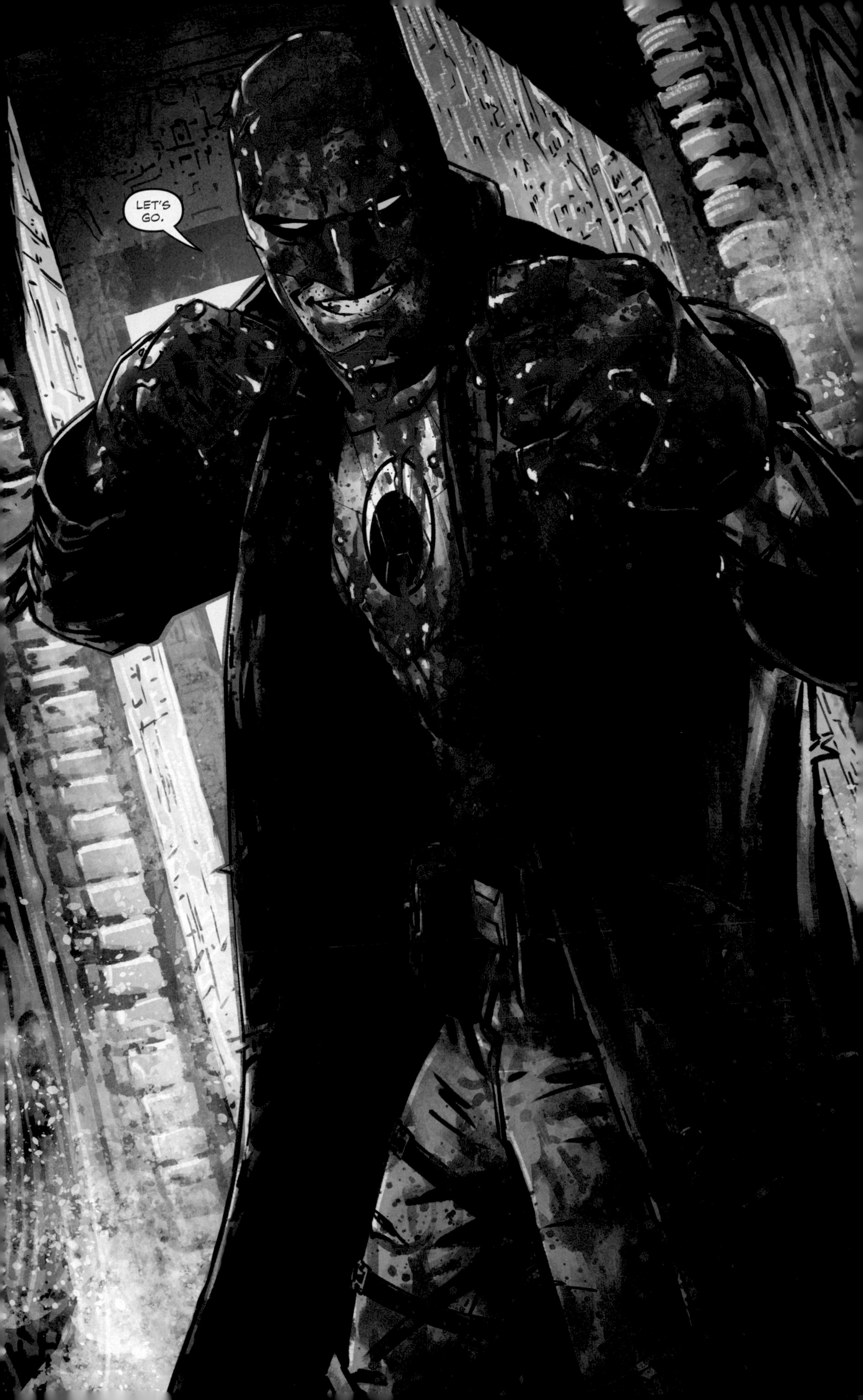
LET'S GO.

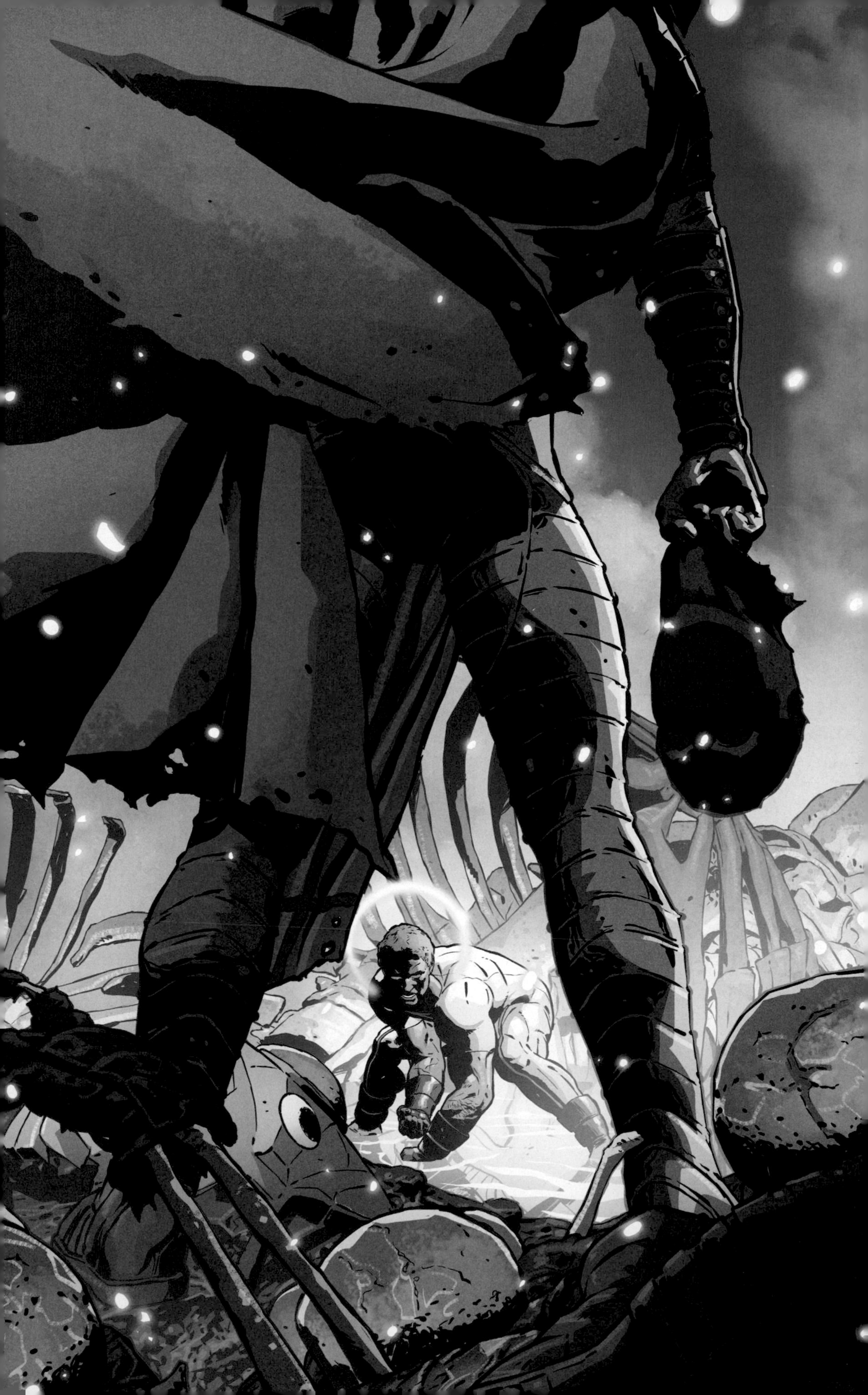

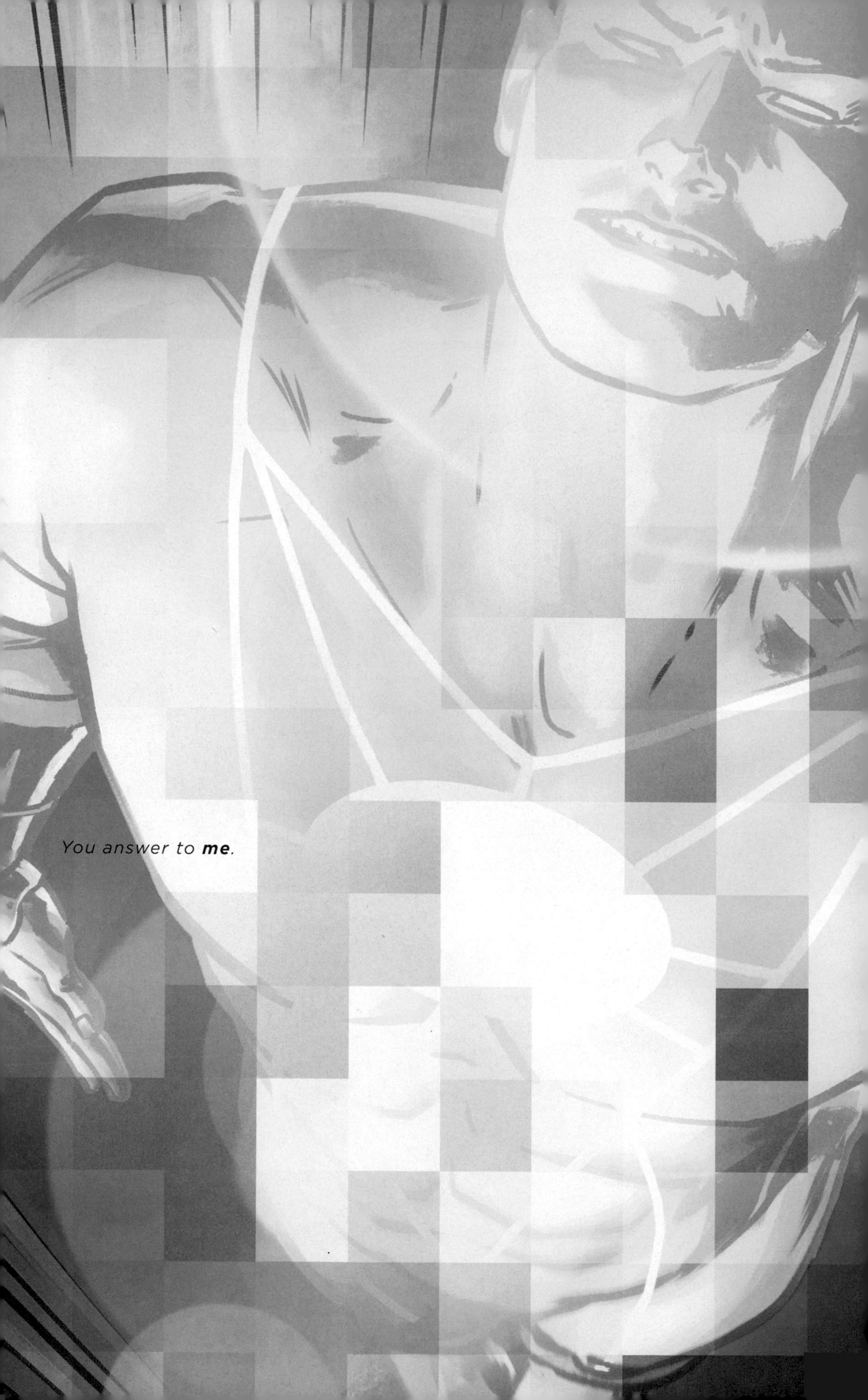
You answer to *me*.

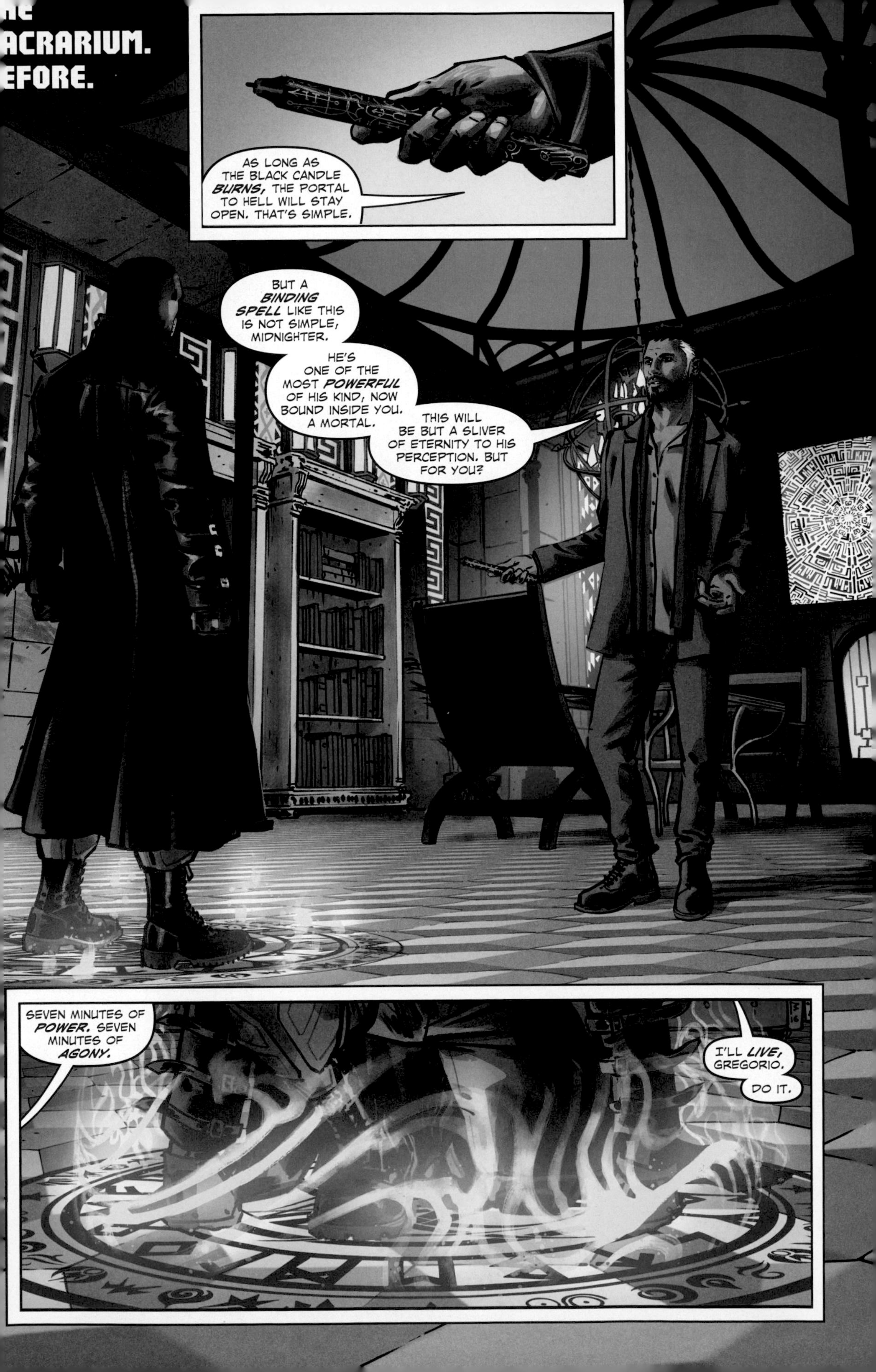
ACRARIUM.
EFORE.
AS LONG AS THE BLACK CANDLE BURNS, THE PORTAL TO HELL WILL STAY OPEN. THAT'S SIMPLE.
BUT A BINDING SPELL LIKE THIS IS NOT SIMPLE, MIDNIGHTER.
HE'S ONE OF THE MOST POWERFUL OF HIS KIND, NOW BOUND INSIDE YOU. A MORTAL.
THIS WILL BE BUT A SLIVER OF ETERNITY TO HIS PERCEPTION. BUT FOR YOU?
SEVEN MINUTES OF POWER. SEVEN MINUTES OF AGONY.
I'LL LIVE, GREGORIO.
DO IT.

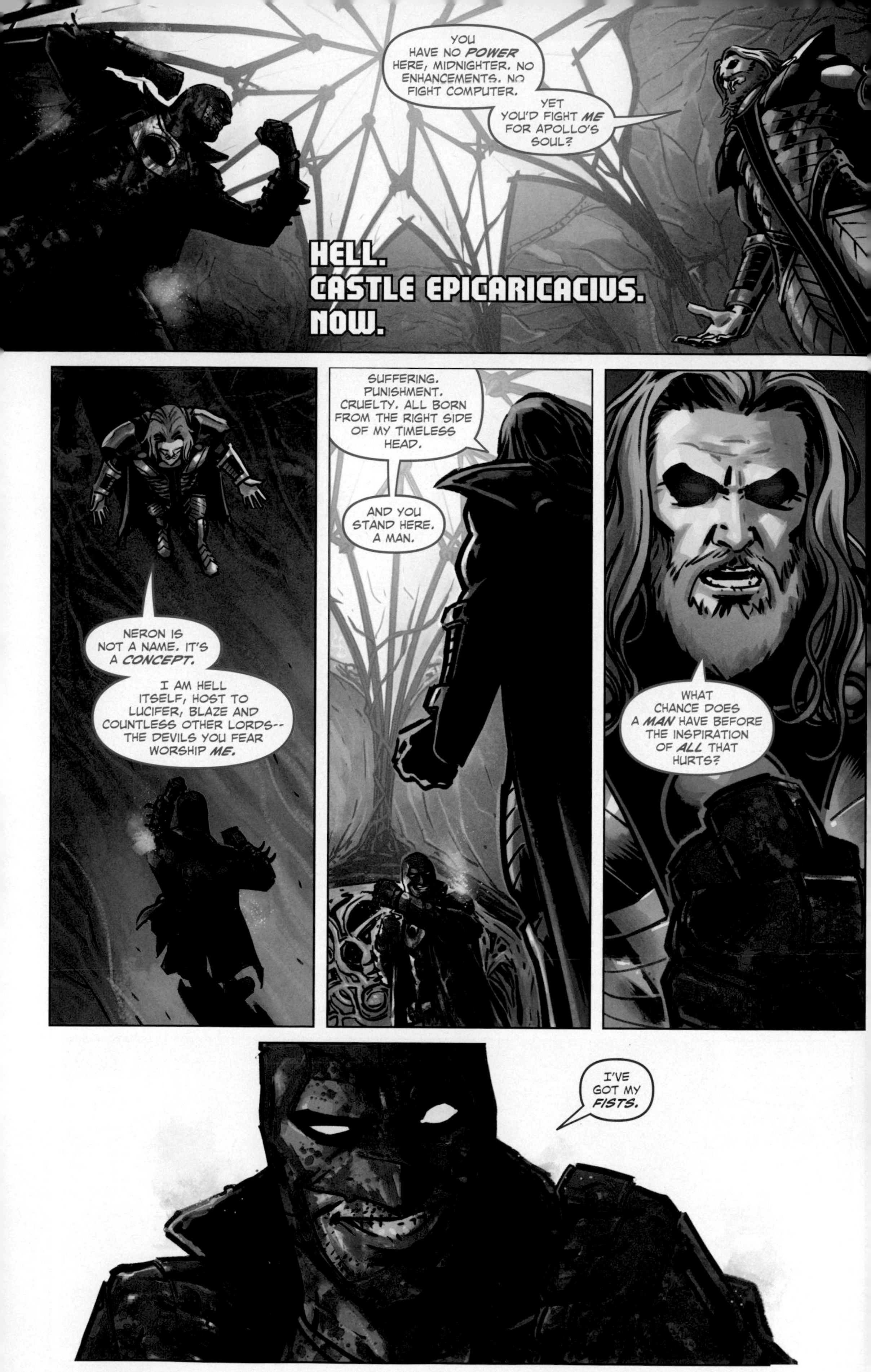

YOU HAVE NO POWER HERE, MIDNIGHTER. NO ENHANCEMENTS. NO FIGHT COMPUTER.
YET YOU'D FIGHT ME FOR APOLLO'S SOUL?
HELL. CASTLE EPICARICACIUS. NOW.
NERON IS NOT A NAME. IT'S A CONCEPT.
I AM HELL ITSELF, HOST TO LUCIFER, BLAZE AND COUNTLESS OTHER LORDS-- THE DEVILS YOU FEAR WORSHIP ME.
SUFFERING. PUNISHMENT. CRUELTY. ALL BORN FROM THE RIGHT SIDE OF MY TIMELESS HEAD.
AND YOU STAND HERE. A MAN.
WHAT CHANCE DOES A MAN HAVE BEFORE THE INSPIRATION OF ALL THAT HURTS?
I'VE GOT MY FISTS.

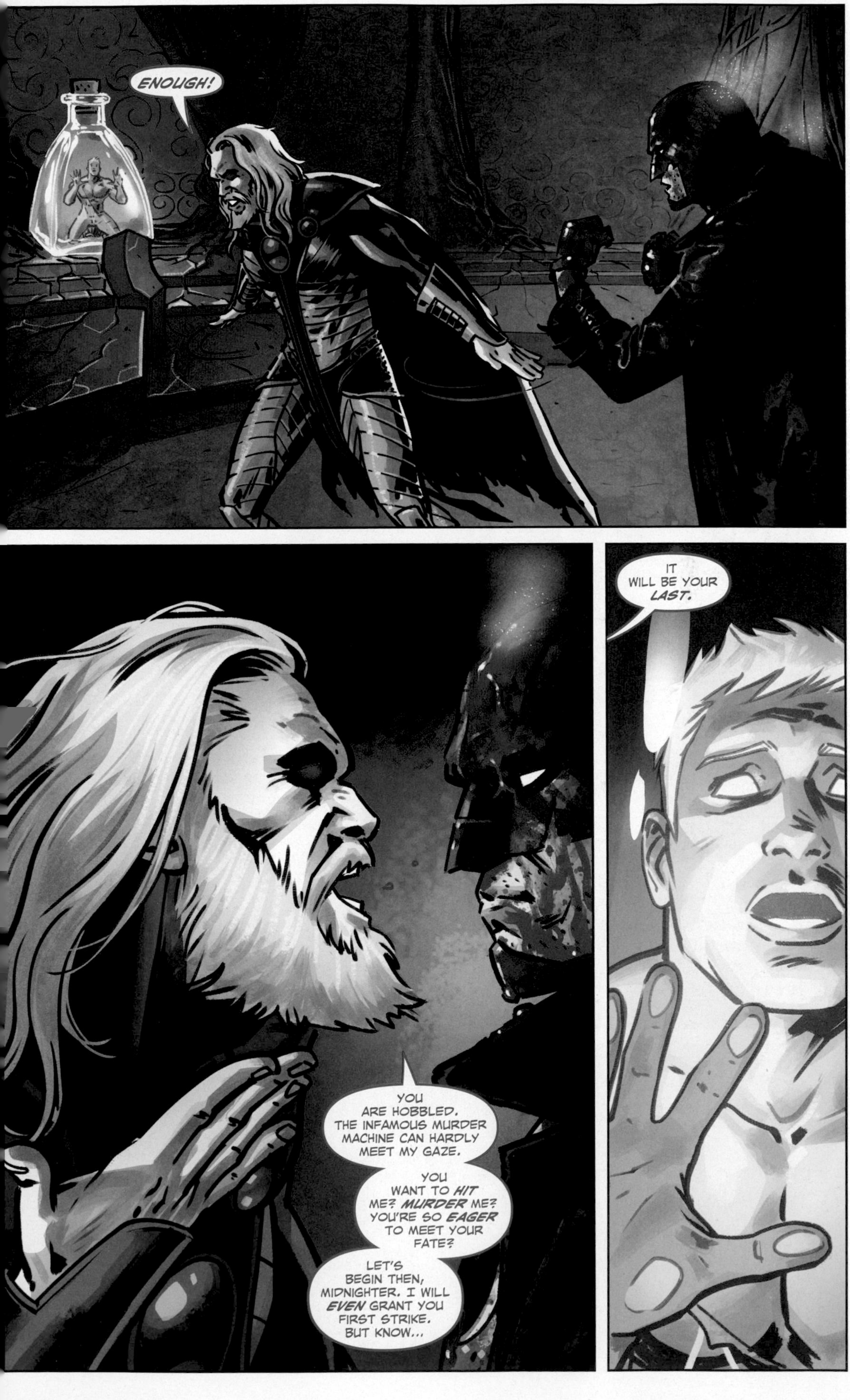
ENOUGH!
YOU ARE HOBBLED. THE INFAMOUS MURDER MACHINE CAN HARDLY MEET MY GAZE.
YOU WANT TO HIT ME? MURDER ME? YOU'RE SO EAGER TO MEET YOUR FATE?
LET'S BEGIN THEN, MIDNIGHTER. I WILL EVEN GRANT YOU FIRST STRIKE. BUT KNOW...
IT WILL BE YOUR LAST.

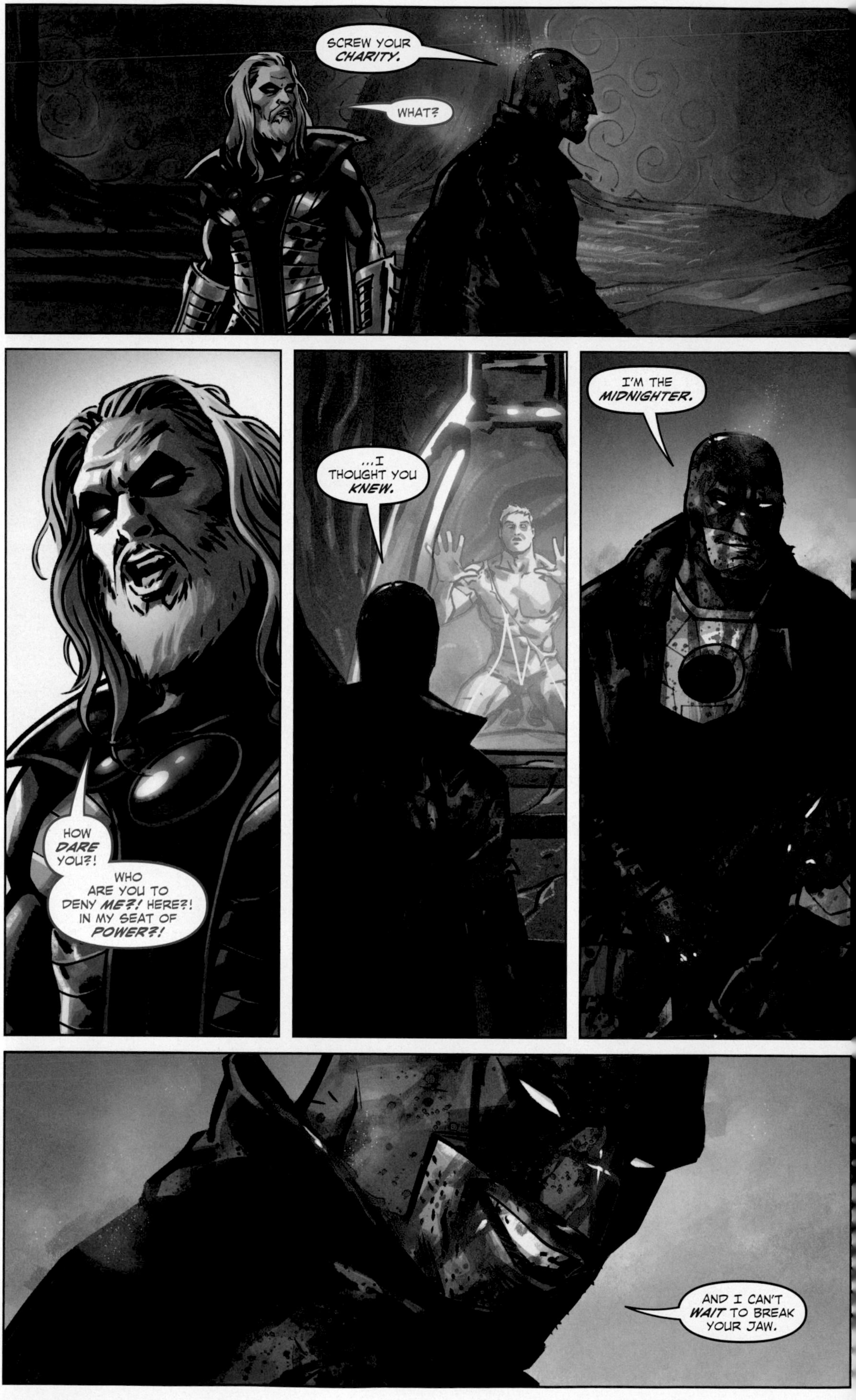

SCREW YOUR *CHARITY.*
WHAT?
HOW *DARE* YOU?!
WHO ARE YOU TO DENY *ME?!* HERE?! IN MY SEAT OF *POWER?!*
...I THOUGHT YOU *KNEW.*
I'M THE *MIDNIGHTER.*
AND I CAN'T *WAIT* TO BREAK YOUR JAW.

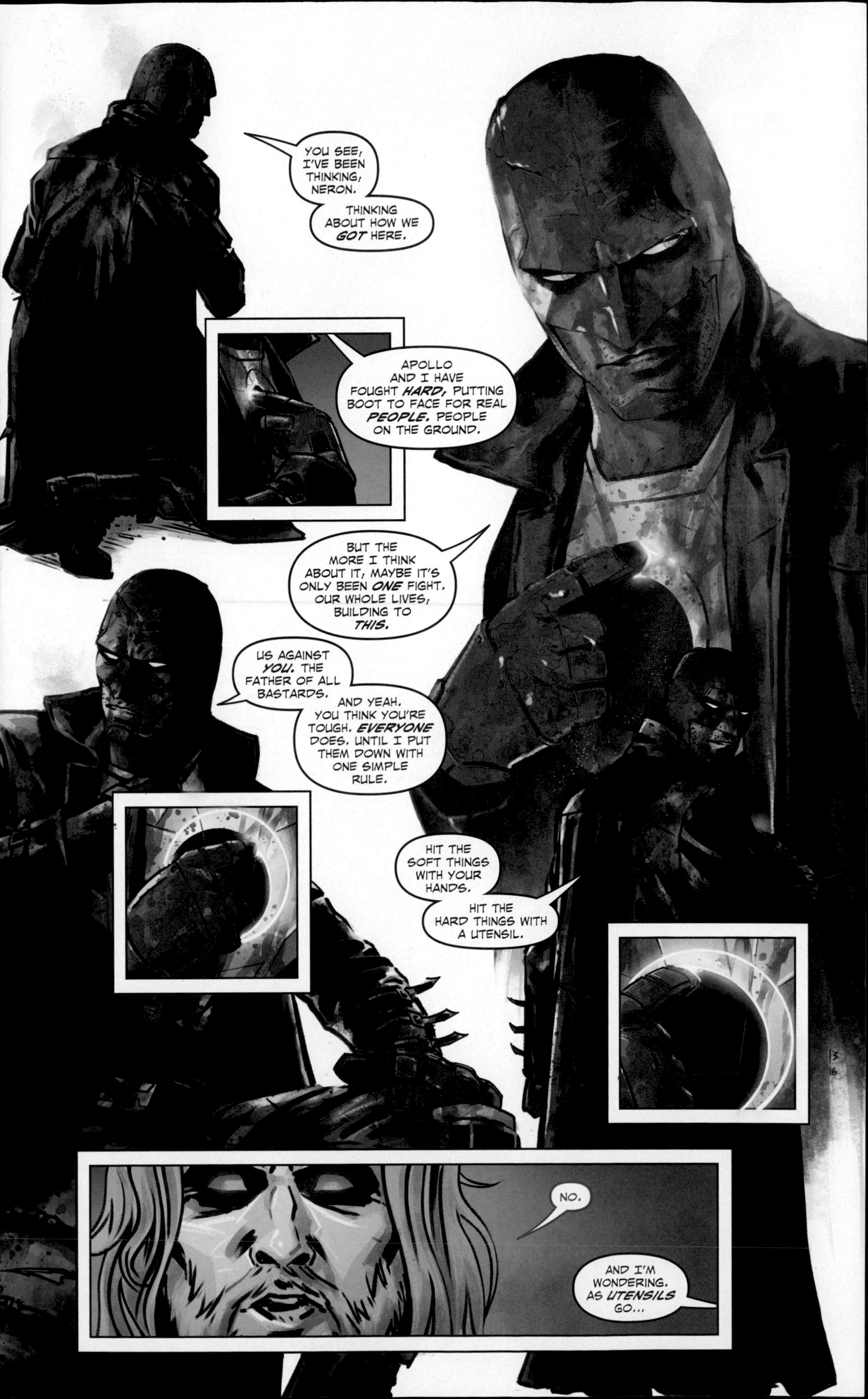
YOU SEE, I'VE BEEN THINKING, NERON.
THINKING ABOUT HOW WE GOT HERE.
APOLLO AND I HAVE FOUGHT HARD, PUTTING BOOT TO FACE FOR REAL PEOPLE. PEOPLE ON THE GROUND.
BUT THE MORE I THINK ABOUT IT, MAYBE IT'S ONLY BEEN ONE FIGHT. OUR WHOLE LIVES, BUILDING TO THIS.
US AGAINST YOU. THE FATHER OF ALL BASTARDS.
AND YEAH. YOU THINK YOU'RE TOUGH. EVERYONE DOES. UNTIL I PUT THEM DOWN WITH ONE SIMPLE RULE.
HIT THE SOFT THINGS WITH YOUR HANDS.
HIT THE HARD THINGS WITH A UTENSIL.
NO.
AND I'M WONDERING. AS UTENSILS GO...

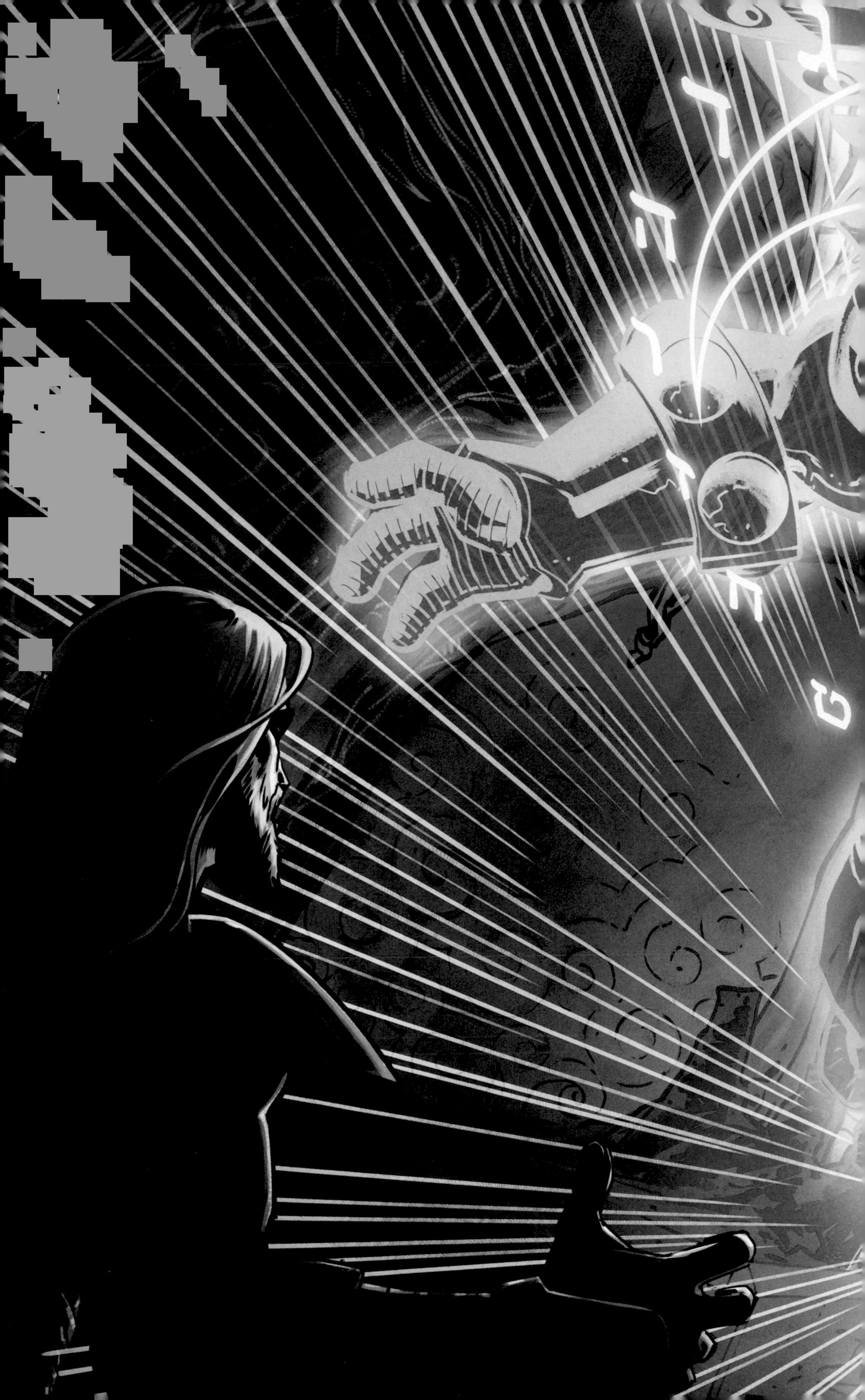

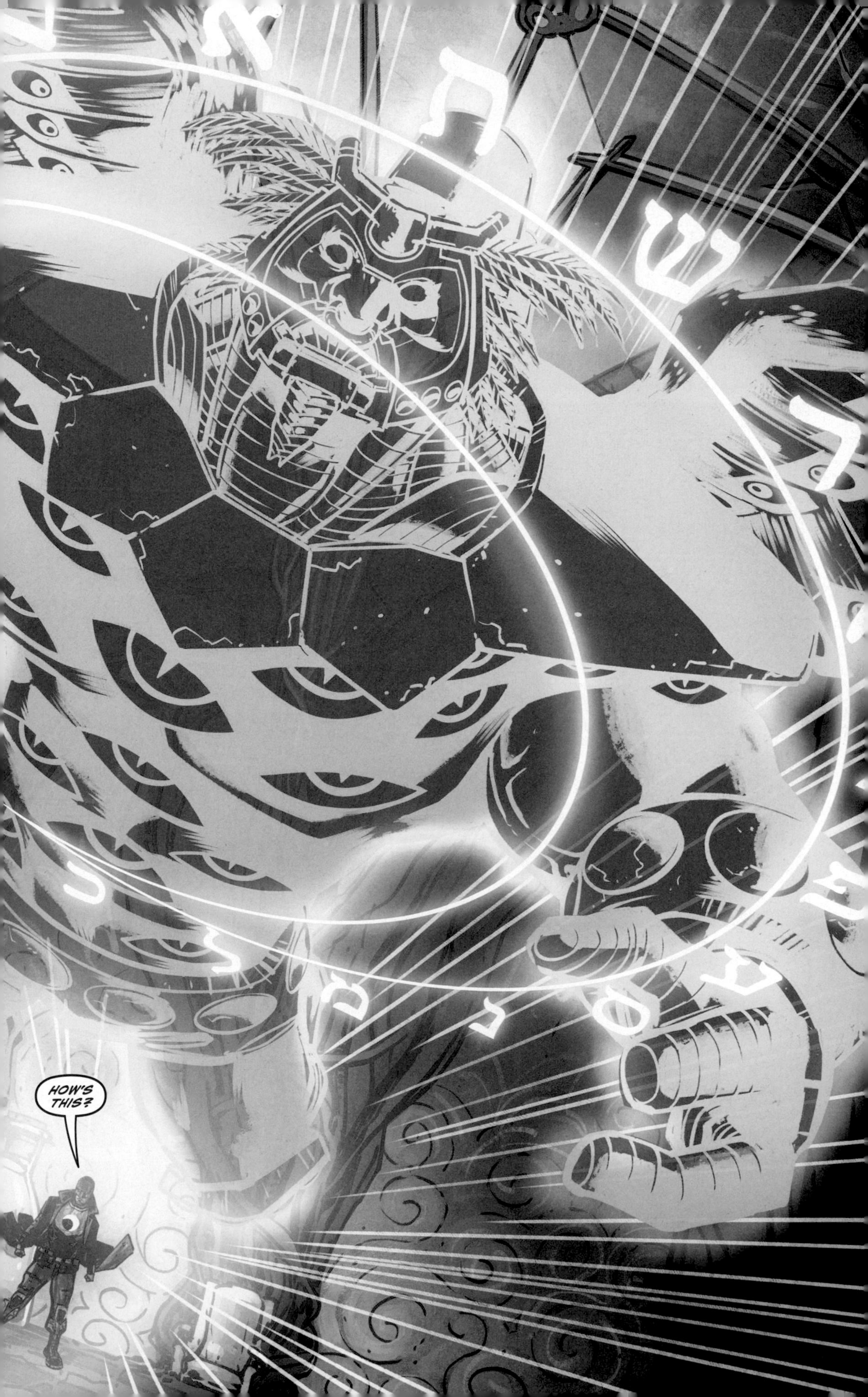
HOW'S THIS?

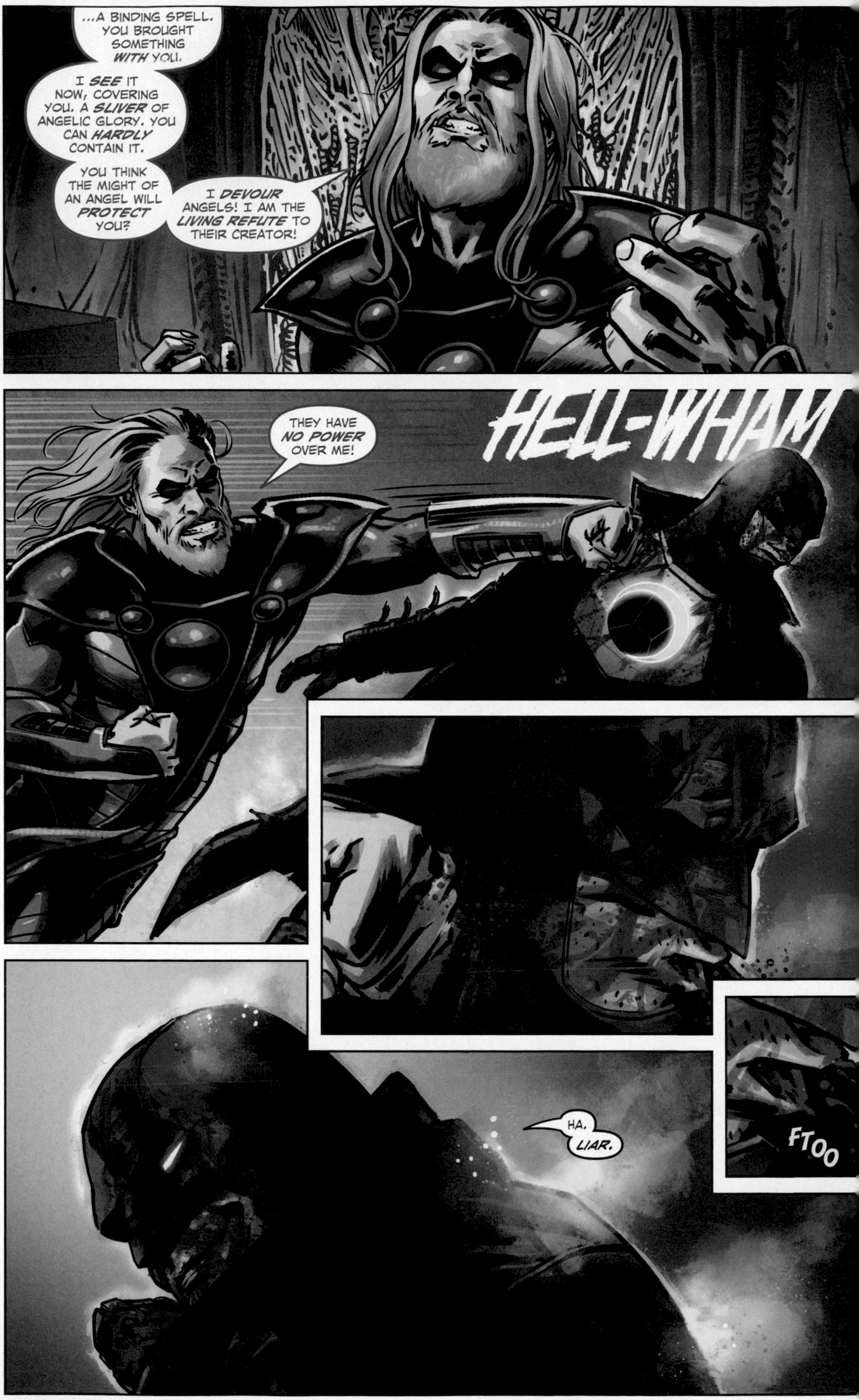

...A BINDING SPELL. YOU BROUGHT SOMETHING WITH YOU.
I SEE IT NOW, COVERING YOU. A SLIVER OF ANGELIC GLORY. YOU CAN HARDLY CONTAIN IT.
YOU THINK THE MIGHT OF AN ANGEL WILL PROTECT YOU?
I DEVOUR ANGELS! I AM THE LIVING REFUTE TO THEIR CREATOR!
THEY HAVE NO POWER OVER ME!
HELL-WHAM
FTOO
HA. LIAR.

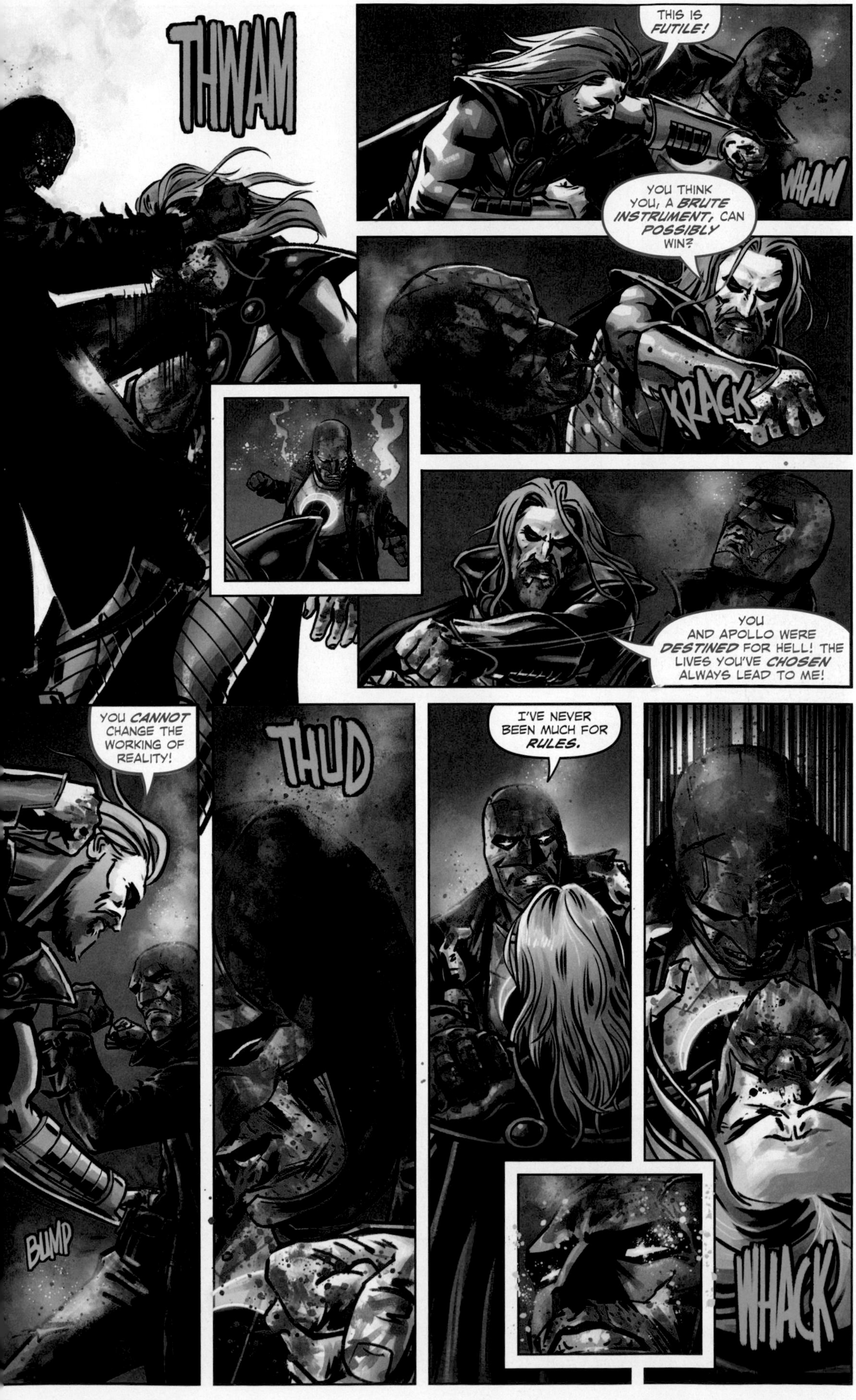
THWAM
THIS IS FUTILE!
WHAM
YOU THINK YOU, A BRUTE INSTRUMENT, CAN POSSIBLY WIN?
KRACK
YOU AND APOLLO WERE DESTINED FOR HELL! THE LIVES YOU'VE CHOSEN ALWAYS LEAD TO ME!
YOU CANNOT CHANGE THE WORKING OF REALITY!
BUMP
THUD
I'VE NEVER BEEN MUCH FOR RULES.
WHACK

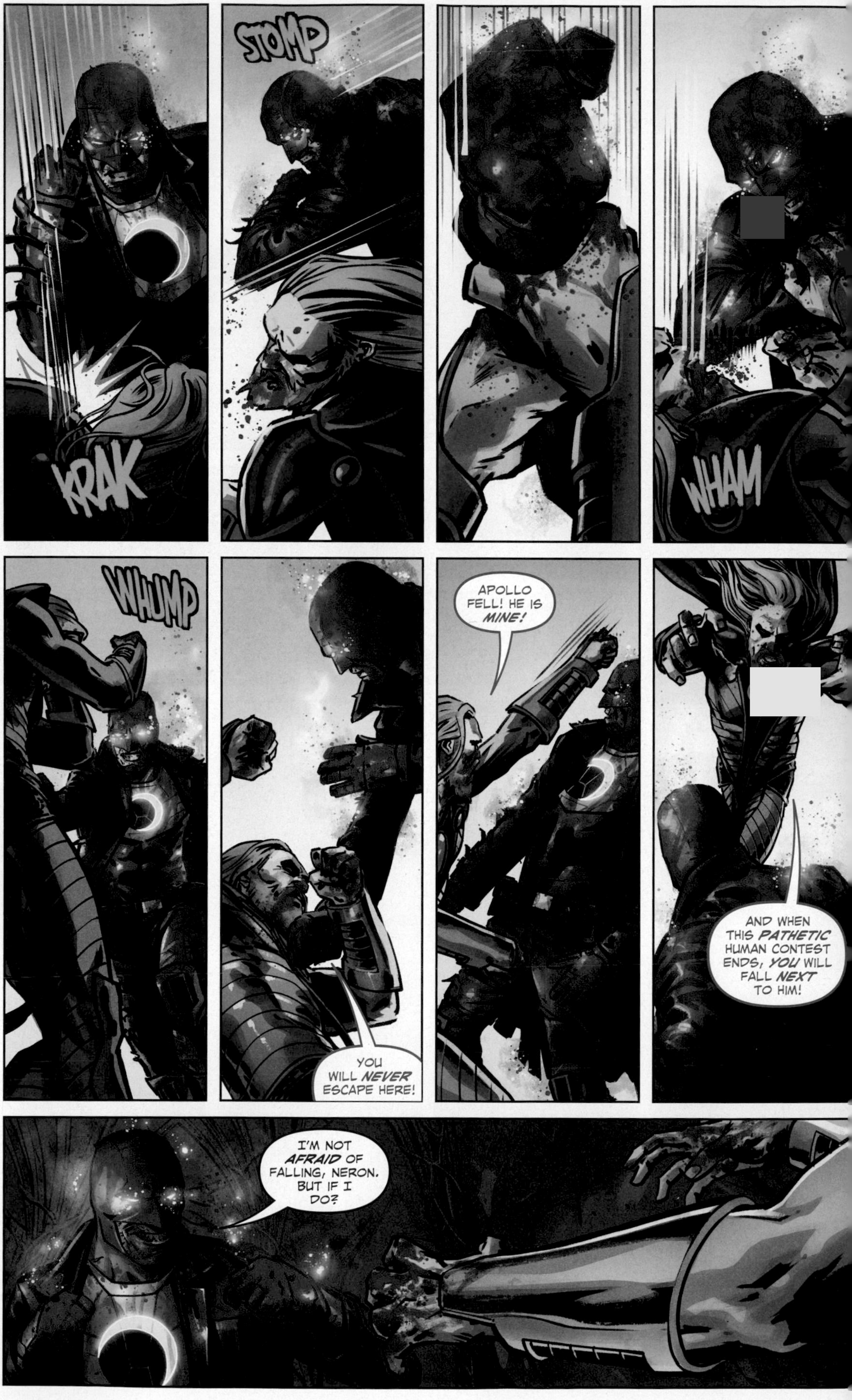
KRAK
STOMP
WHAM
WHUMP
YOU WILL *NEVER* ESCAPE HERE!
APOLLO FELL! HE IS *MINE!*
AND WHEN THIS *PATHETIC* HUMAN CONTEST ENDS, *YOU* WILL FALL *NEXT* TO HIM!
I'M NOT *AFRAID* OF FALLING, NERON. BUT IF I DO?

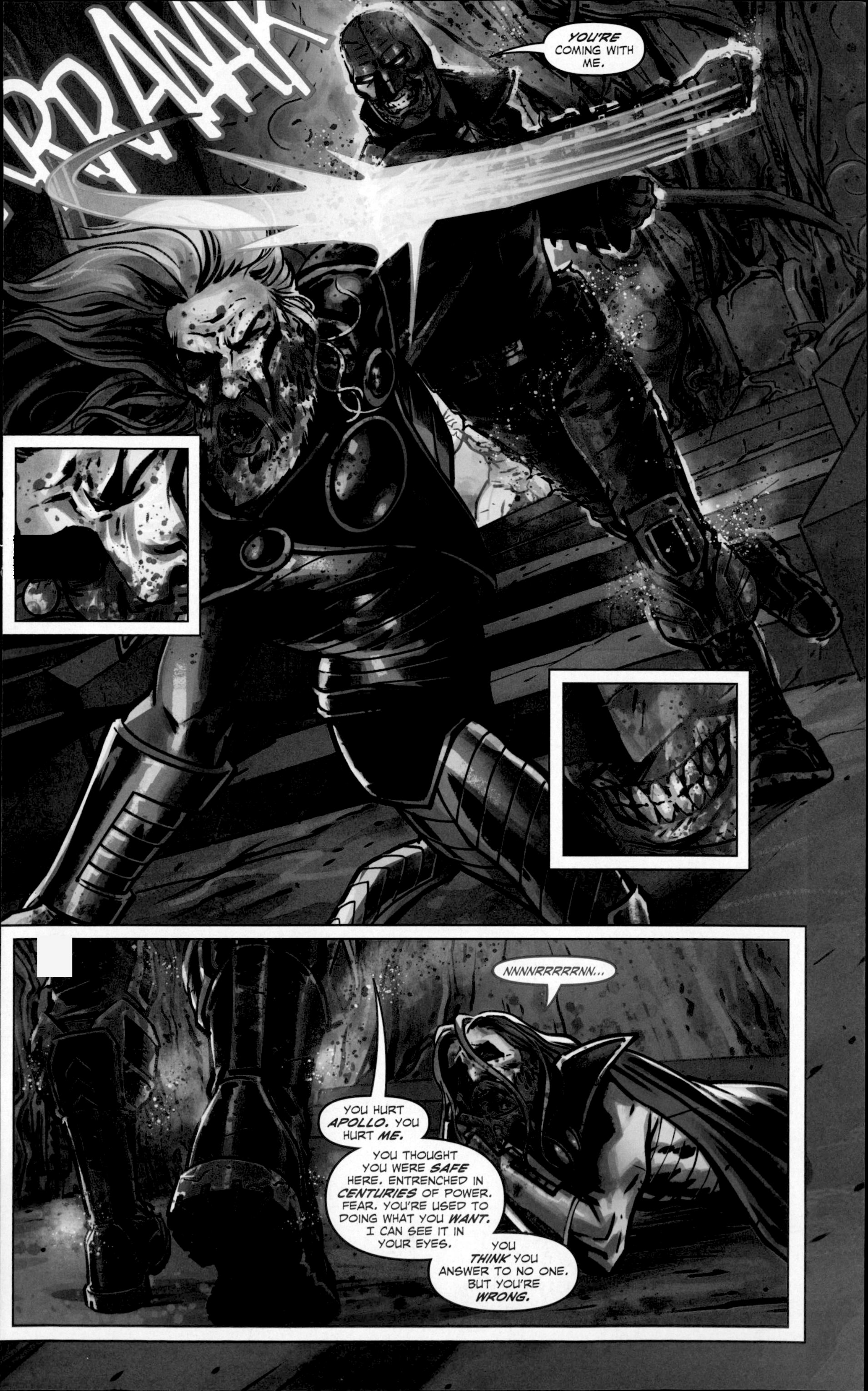
YOU'RE COMING WITH ME.
NNNNRRRRRNN...
YOU HURT APOLLO. YOU HURT ME.
YOU THOUGHT YOU WERE SAFE HERE. ENTRENCHED IN CENTURIES OF POWER. FEAR. YOU'RE USED TO DOING WHAT YOU WANT. I CAN SEE IT IN YOUR EYES.
YOU THINK YOU ANSWER TO NO ONE. BUT YOU'RE WRONG.

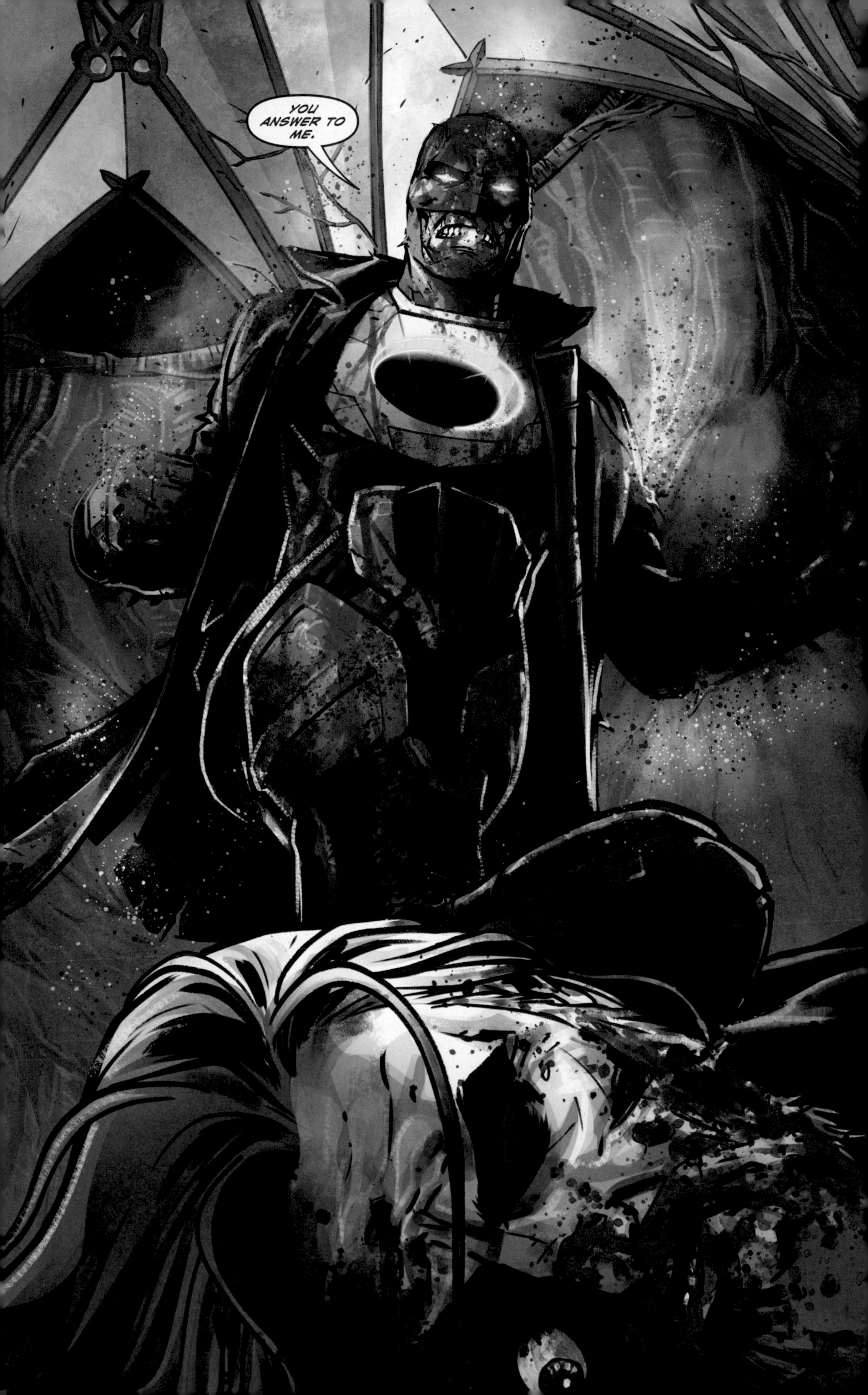
YOU ANSWER TO ME.

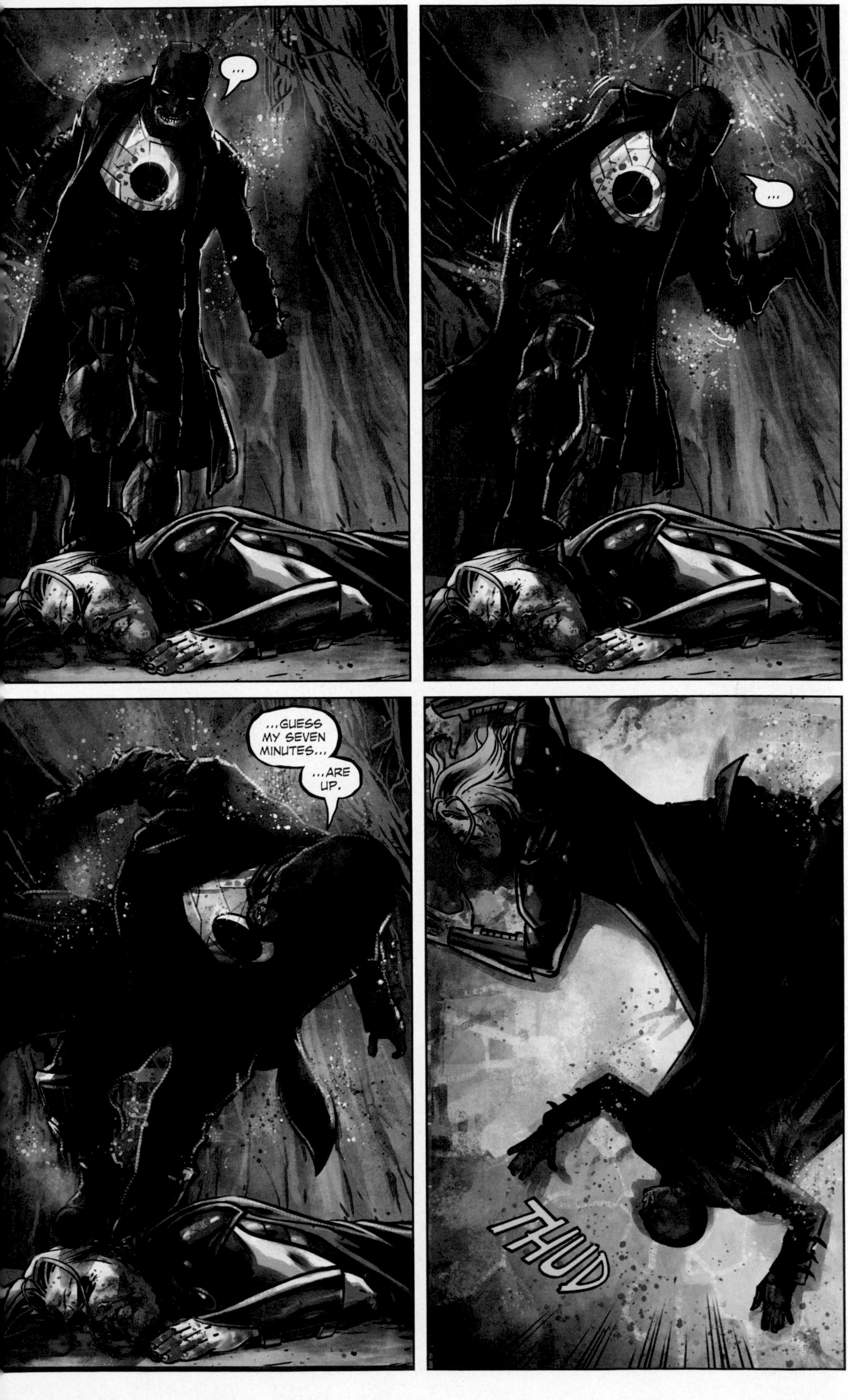
...
...
...GUESS MY SEVEN MINUTES...
...ARE UP.
THUD

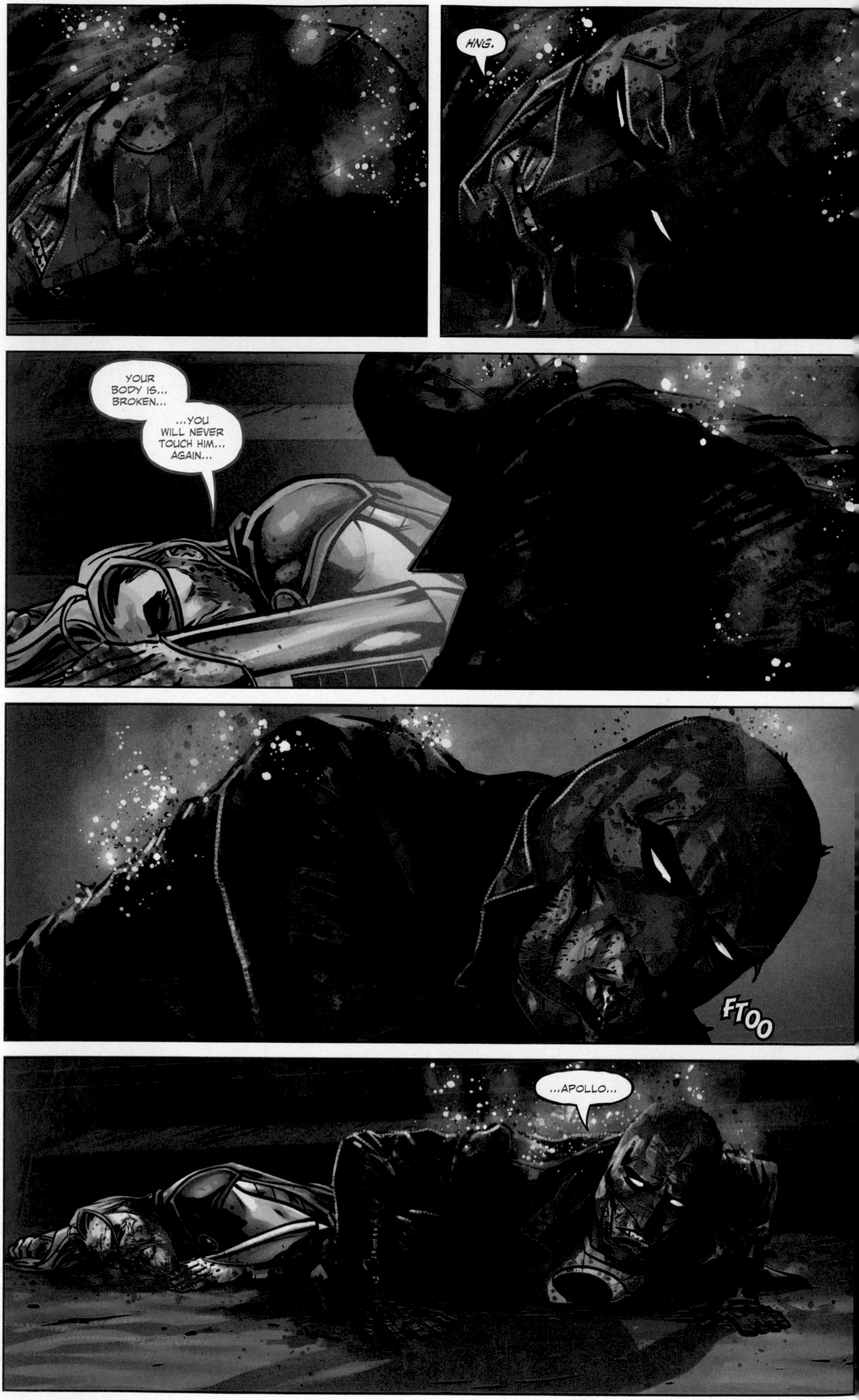
HNG.
YOUR BODY IS... BROKEN...
...YOU WILL NEVER TOUCH HIM... AGAIN...
FTOO
...APOLLO...

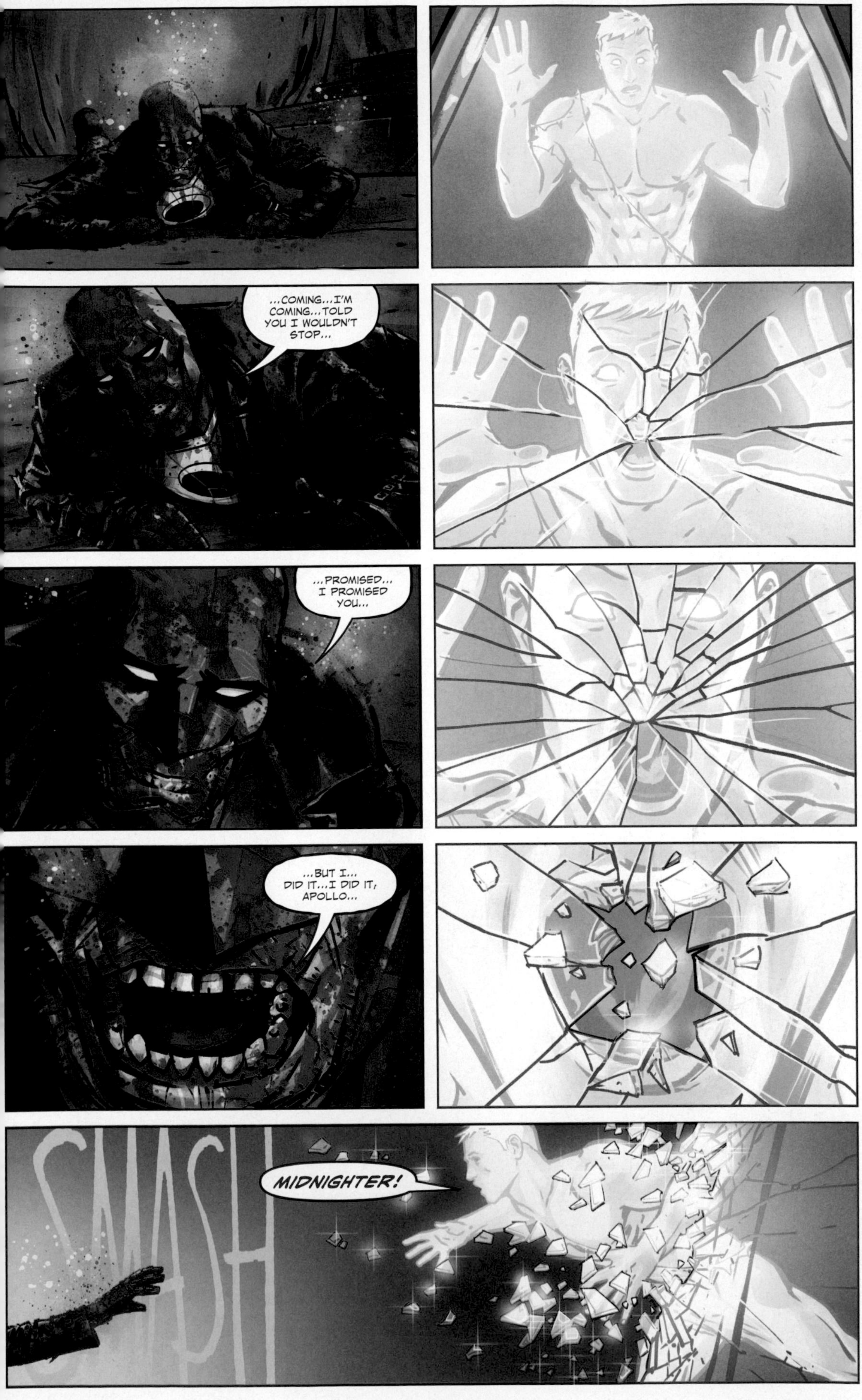
...COMING...I'M COMING...TOLD YOU I WOULDN'T STOP...
...PROMISED... I PROMISED YOU...
...BUT I... DID IT...I DID IT, APOLLO...
SMASH
MIDNIGHTER!

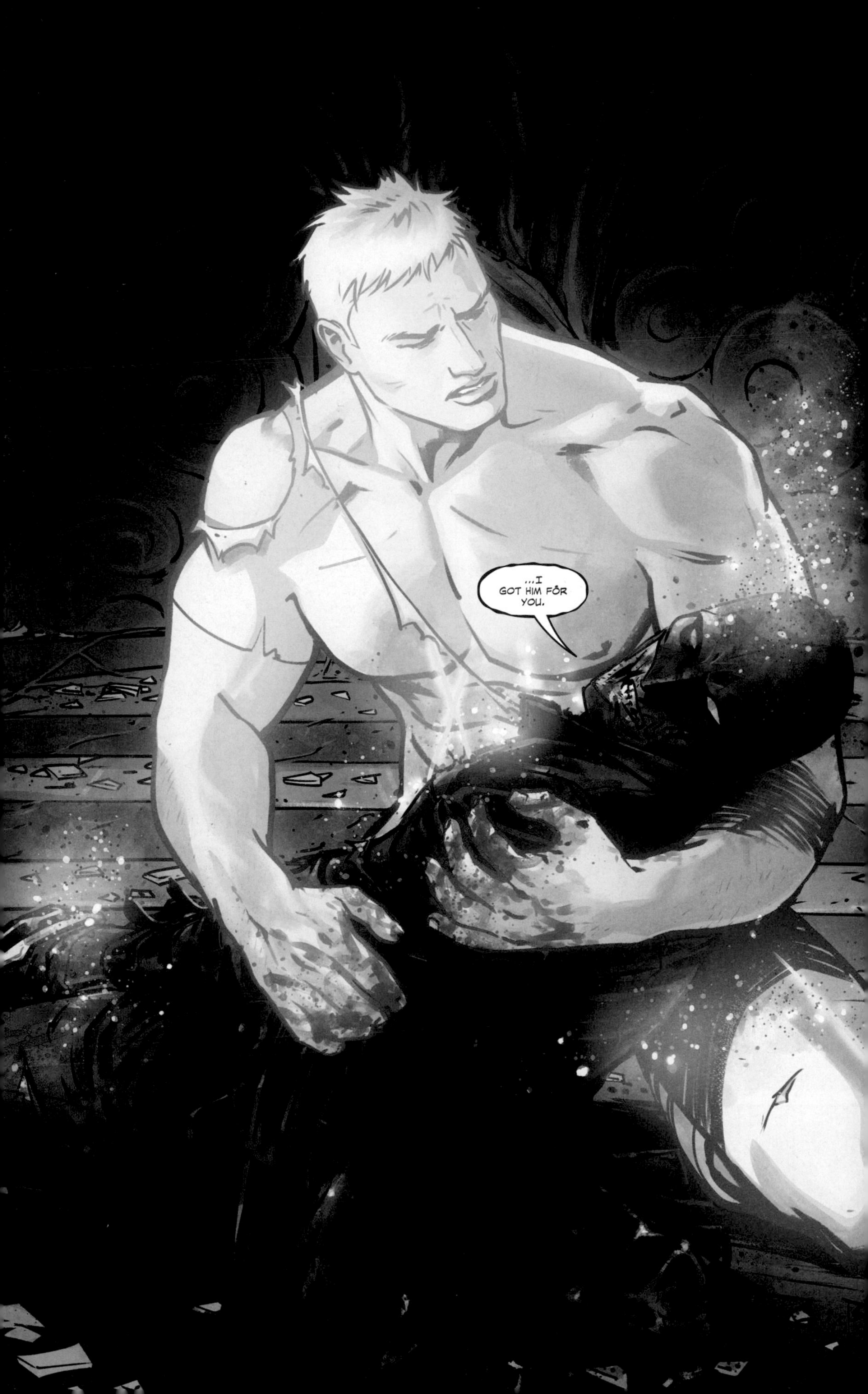
...I GOT HIM FOR YOU.

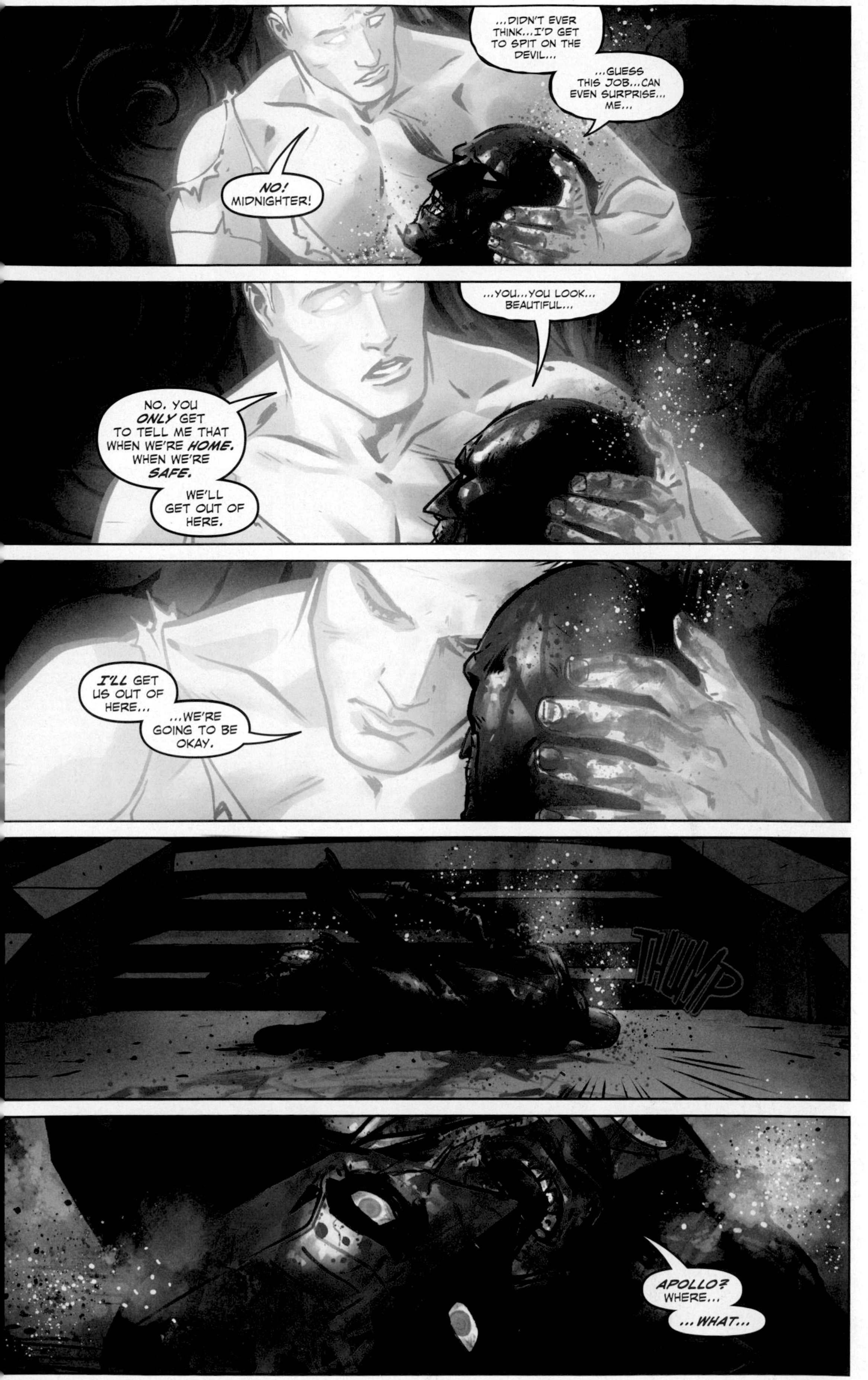
...DIDN'T EVER THINK...I'D GET TO SPIT ON THE DEVIL...
...GUESS THIS JOB...CAN EVEN SURPRISE... ME...
NO! MIDNIGHTER!
...YOU...YOU LOOK... BEAUTIFUL...
NO. YOU ONLY GET TO TELL ME THAT WHEN WE'RE HOME. WHEN WE'RE SAFE.
WE'LL GET OUT OF HERE.
I'LL GET US OUT OF HERE...
...WE'RE GOING TO BE OKAY.
THUMP
APOLLO? WHERE...
...WHAT...

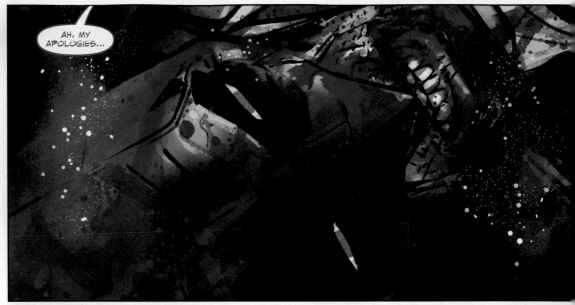

AH, MY APOLOGIES...

...IS *THAT* HOW YOU THOUGHT THIS WOULD END?

YOU ARE IN *MY* REALM, MIDNIGHTER. WHERE I WRITE EXISTENCE. THIS IS WHAT *VICTORY* LOOKS LIKE.

YOU *WON.*

HOW DOES IT *FEEL?*

HE TRIED TO OUTWIT *ME*. HE WAS *WRONG*.

HE *LOST*.

I *COULD* HAVE SAVED HIS SOUL TO TORMENT. BUT I CHOSE OTHERWISE. I *DESTROYED* IT.

SUCH IS MY RIGHT. TO *WASTE* THINGS.

I *SAID* I HAD BEEN WAITING FOR YOU. AND I *WAS*, SURE THAT *NO MATTER* THE OUTCOME OF OUR MEETING...

LIES ARE THE GRAMMAR OF HELL.

AND YOU ARE AN *IDIOT*.

APOLLO *CHALLENGED* ME. A QUESTION--"WHY DID HE TAKE THE NAME APOLLO?"

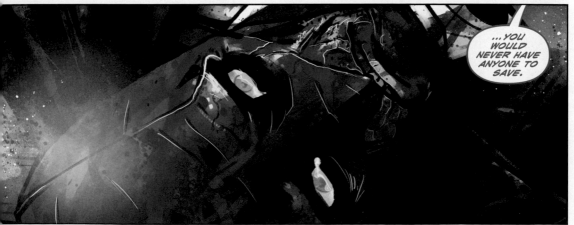
...YOU WOULD NEVER HAVE ANYONE TO SAVE.

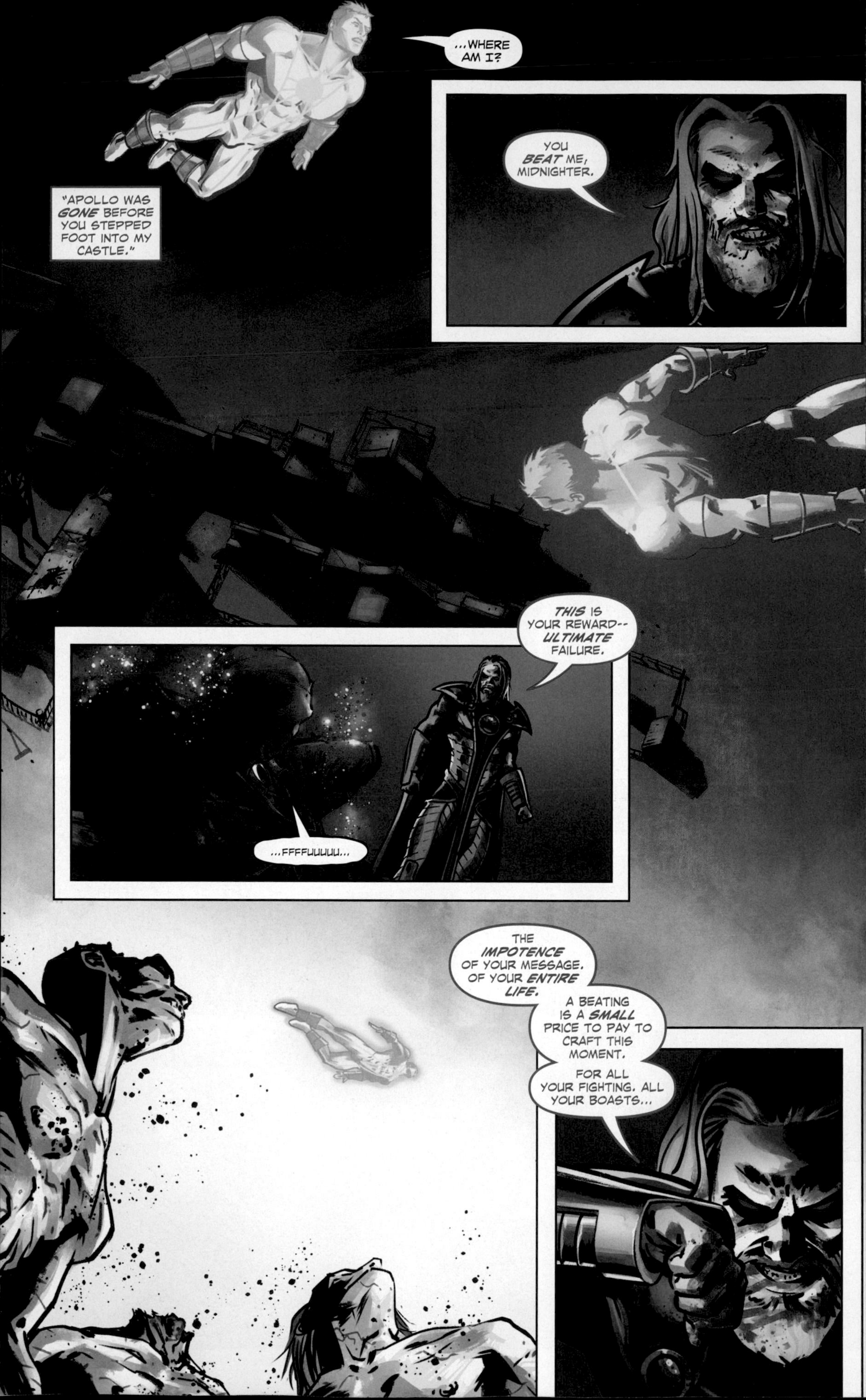
...WHERE AM I?
"APOLLO WAS GONE BEFORE YOU STEPPED FOOT INTO MY CASTLE."
YOU BEAT ME, MIDNIGHTER.
THIS IS YOUR REWARD-- ULTIMATE FAILURE.
...FFFFUUUUU...
THE IMPOTENCE OF YOUR MESSAGE. OF YOUR ENTIRE LIFE.
A BEATING IS A SMALL PRICE TO PAY TO CRAFT THIS MOMENT.
FOR ALL YOUR FIGHTING. ALL YOUR BOASTS...

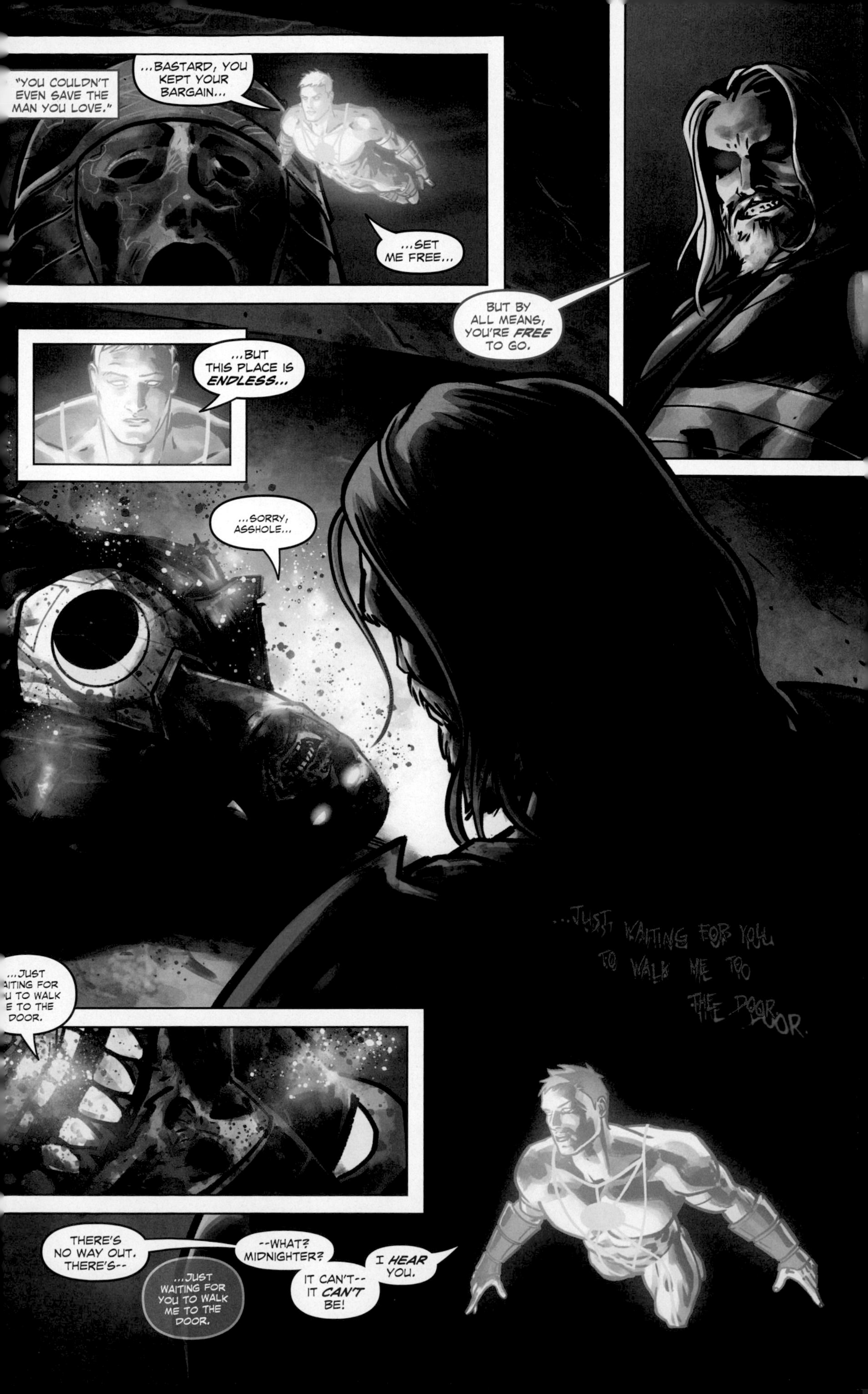

"YOU COULDN'T EVEN SAVE THE MAN YOU LOVE."
...BASTARD, YOU KEPT YOUR BARGAIN...
...SET ME FREE...
BUT BY ALL MEANS, YOU'RE *FREE* TO GO.
...BUT THIS PLACE IS *ENDLESS...*
...SORRY, ASSHOLE...
...JUST WAITING FOR YOU TO WALK ME TO THE DOOR.
...JUST AITING FOR U TO WALK E TO THE DOOR.
THERE'S NO WAY OUT. THERE'S--
...JUST WAITING FOR YOU TO WALK ME TO THE DOOR.
--WHAT? MIDNIGHTER?
IT CAN'T-- IT *CAN'T* BE!
I *HEAR* YOU.

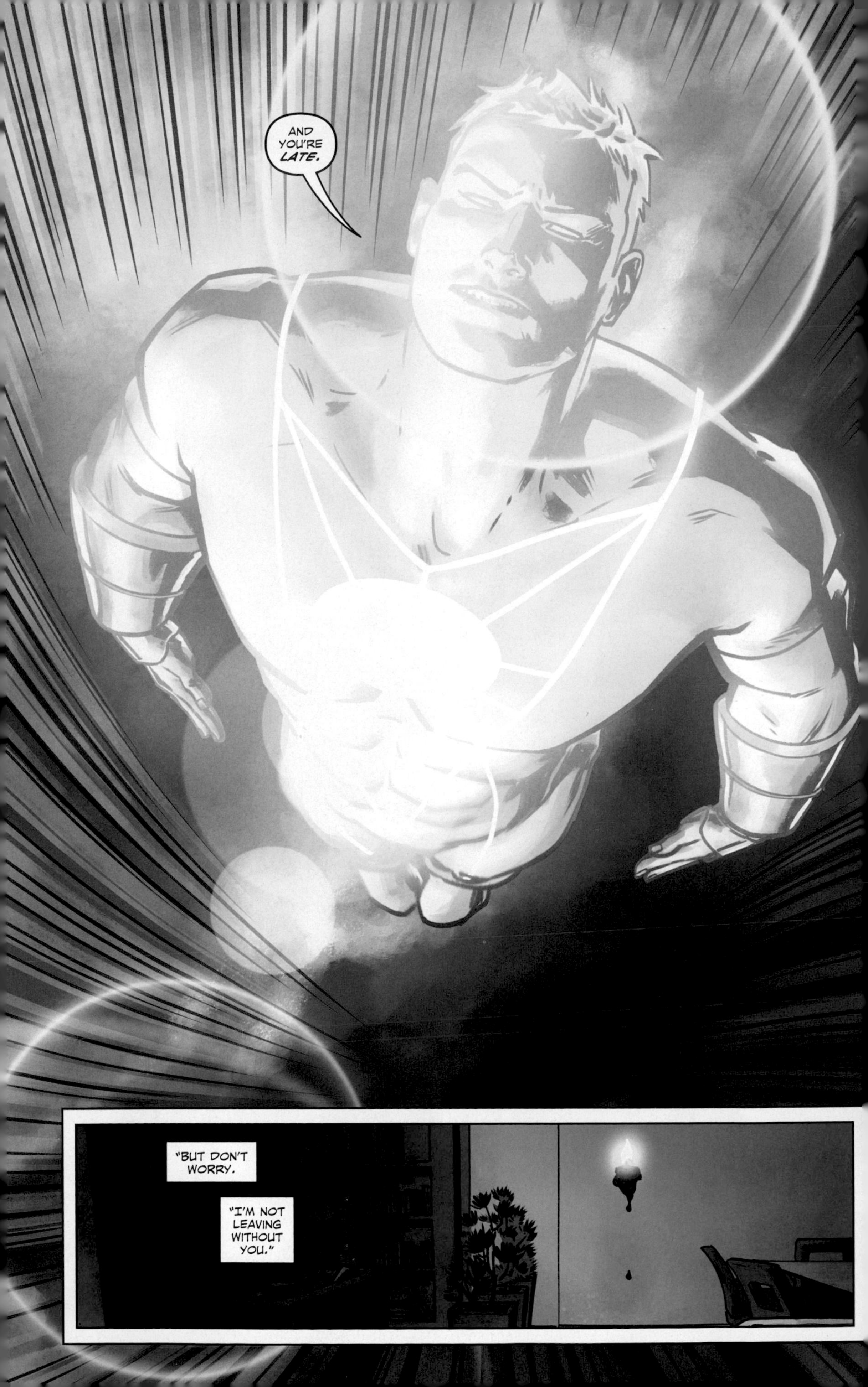
AND YOU'RE *LATE.*
"BUT DON'T WORRY.
"I'M NOT LEAVING WITHOUT YOU."

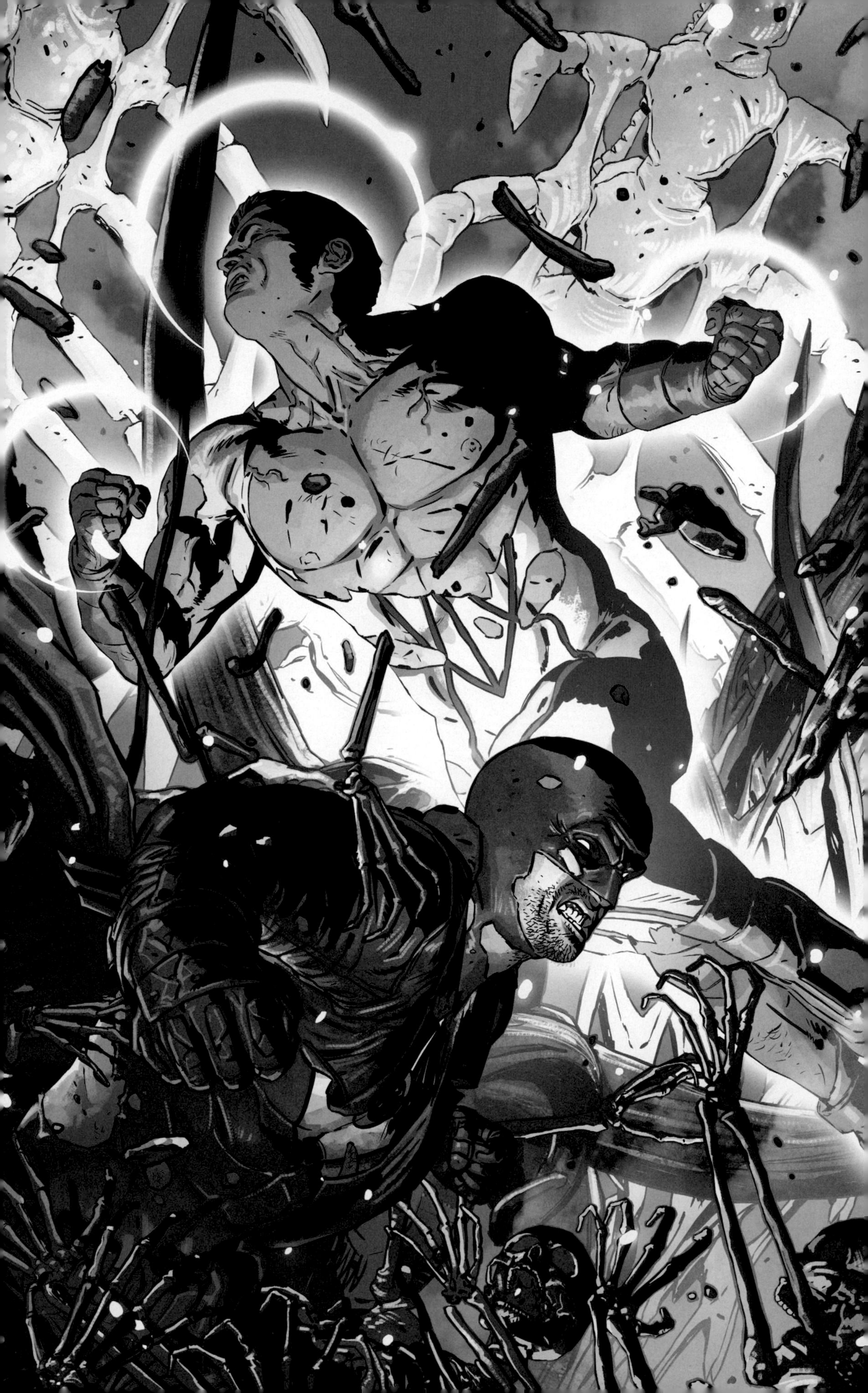

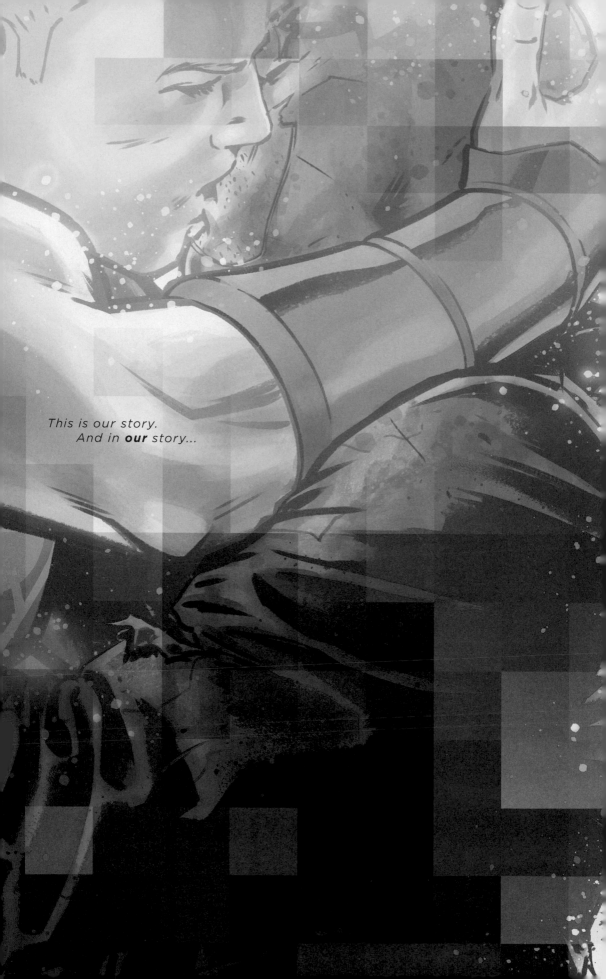

This is our story.
And in **our** story...

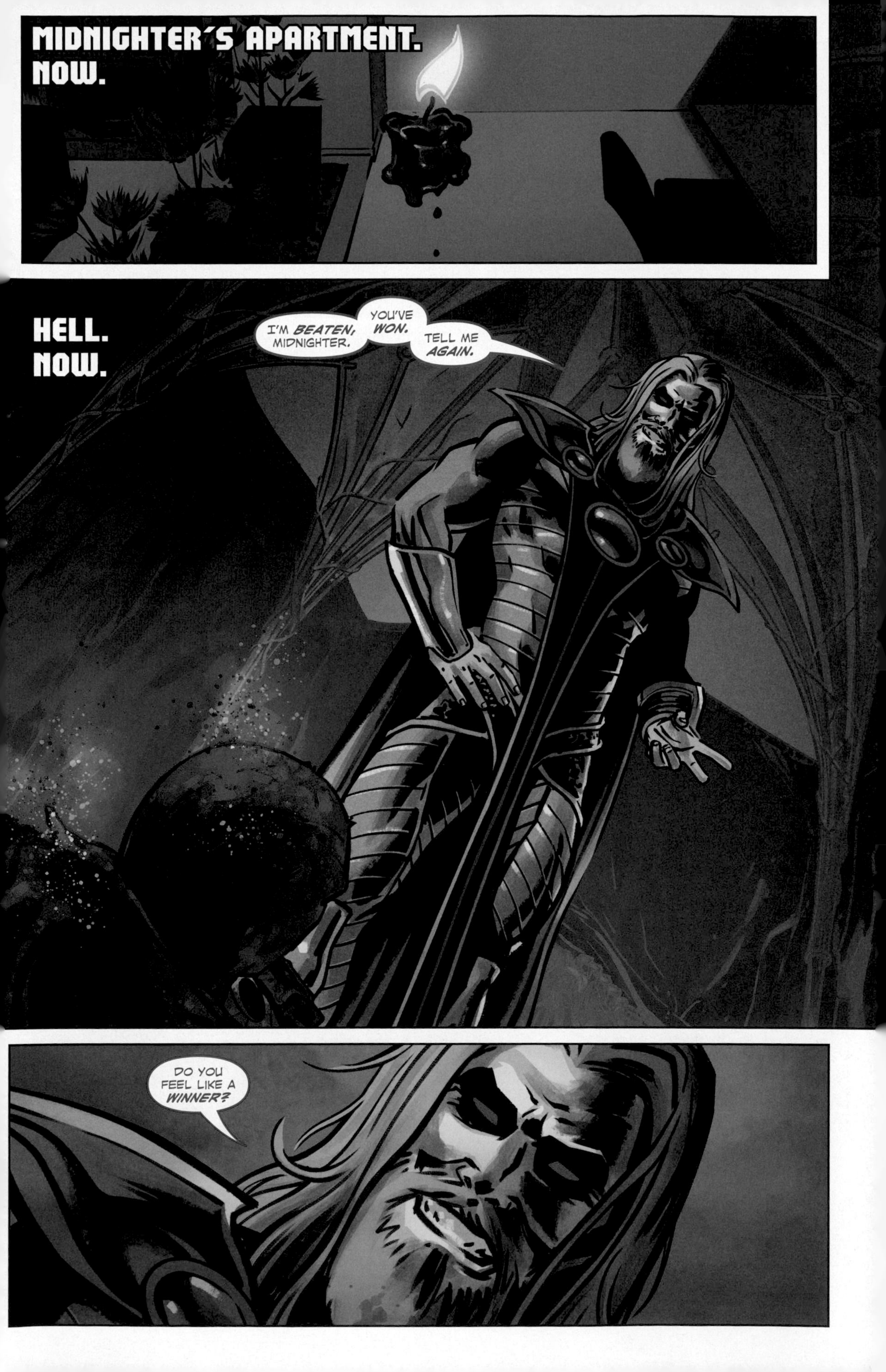
MIDNIGHTER'S APARTMENT.
NOW.
HELL.
NOW.
I'M BEATEN, MIDNIGHTER.
YOU'VE WON.
TELL ME AGAIN.
DO YOU FEEL LIKE A WINNER?

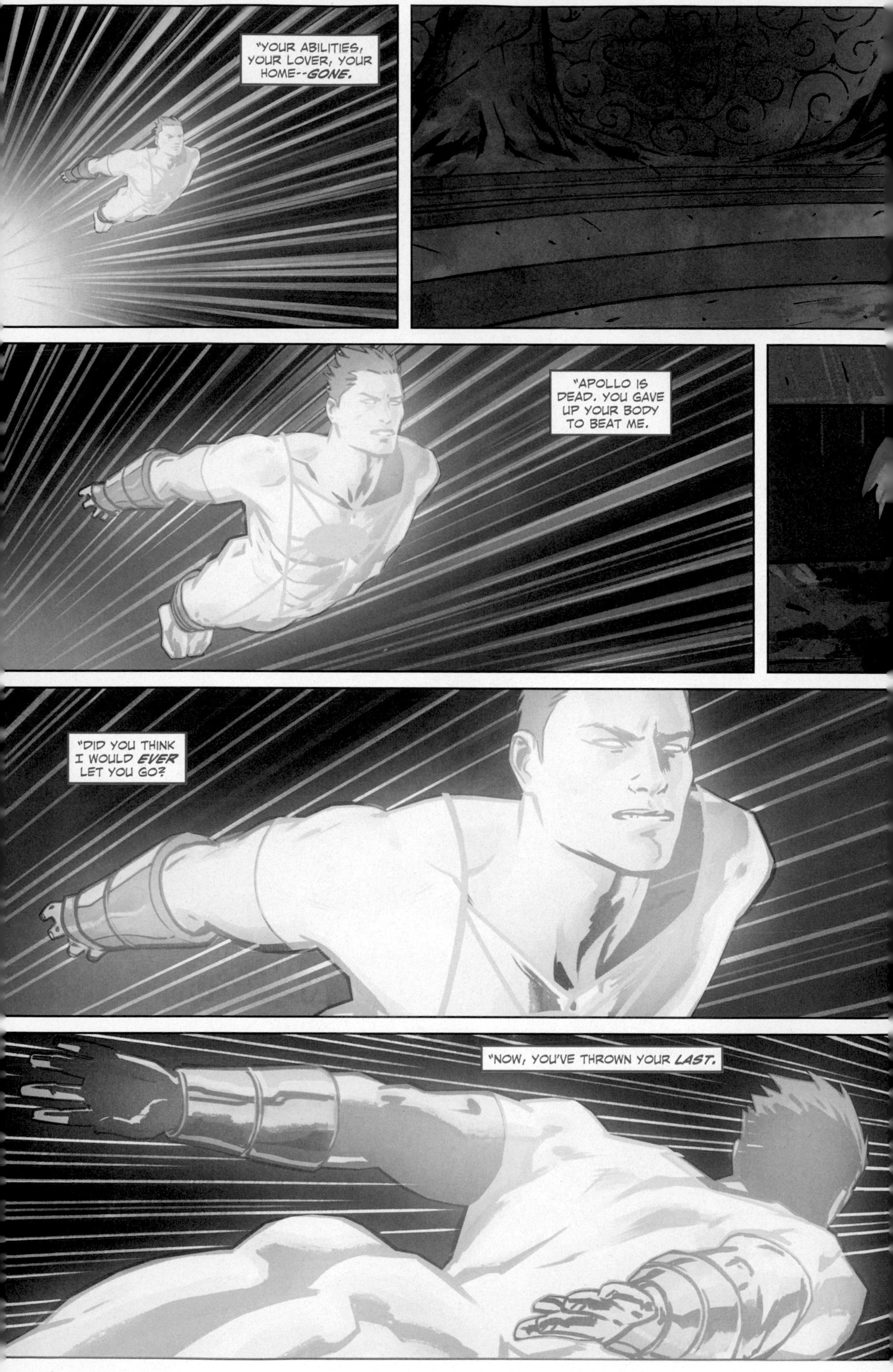
"YOUR ABILITIES, YOUR LOVER, YOUR HOME--GONE.
"APOLLO IS DEAD. YOU GAVE UP YOUR BODY TO BEAT ME.
"DID YOU THINK I WOULD EVER LET YOU GO?
"NOW, YOU'VE THROWN YOUR LAST.

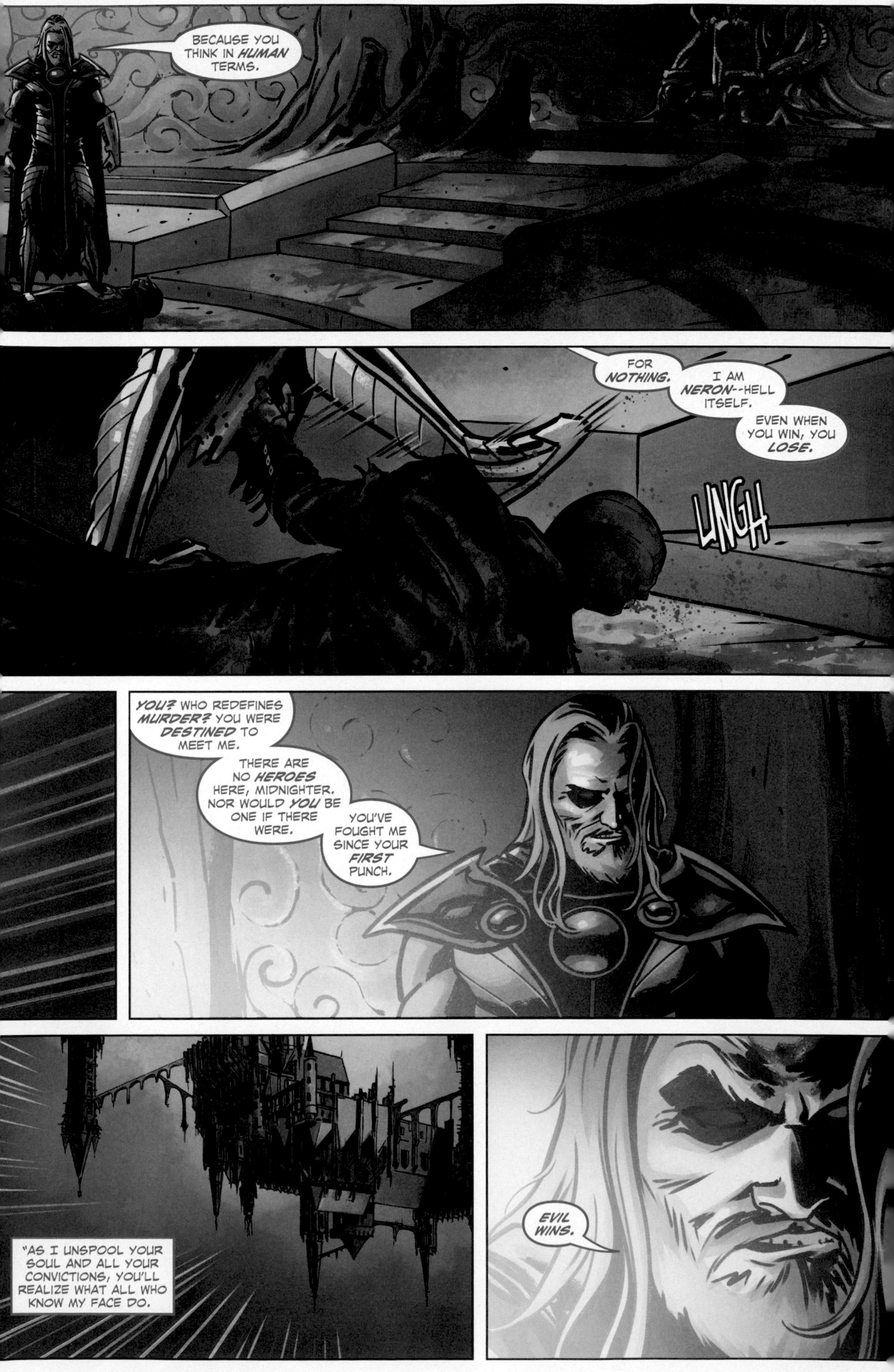
BECAUSE YOU THINK IN HUMAN TERMS.
FOR NOTHING.
I AM NERON--HELL ITSELF.
EVEN WHEN YOU WIN, YOU LOSE.
UNGH
YOU? WHO REDEFINES MURDER? YOU WERE DESTINED TO MEET ME.
THERE ARE NO HEROES HERE, MIDNIGHTER. NOR WOULD YOU BE ONE IF THERE WERE.
YOU'VE FOUGHT ME SINCE YOUR FIRST PUNCH.
"AS I UNSPOOL YOUR SOUL AND ALL YOUR CONVICTIONS, YOU'LL REALIZE WHAT ALL WHO KNOW MY FACE DO.
EVIL WINS.

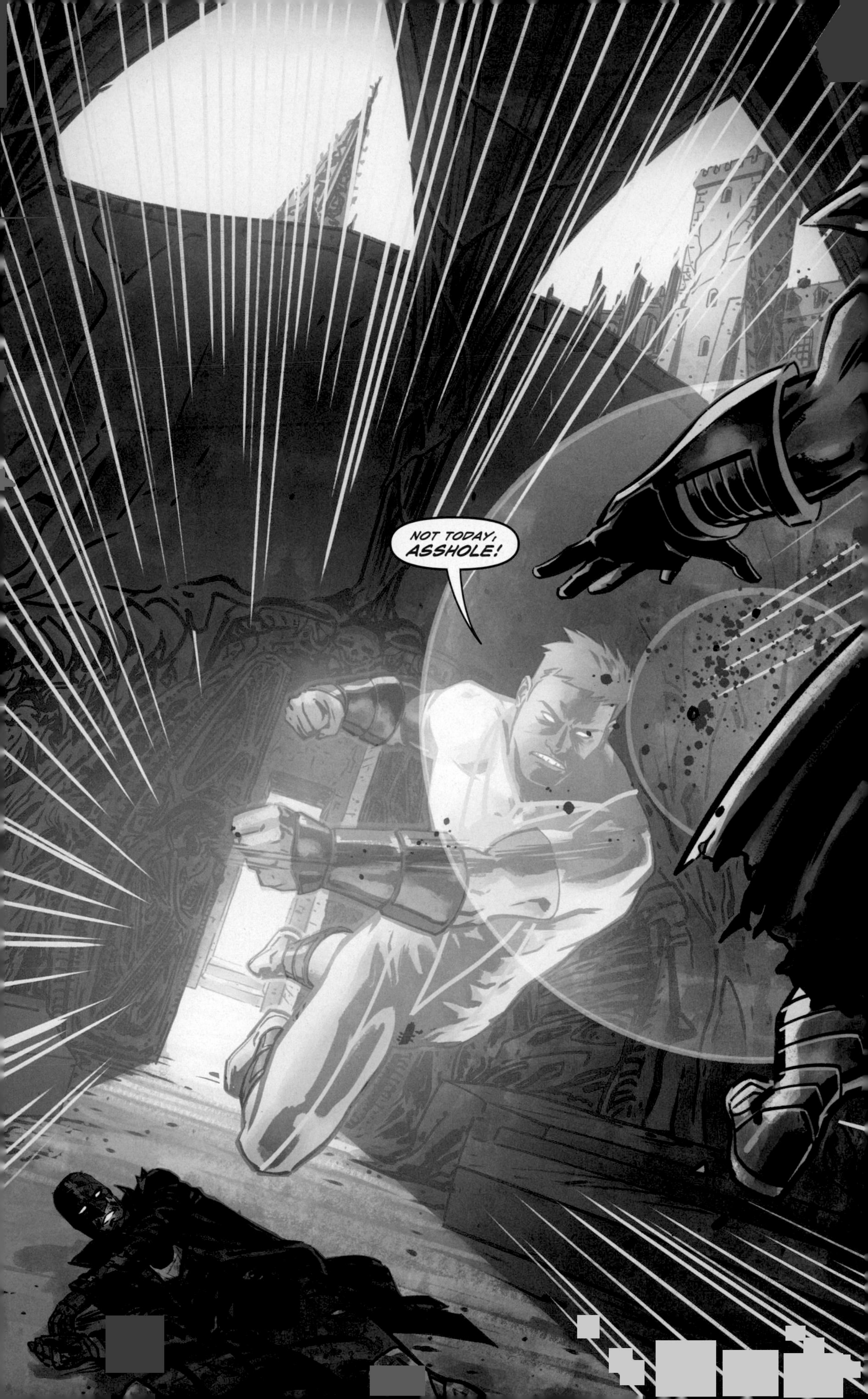
NOT TODAY, ASSHOLE!

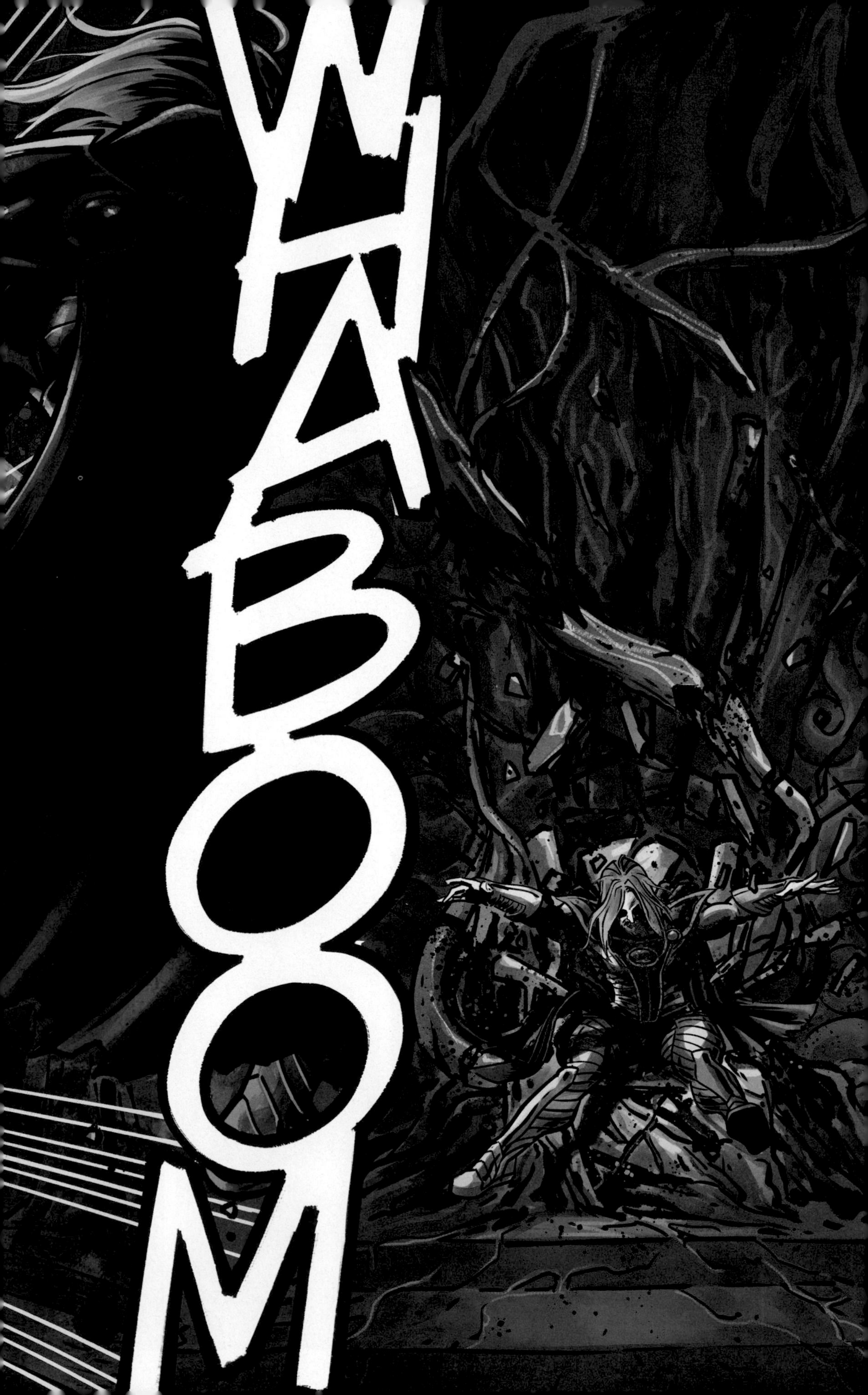
WHABOOM

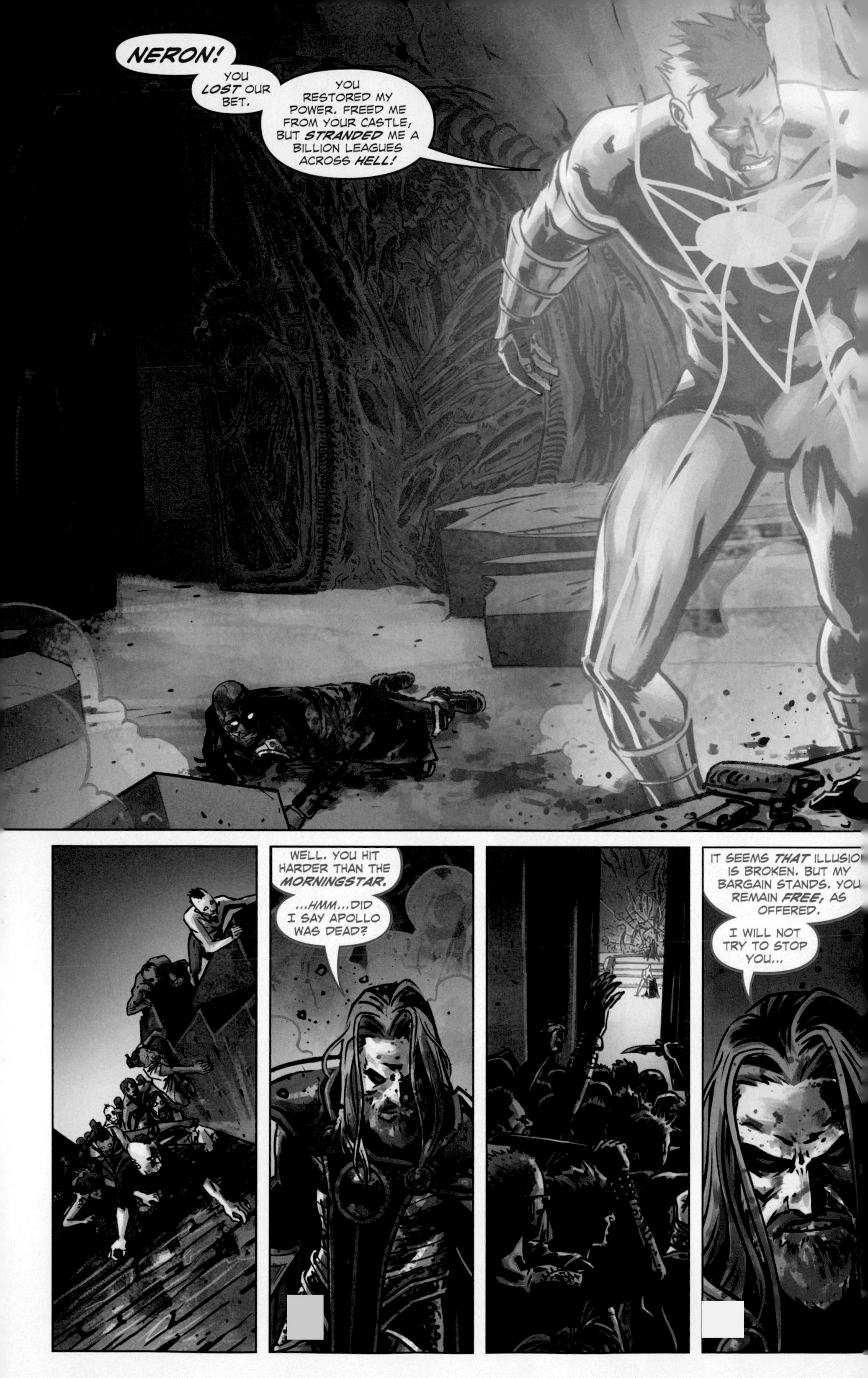
NERON!
YOU LOST OUR BET.
YOU RESTORED MY POWER. FREED ME FROM YOUR CASTLE, BUT STRANDED ME A BILLION LEAGUES ACROSS HELL!
WELL. YOU HIT HARDER THAN THE MORNINGSTAR.
...HMM...DID I SAY APOLLO WAS DEAD?
IT SEEMS THAT ILLUSIO IS BROKEN. BUT MY BARGAIN STANDS. YOU REMAIN FREE, AS OFFERED.
I WILL NOT TRY TO STOP YOU...

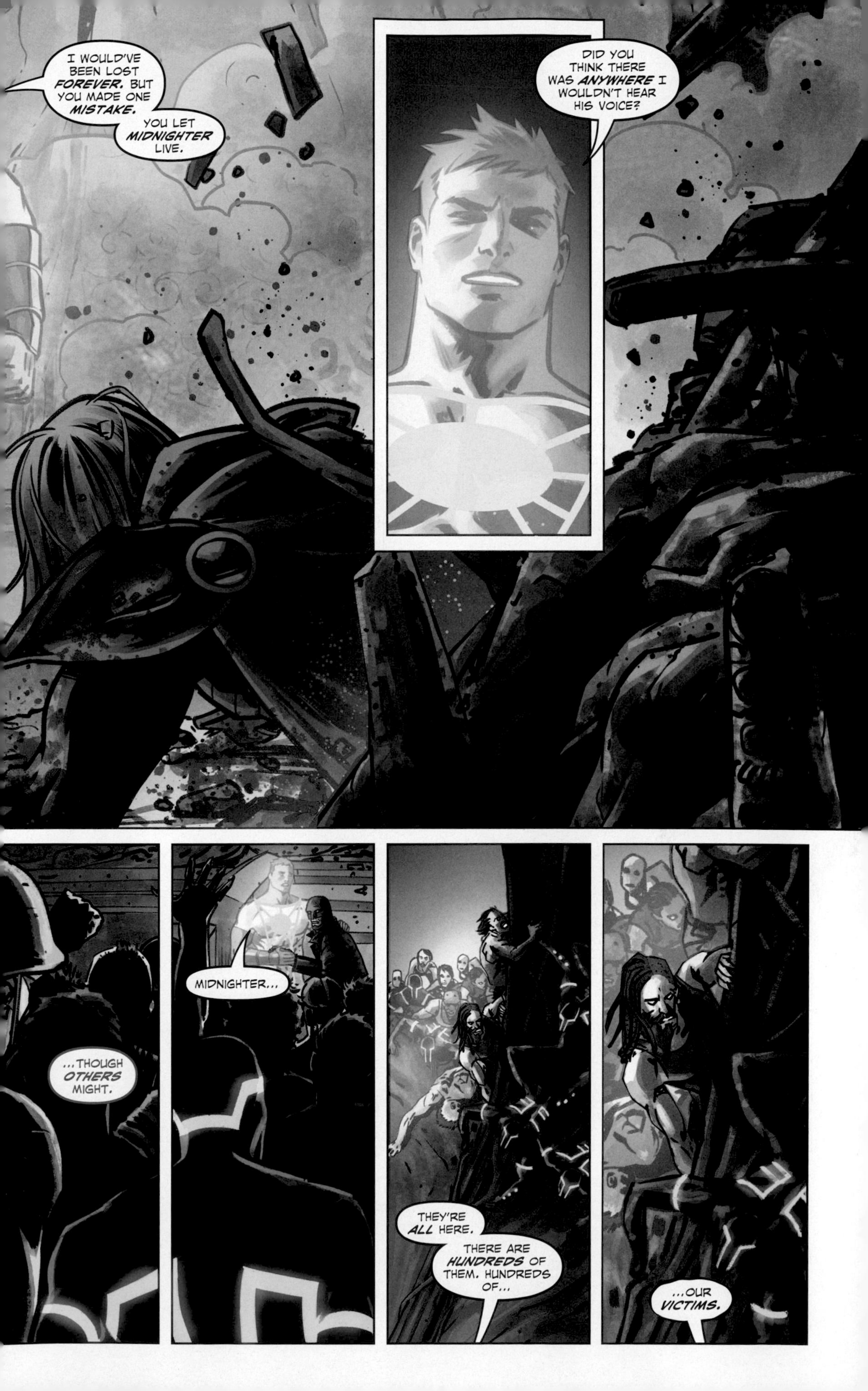
I WOULD'VE BEEN LOST FOREVER. BUT YOU MADE ONE MISTAKE.
YOU LET MIDNIGHTER LIVE.
DID YOU THINK THERE WAS ANYWHERE I WOULDN'T HEAR HIS VOICE?
...THOUGH OTHERS MIGHT.
MIDNIGHTER...
THEY'RE ALL HERE.
THERE ARE HUNDREDS OF THEM. HUNDREDS OF...
...OUR VICTIMS.

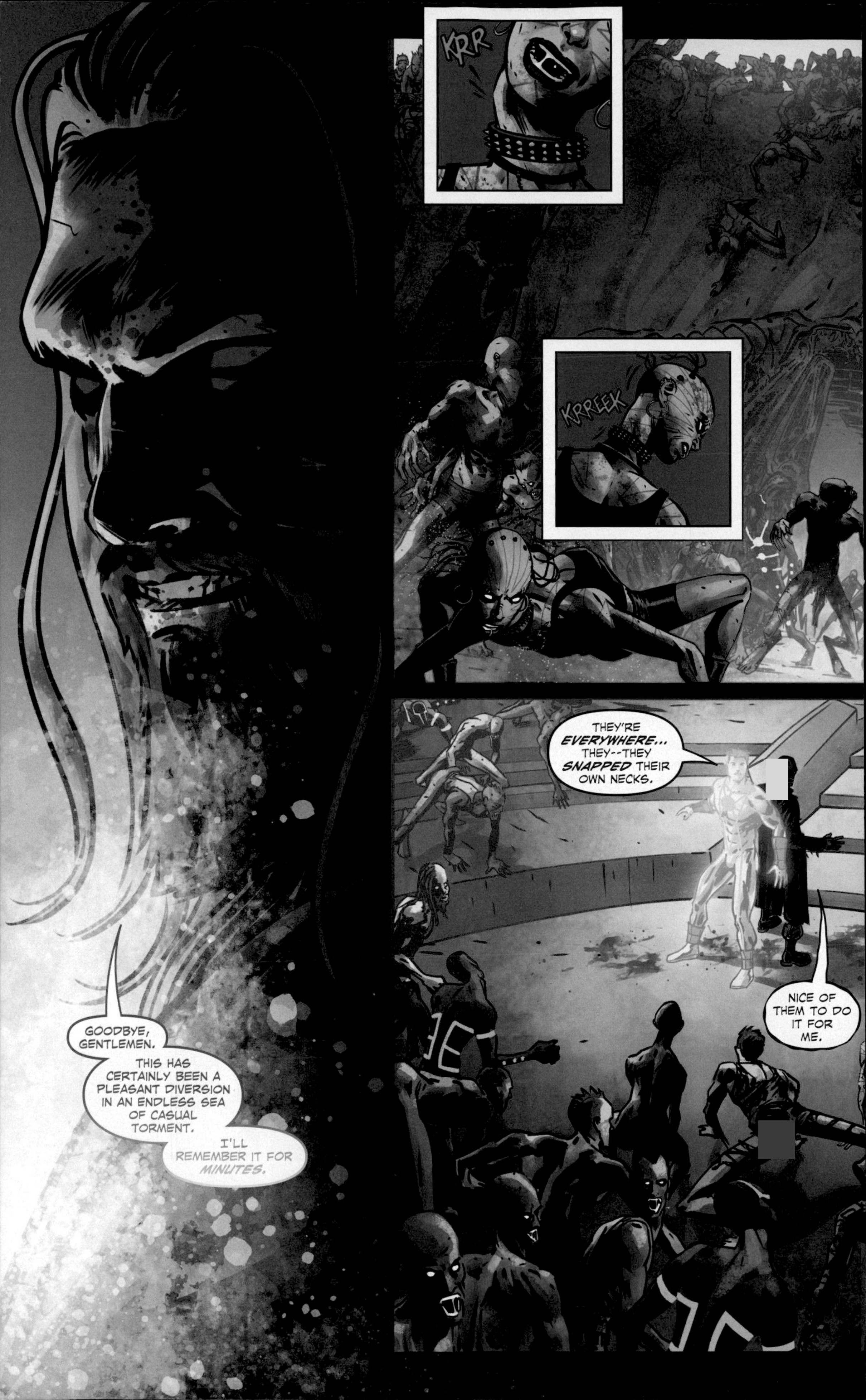
GOODBYE, GENTLEMEN.
THIS HAS CERTAINLY BEEN A PLEASANT DIVERSION IN AN ENDLESS SEA OF CASUAL TORMENT.
I'LL REMEMBER IT FOR *MINUTES.*
KRR
KRREEK
THEY'RE *EVERYWHERE...* THEY--THEY *SNAPPED* THEIR OWN NECKS.
NICE OF THEM TO DO IT FOR ME.

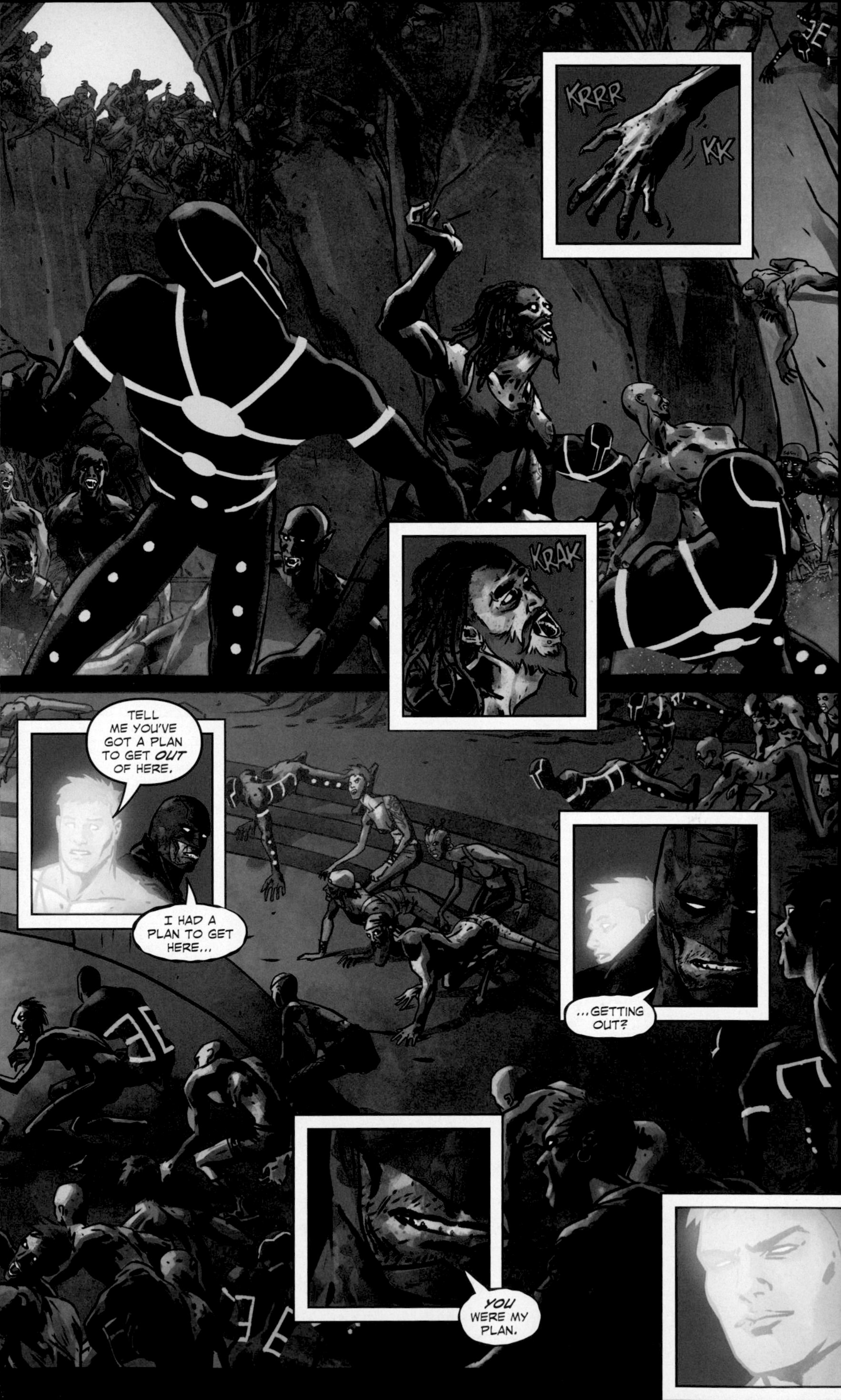
KRRR
KK
KRAK
TELL ME YOU'VE GOT A PLAN TO GET OUT OF HERE.
I HAD A PLAN TO GET HERE...
...GETTING OUT?
YOU WERE MY PLAN.

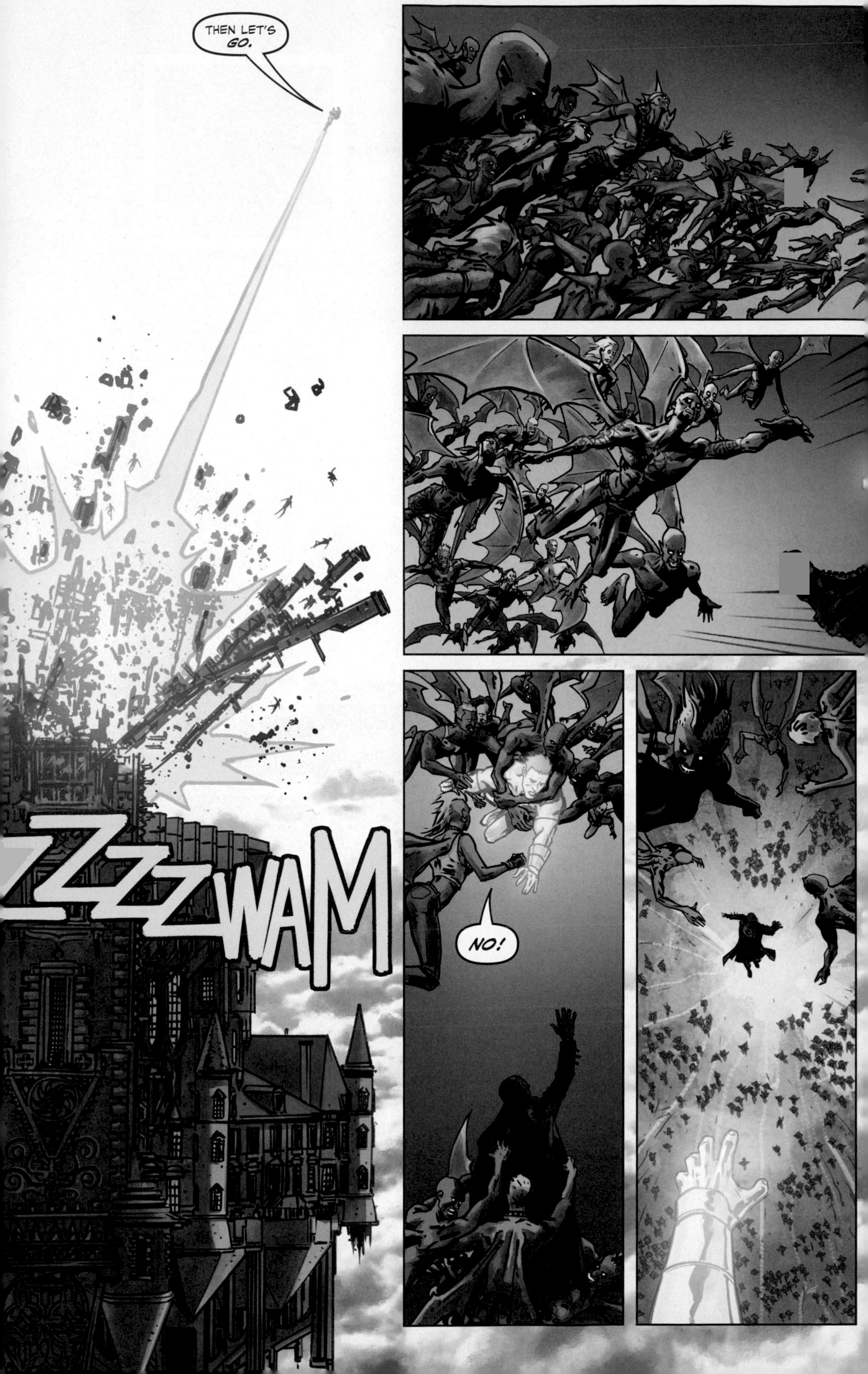
THEN LET'S GO.
ZZZWAM
NO!

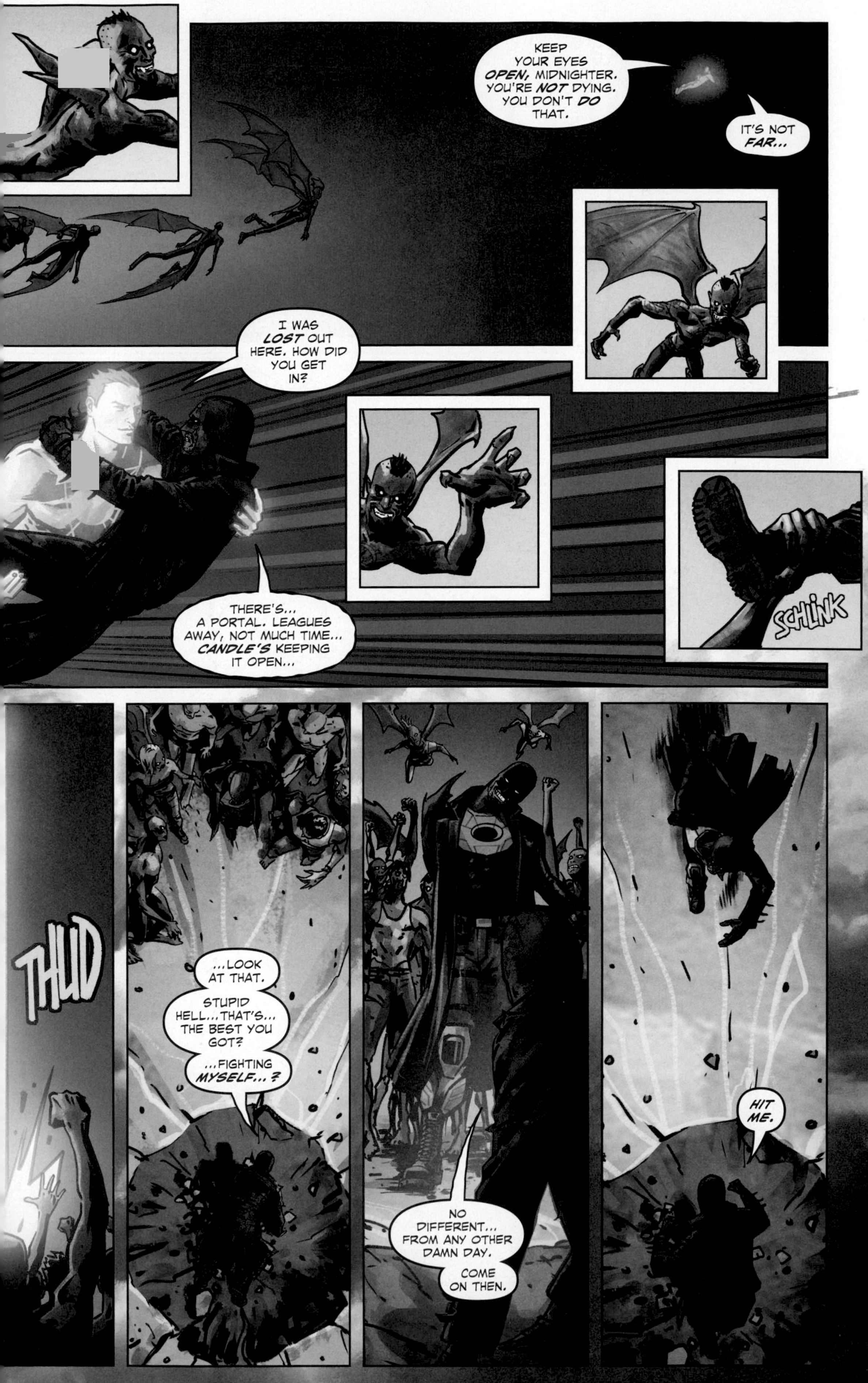
KEEP YOUR EYES OPEN, MIDNIGHTER. YOU'RE NOT DYING. YOU DON'T DO THAT.
IT'S NOT FAR...
I WAS LOST OUT HERE. HOW DID YOU GET IN?
THERE'S... A PORTAL. LEAGUES AWAY, NOT MUCH TIME... CANDLE'S KEEPING IT OPEN...
SCHLINK
THUD
...LOOK AT THAT.
STUPID HELL...THAT'S... THE BEST YOU GOT?
...FIGHTING MYSELF...?
NO DIFFERENT... FROM ANY OTHER DAMN DAY.
COME ON THEN.
HIT ME.

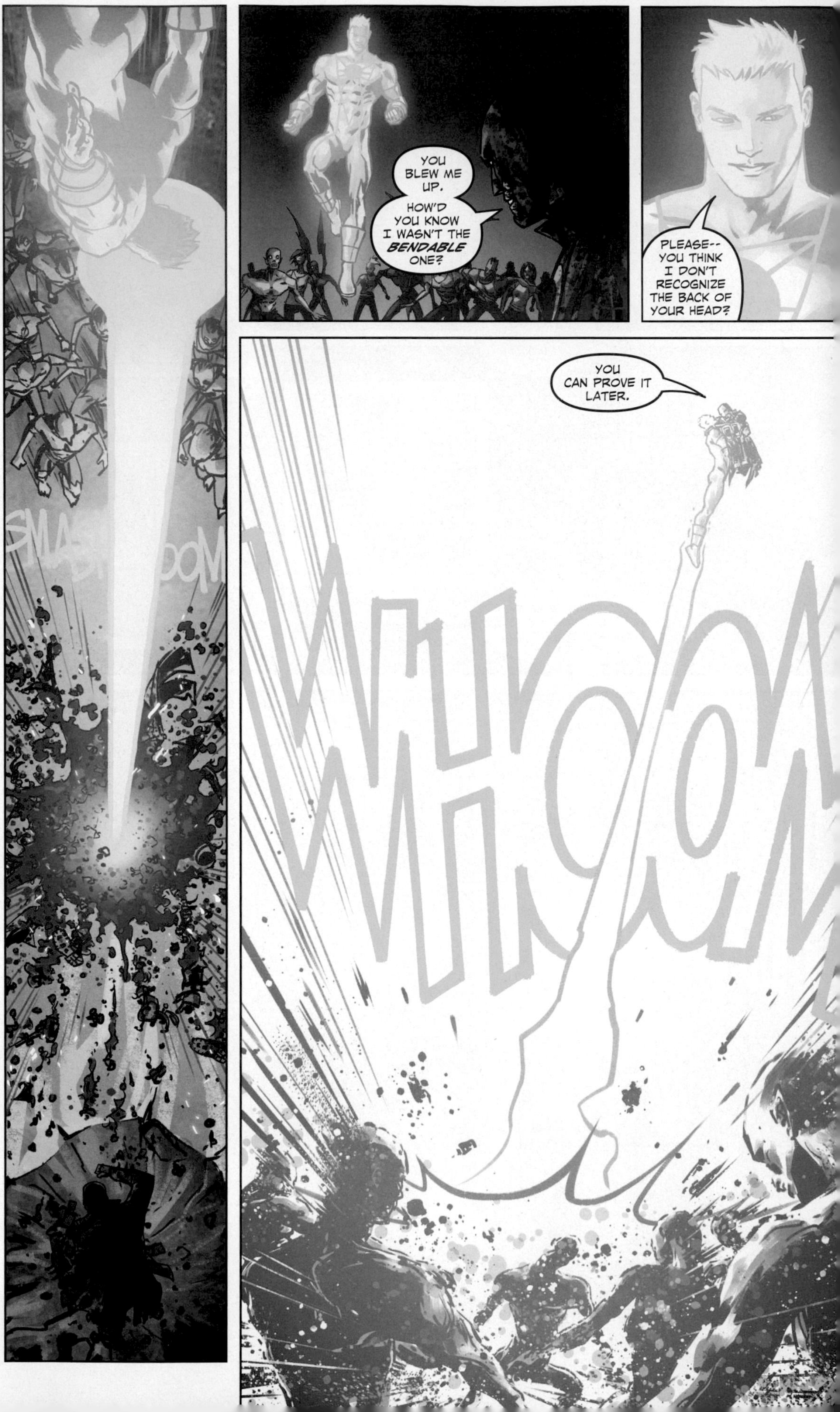
SMASH BOOM
YOU BLEW ME UP.
HOW'D YOU KNOW I WASN'T THE BENDABLE ONE?
PLEASE-- YOU THINK I DON'T RECOGNIZE THE BACK OF YOUR HEAD?
YOU CAN PROVE IT LATER.
WHOOM

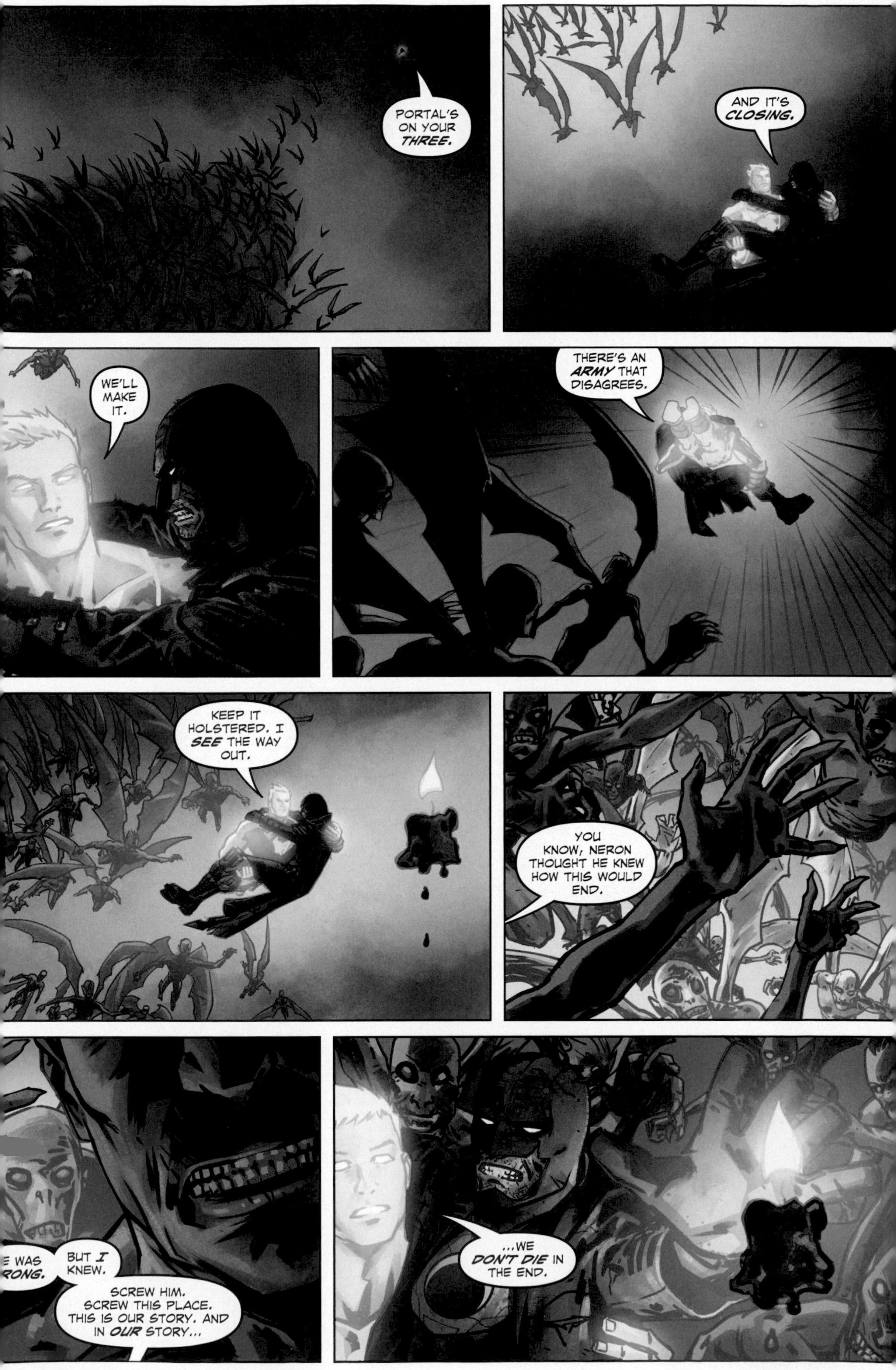

PORTAL'S ON YOUR *THREE.*
AND IT'S *CLOSING.*
WE'LL MAKE IT.
THERE'S AN *ARMY* THAT DISAGREES.
KEEP IT HOLSTERED. I *SEE* THE WAY OUT.
YOU KNOW, NERON THOUGHT HE KNEW HOW THIS WOULD END.
E WAS RONG.
BUT *I* KNEW.
SCREW HIM. SCREW THIS PLACE. THIS IS OUR STORY. AND IN *OUR* STORY...
...WE *DON'T DIE* IN THE END.

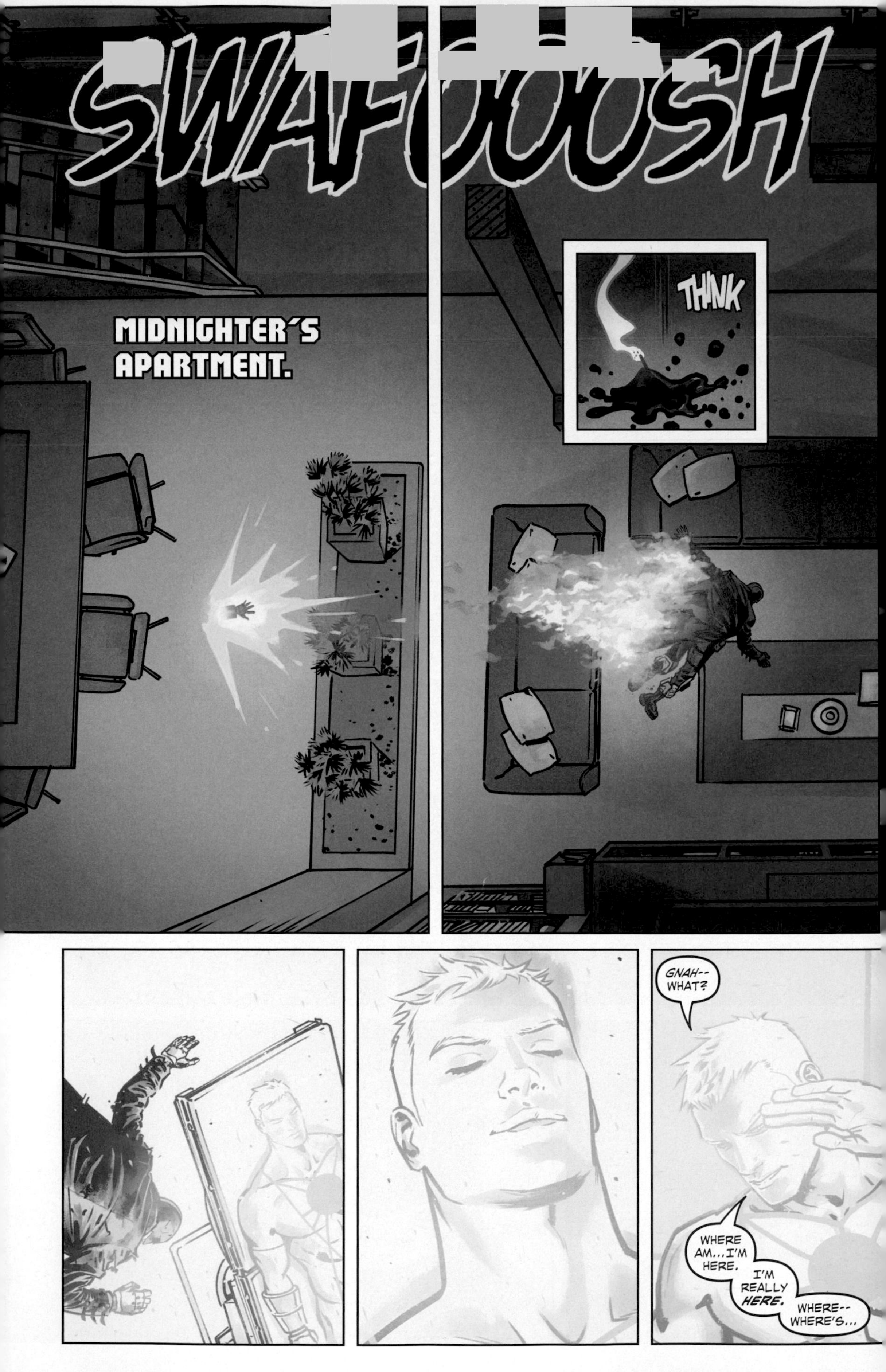
SWAFOOOSH
MIDNIGHTER´S APARTMENT.
THINK
GNAH-- WHAT?
WHERE AM...I'M HERE.
I'M REALLY *HERE.*
WHERE-- WHERE'S...

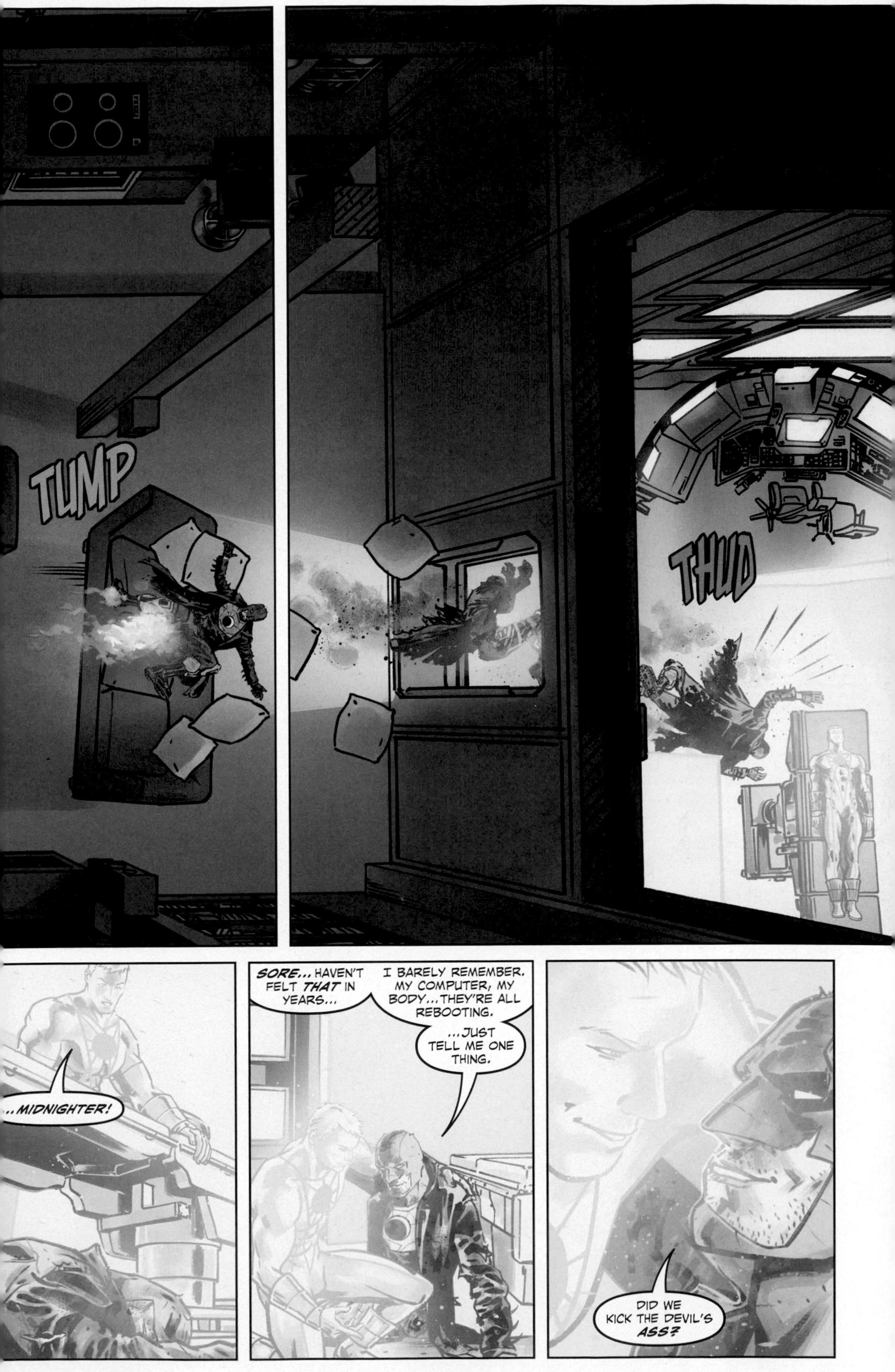
TUMP
THUD
...MIDNIGHTER!
SORE... HAVEN'T FELT THAT IN YEARS...
I BARELY REMEMBER. MY COMPUTER, MY BODY...THEY'RE ALL REBOOTING.
...JUST TELL ME ONE THING.
DID WE KICK THE DEVIL'S ASS?

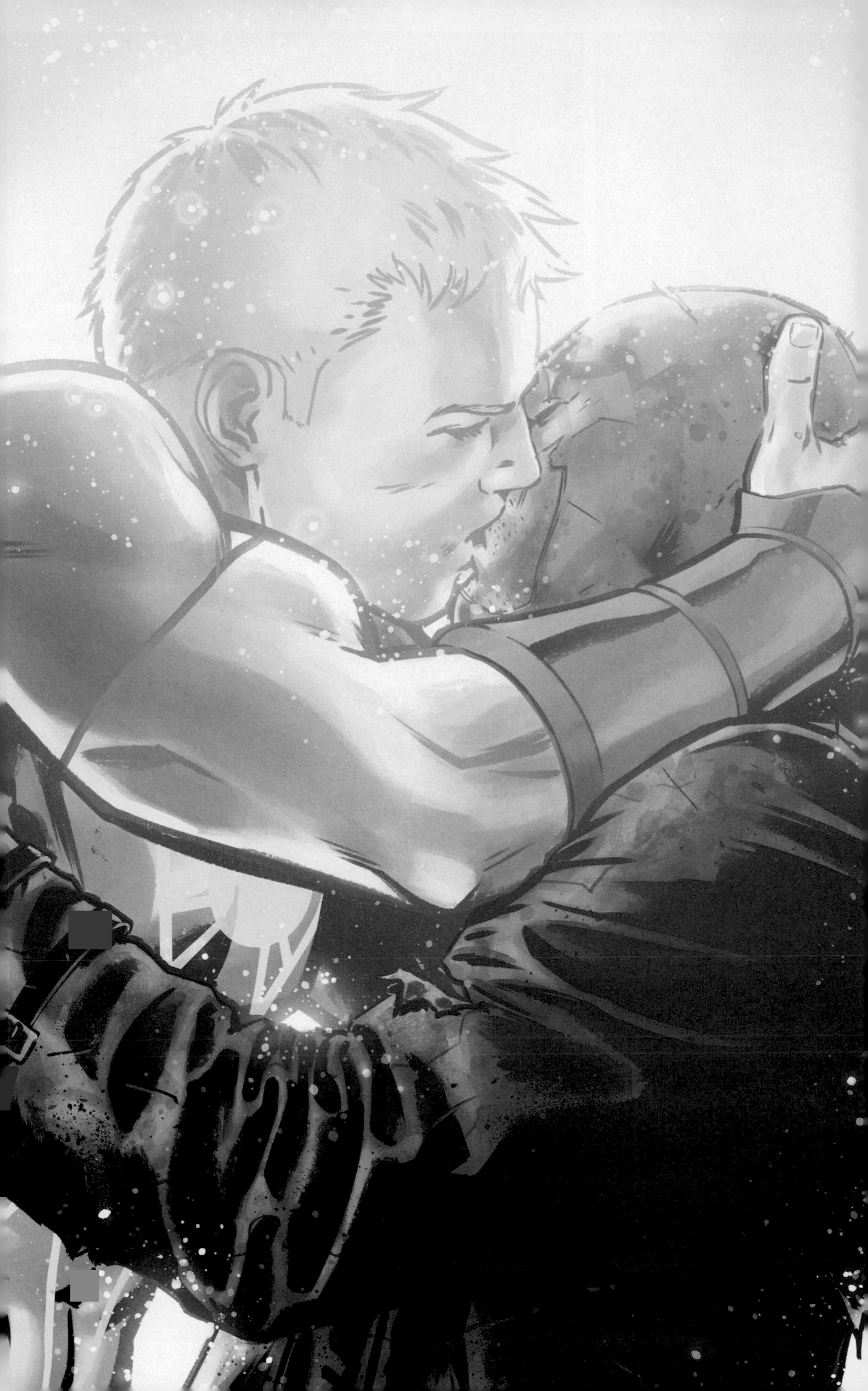

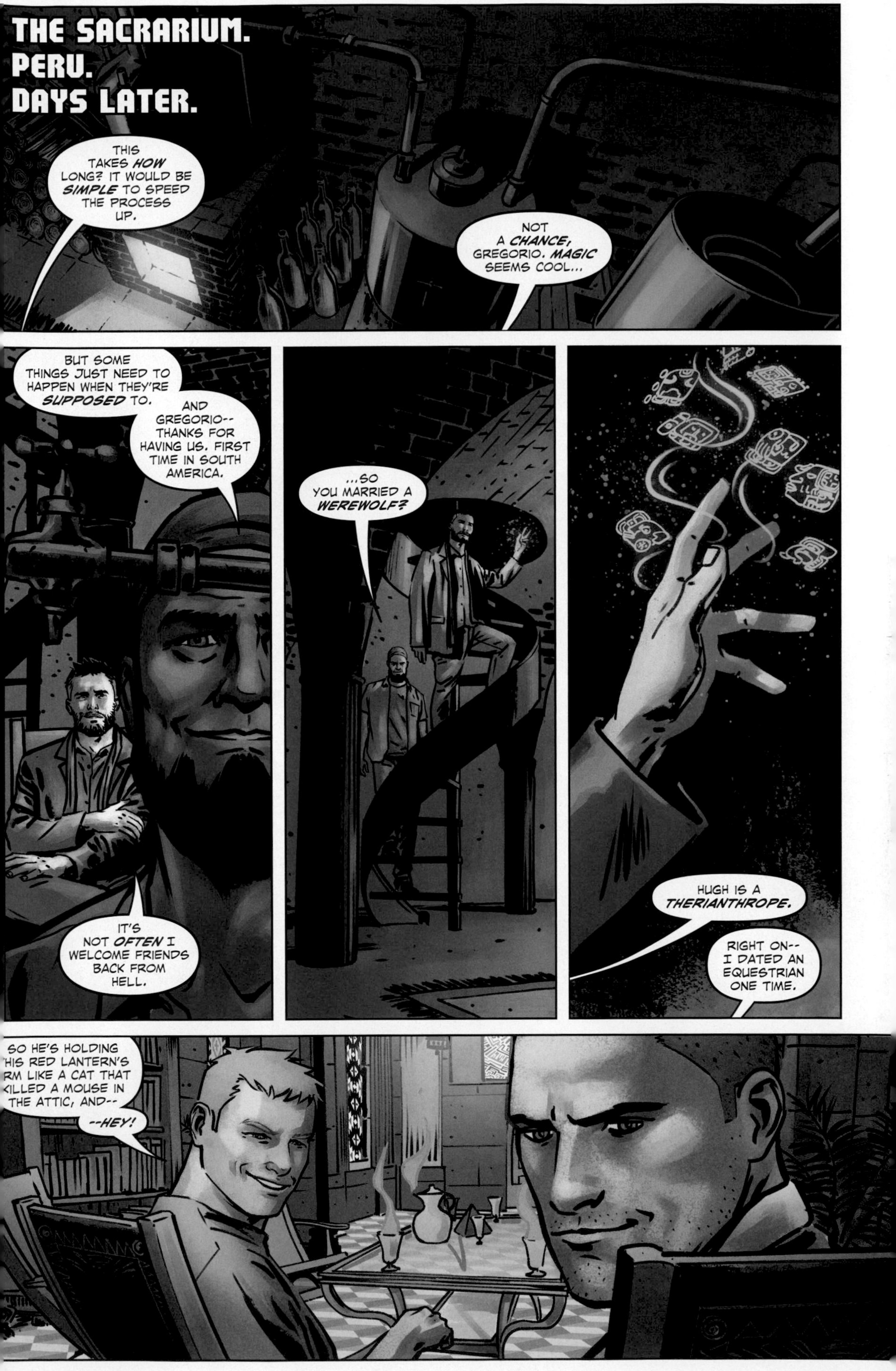
THE SACRARIUM.
PERU.
DAYS LATER.
THIS TAKES HOW LONG? IT WOULD BE SIMPLE TO SPEED THE PROCESS UP.
NOT A CHANCE, GREGORIO. MAGIC SEEMS COOL...
BUT SOME THINGS JUST NEED TO HAPPEN WHEN THEY'RE SUPPOSED TO.
AND GREGORIO--THANKS FOR HAVING US. FIRST TIME IN SOUTH AMERICA.
IT'S NOT OFTEN I WELCOME FRIENDS BACK FROM HELL.
...SO YOU MARRIED A WEREWOLF?
HUGH IS A THERIANTHROPE.
RIGHT ON--I DATED AN EQUESTRIAN ONE TIME.
SO HE'S HOLDING HIS RED LANTERN'S RM LIKE A CAT THAT KILLED A MOUSE IN THE ATTIC, AND--
--HEY!

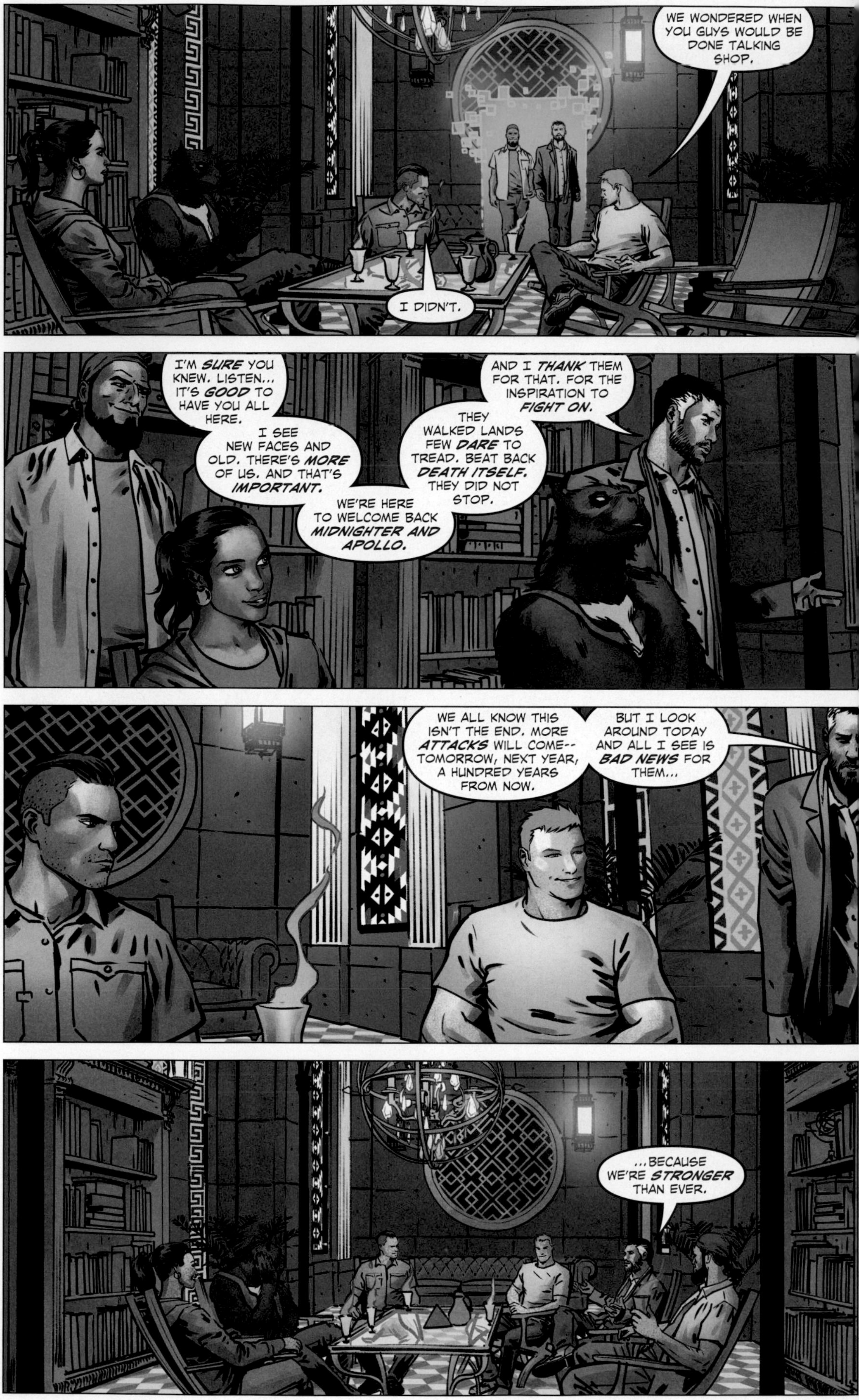
WE WONDERED WHEN YOU GUYS WOULD BE DONE TALKING SHOP.
I DIDN'T.
I'M SURE YOU KNEW. LISTEN... IT'S GOOD TO HAVE YOU ALL HERE.
I SEE NEW FACES AND OLD. THERE'S MORE OF US. AND THAT'S IMPORTANT.
WE'RE HERE TO WELCOME BACK MIDNIGHTER AND APOLLO.
THEY WALKED LANDS FEW DARE TO TREAD. BEAT BACK DEATH ITSELF. THEY DID NOT STOP.
AND I THANK THEM FOR THAT. FOR THE INSPIRATION TO FIGHT ON.
WE ALL KNOW THIS ISN'T THE END. MORE ATTACKS WILL COME-- TOMORROW, NEXT YEAR, A HUNDRED YEARS FROM NOW.
BUT I LOOK AROUND TODAY AND ALL I SEE IS BAD NEWS FOR THEM...
...BECAUSE WE'RE STRONGER THAN EVER.

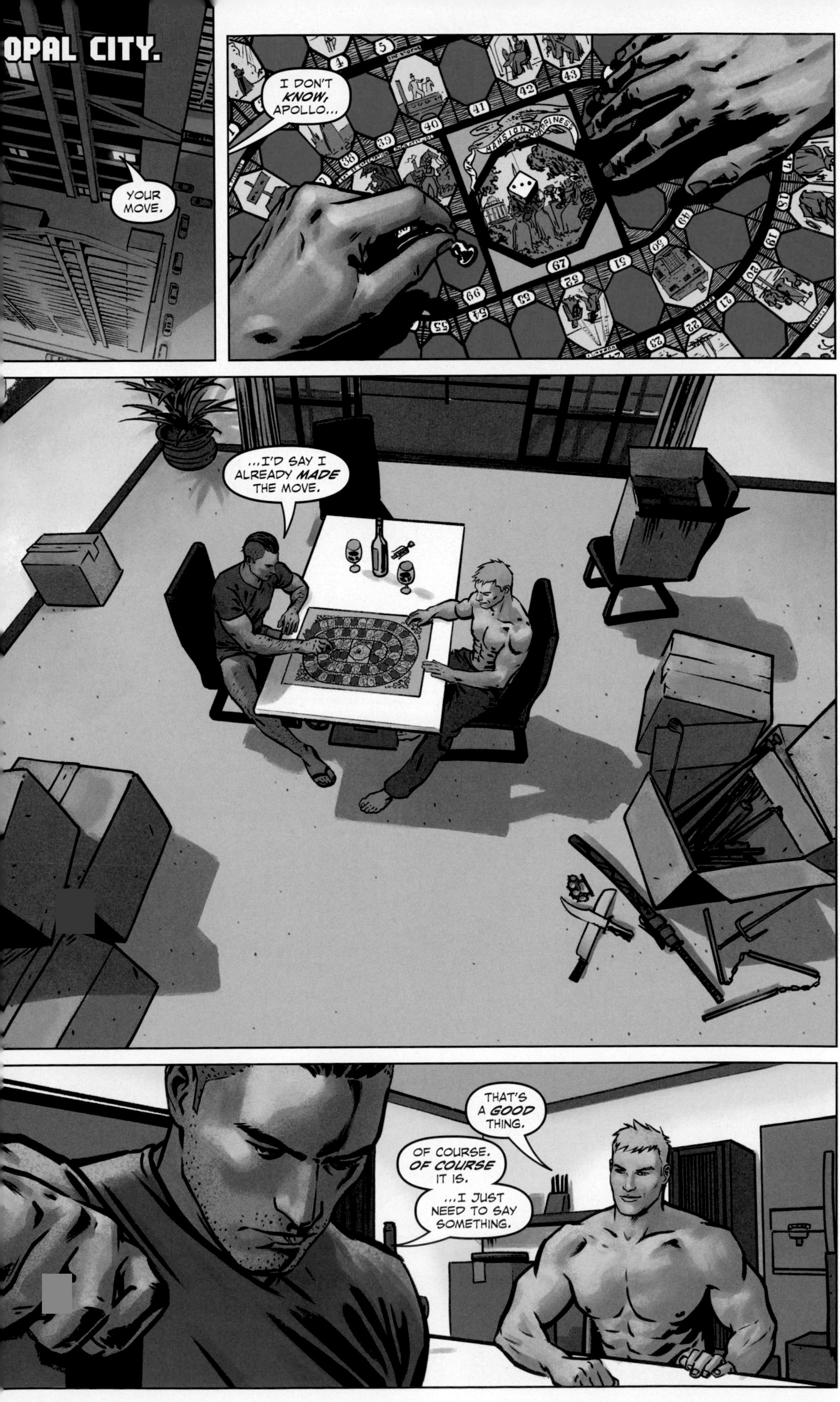
OPAL CITY.
YOUR MOVE.
I DON'T KNOW, APOLLO...
...I'D SAY I ALREADY MADE THE MOVE.
THAT'S A GOOD THING.
OF COURSE. OF COURSE IT IS.
...I JUST NEED TO SAY SOMETHING.

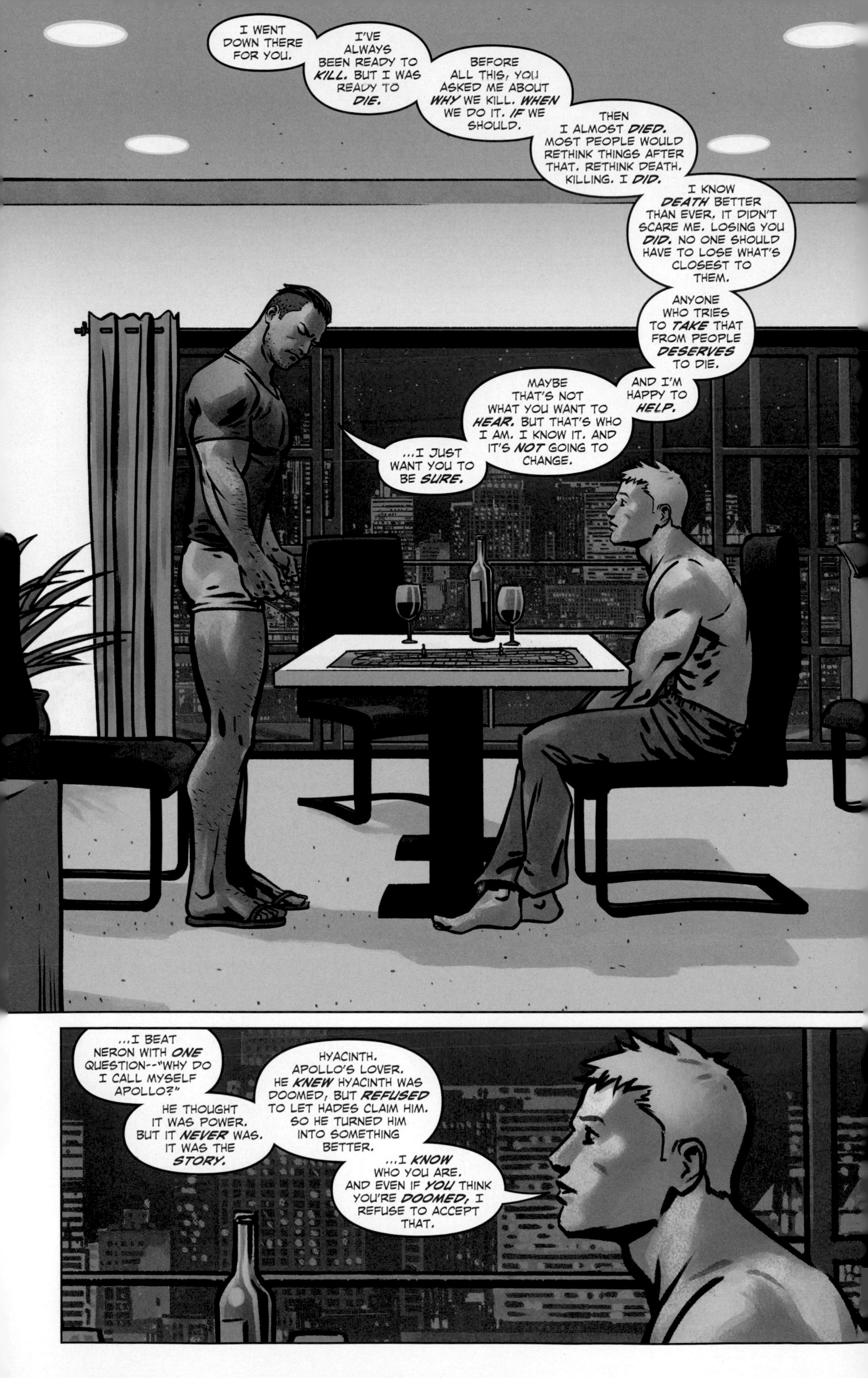
I WENT DOWN THERE FOR YOU.
I'VE ALWAYS BEEN READY TO KILL. BUT I WAS READY TO DIE.
BEFORE ALL THIS, YOU ASKED ME ABOUT WHY WE KILL. WHEN WE DO IT. IF WE SHOULD.
THEN I ALMOST DIED. MOST PEOPLE WOULD RETHINK THINGS AFTER THAT. RETHINK DEATH. KILLING. I DID.
I KNOW DEATH BETTER THAN EVER. IT DIDN'T SCARE ME. LOSING YOU DID. NO ONE SHOULD HAVE TO LOSE WHAT'S CLOSEST TO THEM.
ANYONE WHO TRIES TO TAKE THAT FROM PEOPLE DESERVES TO DIE.
AND I'M HAPPY TO HELP.
MAYBE THAT'S NOT WHAT YOU WANT TO HEAR. BUT THAT'S WHO I AM. I KNOW IT. AND IT'S NOT GOING TO CHANGE.
...I JUST WANT YOU TO BE SURE.
...I BEAT NERON WITH ONE QUESTION--"WHY DO I CALL MYSELF APOLLO?"
HE THOUGHT IT WAS POWER. BUT IT NEVER WAS. IT WAS THE STORY.
HYACINTH. APOLLO'S LOVER. HE KNEW HYACINTH WAS DOOMED, BUT REFUSED TO LET HADES CLAIM HIM. SO HE TURNED HIM INTO SOMETHING BETTER.
...I KNOW WHO YOU ARE. AND EVEN IF YOU THINK YOU'RE DOOMED, I REFUSE TO ACCEPT THAT.

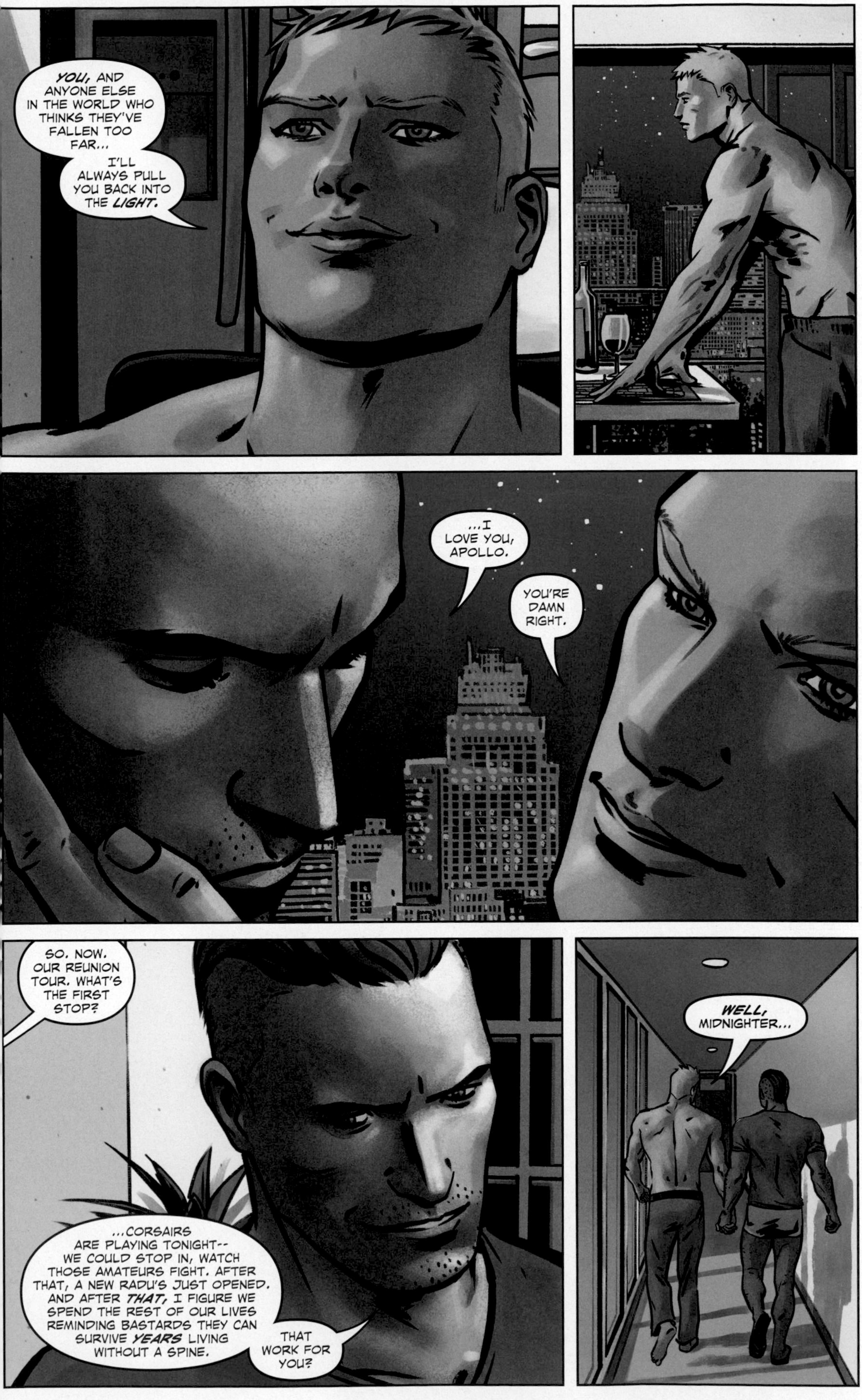
YOU, AND ANYONE ELSE IN THE WORLD WHO THINKS THEY'VE FALLEN TOO FAR...
I'LL ALWAYS PULL YOU BACK INTO THE LIGHT.
...I LOVE YOU, APOLLO.
YOU'RE DAMN RIGHT.
SO. NOW. OUR REUNION TOUR. WHAT'S THE FIRST STOP?
...CORSAIRS ARE PLAYING TONIGHT-- WE COULD STOP IN, WATCH THOSE AMATEURS FIGHT. AFTER THAT, A NEW RADU'S JUST OPENED. AND AFTER THAT, I FIGURE WE SPEND THE REST OF OUR LIVES REMINDING BASTARDS THEY CAN SURVIVE YEARS LIVING WITHOUT A SPINE.
THAT WORK FOR YOU?
WELL, MIDNIGHTER...

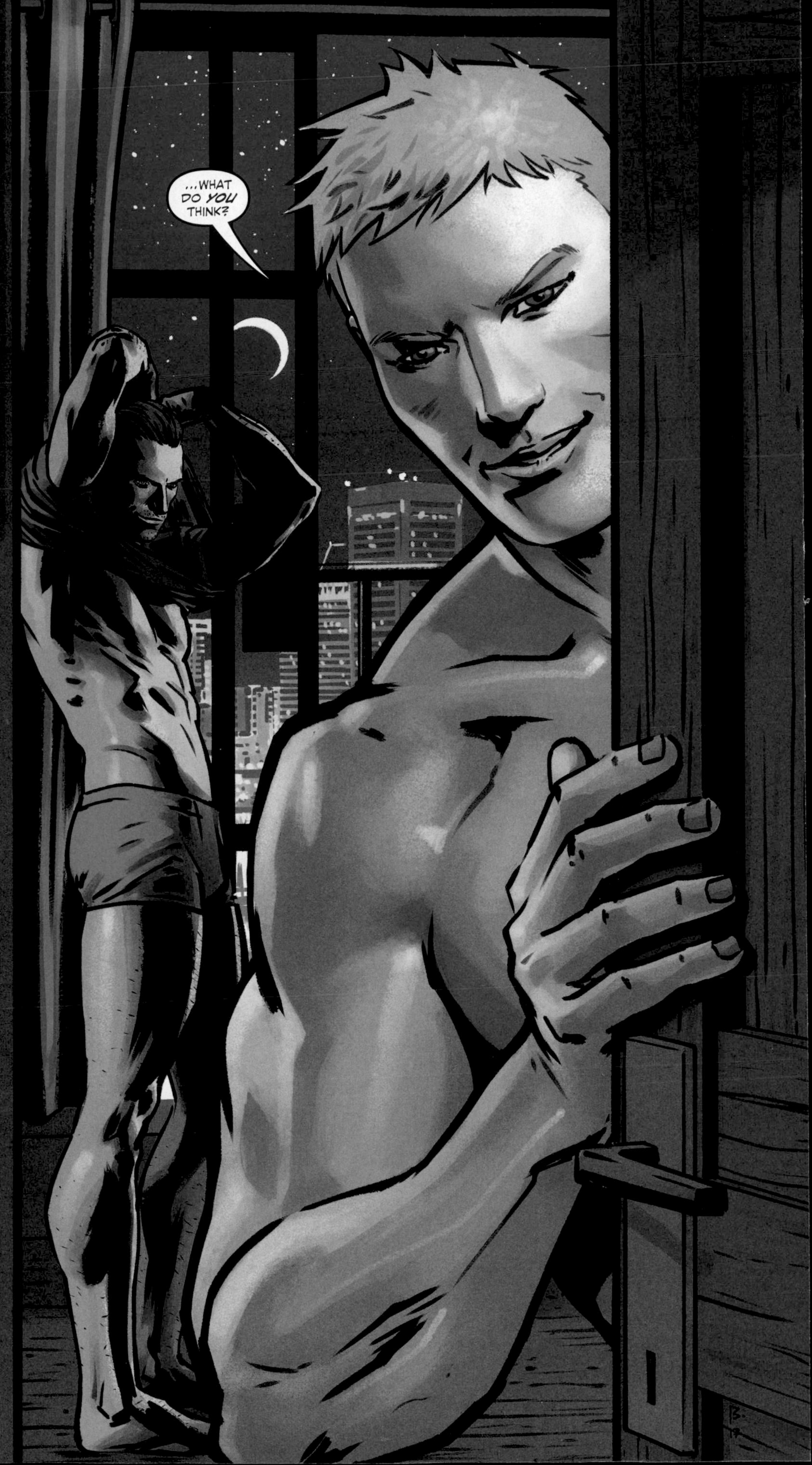
...WHAT DO YOU THINK?

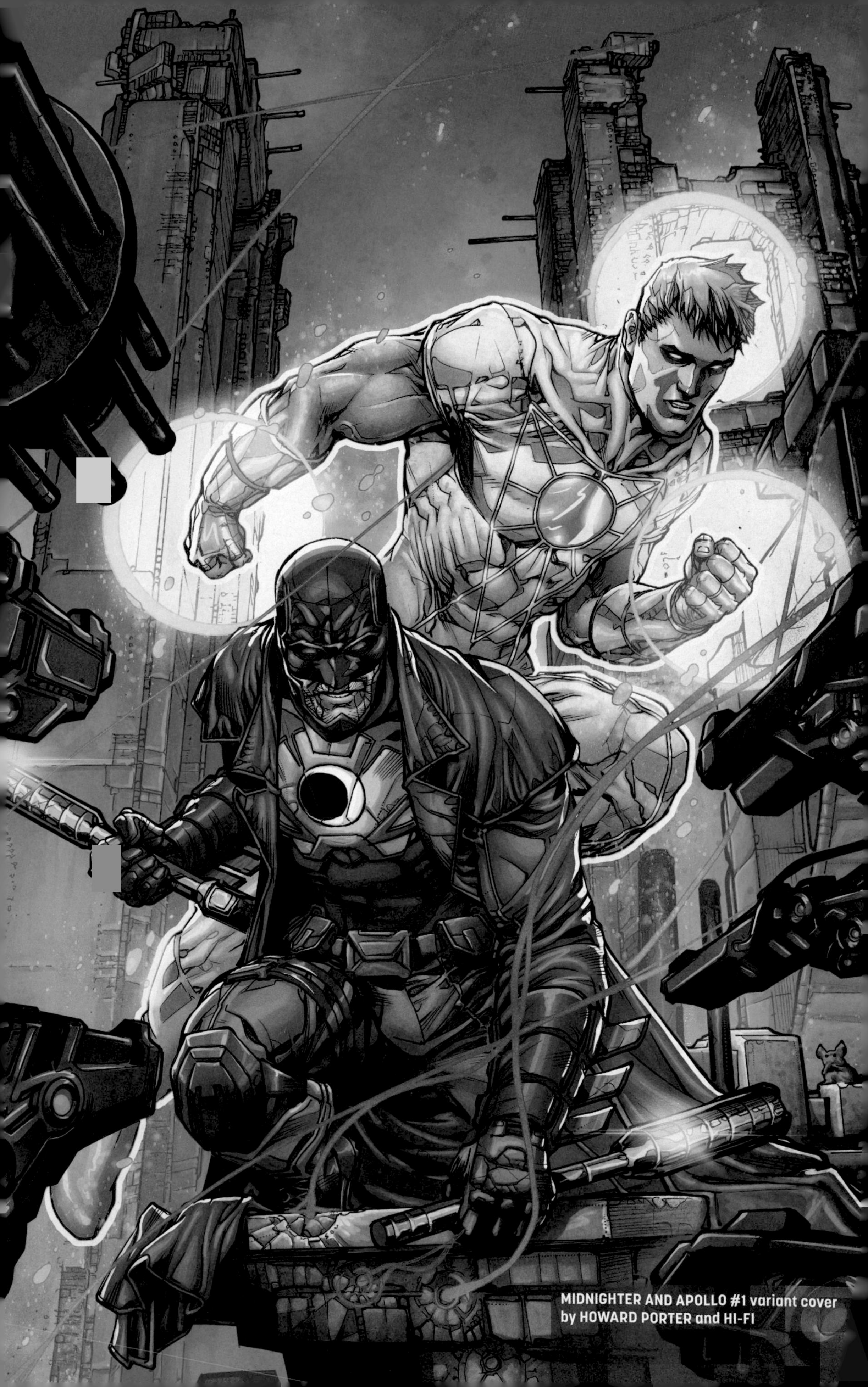

MIDNIGHTER AND APOLLO #1 variant cover
by HOWARD PORTER and HI-FI

CHARACTER DESIGNS by FERNANDO BLANCO

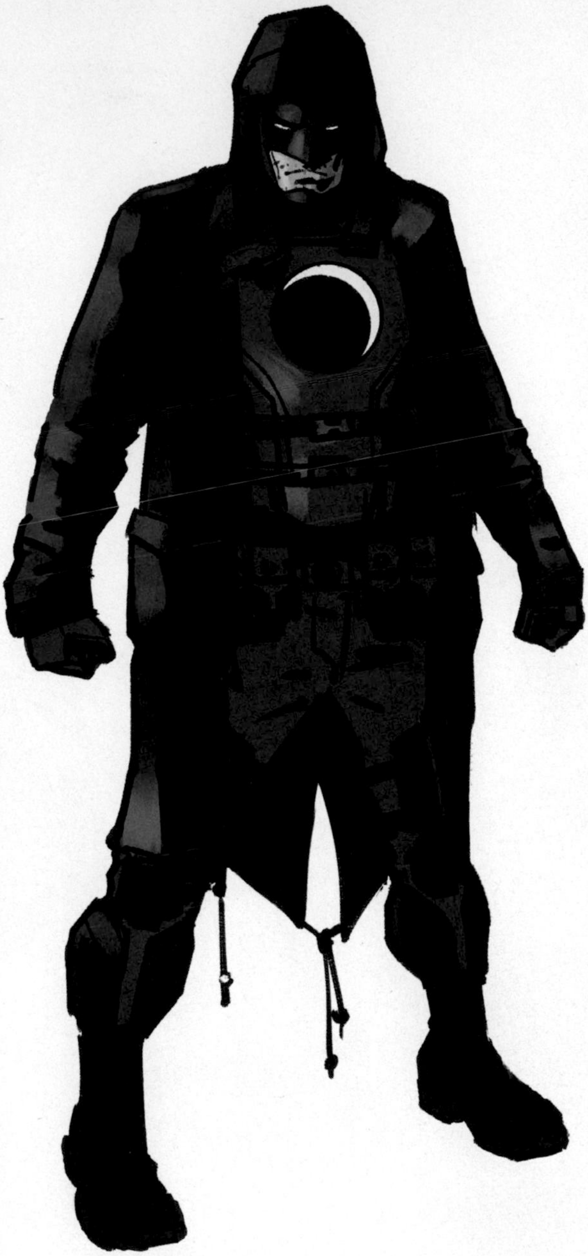

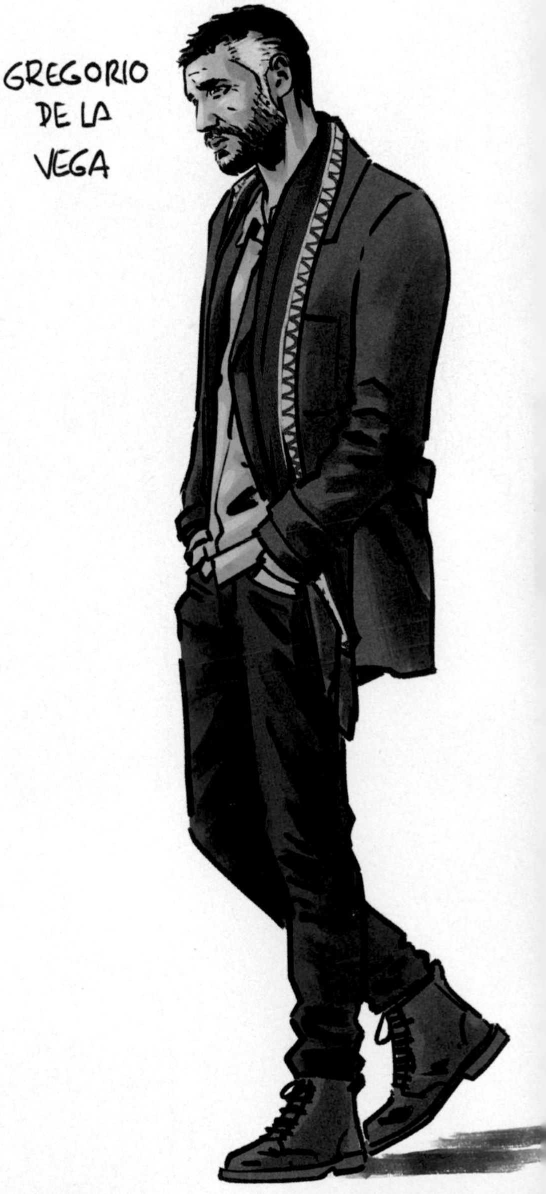
GREGORIO
DE LA
VEGA

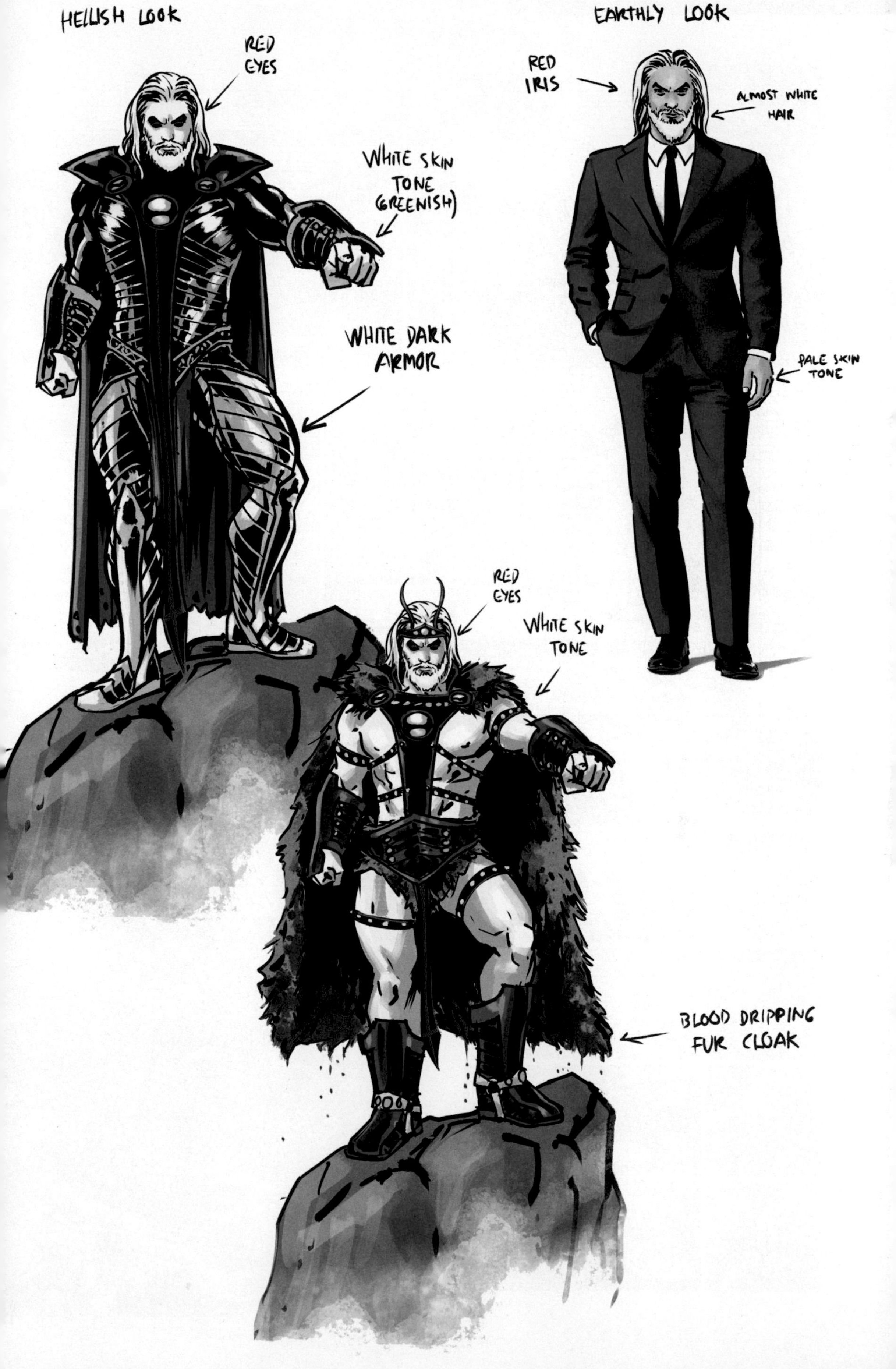
HELLISH LOOK
RED EYES
WHITE SKIN TONE (GREENISH)
WHITE DARK ARMOR
EARTHLY LOOK
RED IRIS
ALMOST WHITE HAIR
PALE SKIN TONE
RED EYES
WHITE SKIN TONE
BLOOD DRIPPING FUR CLOAK

INKS and SKETCHES by FERNANDO BLANCO

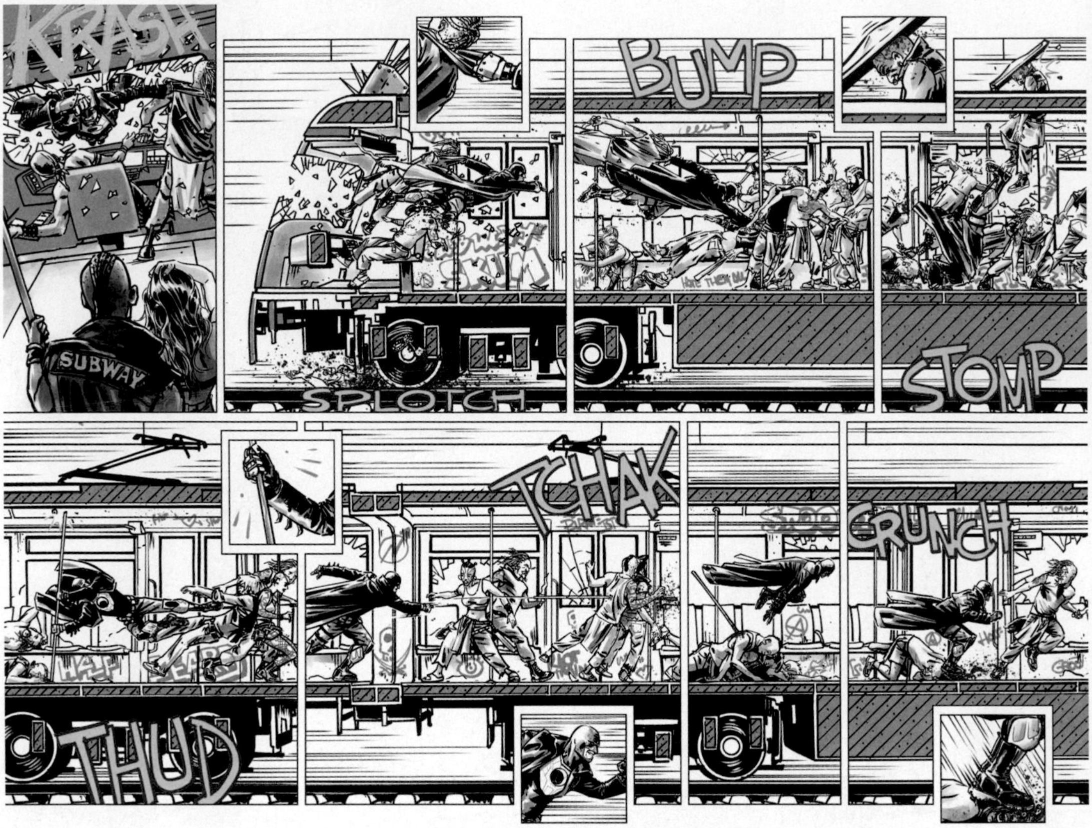
KRASH
SUBWAY
BUMP
SPLOTCH
STOMP
TCHAK
CRUNCH
THUD

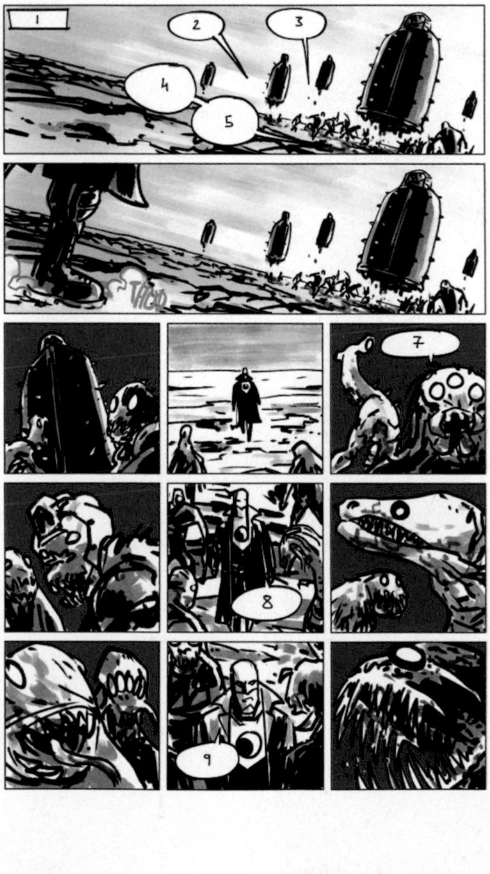
1
2
3
4
5
THUD
7
8
9

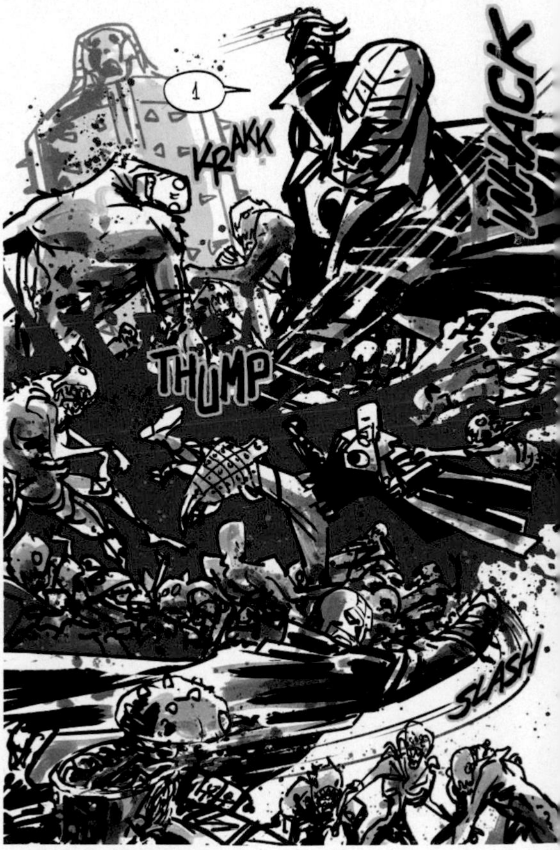
1
KRAKK
WHACK
THUMP
SLASH